Piled Higher and Deeper
The Folklore of Student Life

Piled Higher and Deeper

The Folklore of Student Life

Simon J. Bronner

August House Publishers, Inc.
LITTLE ROCK

Published by August House, Inc.,
P.O.Box 3223, Little Rock, Arkansas, 72203

Printed in the United States of America

10 9 8 7 6 5 4 3 2

LIBRARY OF CONGRESS CATALOGING-IN-PUBLICATION DATA

Piled higher and deeper: the folklore of student life

Simon J. Bronner - 1st ed.
p.   cm.

ISBN 0-87483-433-0 (PB): $14.95

1. College students—United States.
2. College students—United States–Social life and customs
3. Universities and colleges–United States–Case studies. I. Title
LA229.B66   1995
378.1'89'0973—dc20   95-23120
CIP

Executive editor: Ted Parkhurst
Project editor: Judith Faust
Design director: Ted Parkhurst

This book is printed on archival-quality paper that meets the
guidelines for performance and durability of the Committee on
Production Guidelines for Book Longevity of the
Council on Library Resources.

AUGUST HOUSE, INC.   PUBLISHERS   LITTLE ROCK

For Ron and Cathy Baker,
and for my students

Contents

Acknowledgments

I had barely made the transition from student to teacher when an esteemed professor of education at Penn State, Stanley Miller, challenged me to apply my cultural studies to college students and present my findings to the university community. I made the presentation he asked for and received an enthusiastic response because of what the material revealed about the state of higher education—but in the process of gathering the material, I realized how much more needed to be collected, collated, and interpreted. And so this project began...

Years later, this book arose after my sifting through thousands of surveys, interviews, letters, photographs, artifacts, and publications. And there—organizing, referencing, and making sense of the piles, ever higher and deeper—was Alan Mays, as skilled an archivist as one could ever hope for. A friend and sage, Alan made this book possible.

Liz and Ted Parkhurst believed in the book from the start, and their patience and encouragement nurtured the project through to the end. In between, I had many helpful hands. William Mahar, division head of humanities at Penn State Harrisburg, lent support to the project as did Howard Sachs, associate dean for Research and Graduate Studies. The staff of the Center for Research and Graduate Studies have my unending gratitude for handling the surveys and transcriptions. The staff of the Heindel Library at Penn State Harrisburg were extremely helpful, particularly Ruth Runion Slear in Interlibrary Loan. Janet Widoff, coordinator of Student Activities, additionally gave me a valuable window into the student world. Leon Stout, Penn State's university archivist, opened up the vaults to help me, and was particularly helpful with locating photographs. Darrell Peterson of Penn State Harrisburg lent his photographic expertise, and Donna Horley, secretary for the humanities division, assisted greatly in many ways. Tricia Meley, graduate assistant, deserves special thanks for tending to many details of the project.

I owe many—too many to list here—community relations officers, student activity directors, archivists, historians, and student interns working in colleges across the United States for generously providing me with invaluable materials. Professors at the institutions also came through wonderfully with student papers and commentaries. I want to especially thank Robert Bethke of the

University of Delaware, William Wilson of Brigham Young University, Angus Gillespie of Rutgers, Richard Meyer of Western Oregon State College, Danielle Roemer of Northern Kentucky University, Mac Barrick of Shippensburg University, Jan Harold Brunvand of the University of Utah, William Ferris of the University of Mississippi, Jay Mechling of the University of California at Davis, Kurt Dewhurst and Marsha MacDowell of Michigan State University, Elizabeth Tucker of SUNY at Binghamton, Kenneth Thigpen of Penn State University, and Alan Dundes of the University of California at Berkeley.

In addition, I benefited from the contributions of alumni from universities around the country and even abroad. Some mobilized others to help me. For this and more, I thank Sue Samuelson (Berkeley, UCLA, Penn), Patricia Clawges (Virginia), Thea Hocker (C.W. Post), Henry Koretzky (Penn State), Lynne Stovich Spector (Penn State), Tammie Nicodemus (Hood), and Hope Coulter (Harvard). Special mention also goes to William Aspinall (Penn State, Indiana) and Harry Spector (Richmond, Lebanon Valley) for an initiation or two. I am especially grateful to the students in my classes at Penn State who taught me so well.

Even before this project began, I mounted intellectual debts. Wilhelm Nicolaisen, my first teacher of folklore, had the courage to talk critically about the culture of college students, and Richard Dorson at Indiana University encouraged its serious study. Ronald L. Baker also listened to Dorson and offered groundbreaking folklore collections of his own from Indiana and Illinois toward the understanding of the occupational culture of students. His wife Cathy brought a perspective from educational psychology to the subject. Many conversations among the three of us, and later with folklorist Bill McNeil and Ron and Cathy's children Jill and Jon (collegians every one), informed, indeed inspired, my writing.

Orientation

"Welcome, scholars," the resident assistant barked with some sarcasm as I joined the other wide-eyed freshmen in my first dormitory meeting, far from home.

"You're no longer in high school, you're in college now," this senior student, apparently wise to the ways of higher learning, reminded us, as if we had safely crossed a huge abyss.

"You've come to get your degree, and some of you may even go for the Ph.D." He paused, and his authoritarian air shifted to one more relaxed, as if he were an uncle giving us the low-down on the rest of the family.

"You know what B.S. stands for, don't you?" Heads turned and glances were exchanges anticipating where he was going with this off-color reference. "M.S. is more of the same, and Ph.D.—well, that's it just piled higher and deeper."

As the first bit of lore given us about student life, it was no doubt variously interpreted by the young recruits gathered in the lounge that August day early in the 1970s. The resident assistant, I think, meant it to give us the unofficial cultural perspective on college and its demands, and to put us at ease with humor. For some in the room, it was a refreshing reminder that the job of being a college student is nothing to be afraid of. For others, it was a reminder that if they didn't do well, they needn't feel it was the end of the world. Some mentioned to each other that college involved more than getting the degree: it was largely social. Yet undergirding these views was the assumption drawn from the lore that degrees, represented by those magic letters, hold power.

I must have heard this humorous description of degree initials in one form or another hundreds of times in my college career, and I later discovered that others across the country had heard it, too—for generations. Still, if it had been the only bit of lore recounted during my years, I might have thought little about it. I found, though, a long legacy of tradition supporting my experience of classes and social events.

I heard, for example, that a sculpture of Pegasus over the entrance to the Fine Arts Building would fly off if a virgin walked into the building. (The sculpture is still there.) From students on other campuses I heard of columns collapsing, clocks on towers stopping, and statues altering their poses in the event that a virgin should graduate.

I listened intently as word went around about a popular seer predicting a mass murder would take place at a college like mine. Funny how the story circulated around *several* campuses in the area just before Hallowe'en, along with stories of lover's lane murders and roommates done in because they recklessly defied warnings against going out into the scary night.

I pricked up my ears at stories of straight-A students committing suicide under the pressure of their studies, and of the ghosts of those students returning to warn the living. If my roommate committed suicide, I heard, I would receive a 4.0 for the semester. (I never had a chance to verify that one.)

I was told that once in class, one waited fifteen minutes for a full professor, but only five for an assistant prof. Later, as I set off on the trail to graduate school, I heard the business about the degrees and their meaning again, told this time to take a poke at the growth of graduate education everywhere—and to say maybe it's not such a long, hard road, if it all amounts to the same thing, just piled higher and deeper. With stacks of books and papers neatly rising around us, the lines led us also to reflect on the anal retention the adademic grind requires.

This material is hardly frivolous, for it says much about the fears, joys, and values of America's college students—students who become the nation's professionals and leaders. Add to these stories and beliefs the special vocabulary peculiar to college students, and the customs, games, rituals, and songs college students alone seem to know, and you have a sense of an occupational culture preserved by the bounded settings of college campuses throughout the country. Being a student is a special experience—one that most readily leave behind after a few years, but one alumni look back on with nostalgia.

Being a student assumes lack of power in relation to teachers and administrators, and yet, on the positive side, offers the idealism of the quest for knowledge, skill, and ever more daring escapades. Never again in their lifetimes will adults be so free and open to new experience as they were when they were students.

College students abound in the United States. Put in a world context, the United States ranks first in percentage of the population with post-secondary training, and Canada is second. The figures for America are more than double those of Japan, almost three times Great Britain's, and more than four times the Soviet Union's (Kurian 1984: 368-69). Sixty percent of high school graduates in the United States pursue some form of higher education, although only about half of them tough it out to graduation. The United States boasts more than thirty-three hundred colleges in all, educating more than thirteen million students.

Who are these students? Where do they live and learn? They are usually young; the number of older students is rising, but almost sixty-two percent of undergraduates are still between the ages of eighteen and twenty-four. Though there is a trend toward more part-time students, one still finds that about sixty percent of undergraduates are attending college full-time. By a margin of almost 900,000, more women than men attend America's colleges. The overwhelming majority of students are white, but more than 2.25 million of America's college students represent minorities—native American, Asian, black, and Hispanic—and of these a little more than a million are black.

The map of America's college students looks much like the population map of the United States with some notable exceptions. A large concentration of students live in the megalopolis that runs from Washington, D.C., through Philadelphia, New York, and Boston. According to the census, though, the region with the most students—2.25 million—covers Ohio, Indiana, Illinois, Michigan, and Wisconsin. The single campus with the most students is the University of Minnesota-Twin Cities, with an enrollment of more than 62,000. Other giants are Ohio State University at Columbus (53,115), and the University of Texas at Austin (47,743). More than a hundred campuses claim 20,000 students or more.

The small college tradition is strong, especially in the South, which claims more colleges than any other region. Eighty percent of all institutions nationwide enroll fewer than 5,000 students each.Of the states, New York State has the most colleges with 301, followed by California and Pennsylvania with 290 and 206, respectively.

Judging from what college students study these days, the business of America is business. According to census data, three times more students are enrolled in business and management programs than in the next most popular major of engineering. Other popular majors include biological and physical sciences, social sciences and psychology, education, and communications and English. Students sometimes organize the groups this way: "The business students tell the liberal arts students to find real jobs, and the B.A. students chide the business students for their lack of imagination. Both groups consider the engineers to be eggheads" (Yale 1990: 683).

Priding themselves on offering many choices, America's colleges also list programs that defy easy categorization such as humane studies, applied living, and history of consciousness, not to mention various interdisciplinary combinations and area studies. And yes, one can earn degrees in folklore at several prestigious schools, from the University of Pennsylvania on one coast to the University of California at Los Angeles on the other.

College students can also enroll in many different types of institutions. One can choose a military academy, Bible college, school of technology, or institution specializing in art or music. It may be a two- or four-year institution, either public or private, with sectarian or non-denominational affiliation.

Colleges for blacks and women have in particular been known for their special traditions. Originally established to offer higher education to those groups historically blocked from the white male preserve of early colleges, black and women's colleges commonly instituted customs emphasizing a strong feeling of community among students and faculty (Horowitz 1984; Boas 1971). Partly as a result, their student retention rates are above the national average. And one may still choose a men's college from a small remaining number, including Hampden-Sydney, Wabash, and Morehouse.

Despite this diversity, one can recognize some common characteristics of America's colleges and their students. Most students take an individualized elective curriculum, attend colleges with "campuses," and work on the early semester system (the first semester starting before Labor Day and ending before Christmas, the second semester starting in January and ending in May). Looking back a couple of generations, however, one realizes that much has changed in college life just since World War II, and even more since the first American colleges were established shortly after the Pilgrims arrived in the seventeenth century. This history is the backdrop against which the folklore of student life has taken its cues.

In 1636, the first American college, Harvard, opened its doors, followed by William and Mary in 1693, and a smattering of other schools through the eighteenth century. These early schools were small and struggling; they enrolled on average forty students apiece. By 1776, only one in a thousand Americans had attended college. Those who went came generally from well-to-do white Protestant stock. The colleges educated mostly future clergymen, lawyers, and doctors in a controlled curriculum of Latin, Greek, Hebrew, logic, rhetoric, philosophy, and mathematics. Students aligned themselves with their entering class; all students in the class took the same courses. Tutors read from lessons and students recited assignments from memory.

Designers built Harvard, William and Mary, and Yale on the model of the English quadrangle, although they typically allowed for a more spacious feeling. Princeton distinguished its grounds, a centerpiece building fronted by a large lawn, from Harvard Yard, and with reverence for classical civilization called it a campus (taken from a Latin term for a field used for events in ancient Rome such as games, military exercises, and public meetings). The name and image of the campus have stuck to American colleges since.

Further emulating the English, the colleges organized around residential plans. Under these cloistered conditions, schoolmasters controlled students by strict moral discipline. Acting *in loco parentis* ("in the place of a parent"), they reasoned that students were considered children in need of protection from worldly vice on their way to a professional calling. Masters confined students to campus except on certain days and sent them to bed without supper for infractions of the rules. Their letters and packages, both incoming and outgoing, were subject to inspection by college officials (Schaeper, et al, 1987: 25). The college was a self-contained community, with students housed alongside instructors, and they moved together through a exhausting uniform daily routine of prayers, meals, recitations, and studies (Rudolph 1962: 96-109).

Between the American Revolution and the Civil War, American colleges expanded into the interior of the new republic. European travellers remarked with puzzlement that most of the new colleges were established on the fringes of settlement. As early as 1818, Saint Louis University was established west of the Mississippi, and in 1842, Willamette of Salem, Oregon, was organized on the west coast. More than half the colleges founded before the Civil War were outside the original thirteen colonies. By the 1830s, thirty-seven colleges operated in Ohio alone, a state with three million inhabitants. England, with a population of twenty-three million, had only four universities.

For communities in the United States, the college represented future aspiration rather than ancient lineage. With the college in their midst, communities hoped to make their claim for higher civilization as well as for economic gain. Church leaders also saw in the colleges outposts from which to lead a missionary charge out to the edges of settlement. Many communities with five hundred or fewer residents, isolated from major centers, fought for the right to host a college. In this tradition one sees emerging the common American image of the isolated, bucolic college campus. The communal character of this kind of institution and its intensive round of intellectual work and social life combine to give it the appellation of the "old-time college" (Bledstein 1976).

The antebellum period witnessed the rise of state universities. The University of Georgia was the first to be chartered, and in 1795, the University of North Carolina opened as the first public college. Thomas Jefferson founded the University of Virginia in 1819, and with eight separate colleges under its wing, the school pioneered the multiversity system so common today. Specialized schools for the military and technical trades also opened during this period: Rensselaer Polytechnic Institute in 1824, and academies for the army and navy in 1802 and 1845, respectively. During the late 1850s, agriculture received its due at colleges such as Michigan State and Penn State. Schools were now available for the sons of merchants and farmers as well as for the upper classes.

In the midst of this expansion—and during a time of national ambition and growth—students fought faculty for reform. Feeling the expanded opportunities in this new nation, and with the memory of colonial rebellion fresh in their minds, youth resisted being treated like children.

At Harvard, students planted bombs in classrooms, and at Yale they smashed windows in an out-of-control rage (Bledstein 1976: 228-34). Secret societies, forerunners of the fraternities, emerged among the students. They aired complaints about vindictive faculty, prison-like conditions, and rotten food. Reports circulated widely in the 1830s of students fighting, burning, and looting; a common student ploy was to lock out faculty from their residences and classrooms (Rudolph 1962: 97-98).

Although faculty did reassert control in this period, the unrest ushered reforms into the old-time college. The classical curriculum cautiously opened up to include practical and modern subjects—science, English, economics, and geography. More lay scholars filled the ranks of the faculty, and, in a peculiarly American hierarchy, they divided by rank into assistant, associate, and full professors (Forrest 1940: 445). Schools eased requirements for attendance at morning and evening prayers, and relaxed rules for confinement of students to dorms. Oberlin became the first college to admit women, and Amherst graduated the first black.

Some schools introduced athletics and class "scraps" (organized battles between the freshmen and sophomores) to redirect the aggressive energies of students. Harvard and Yale began intercollegiate sports with a crew race in 1852, and other extracurricular activities gave students social outlets—or "a life," as some would observe.

Change accelerated between the Civil War and World War I. A boost came from the Morrill Act of 1862, which established land grant colleges. The act resulted in the creation of seventy-two new schools. They typically enrolled both men and women, were independent of church control, and offered a wide range of courses from the classics and humanities to agricultural and mechanical studies. The number of colleges hit two thousand by World War I, a tenfold increase since the Civil War. By 1870, the young United States claimed more colleges than existed in all of Europe. After modest increases in graduates through the nineteenth century, college enrollment almost doubled during the 1880s and 1890s.

The German model of education—the basis for America's research universities today, and for the appellation of the "modern university"—drew wider acceptance before World War I. Bureaucratically structured into departments, this model emphasized research to aid instruction and graduate study to advance knowledge in specific fields. Students took a field as a "major" and elected to take courses in other subjects or departments. The expansion of this model meant that the emphasis on class loyalty common in the old-time college was gradually replaced by connection to the major. Study became more individualized and research-oriented.

As strict administrative control of the student's routine subsided and more students entered colleges during the late nineteenth century, an extra-curricular social life revolving around the collegiate experience emerged with greater strength. Greek-letter fraternities serving student needs had been around since 1825, when Kappa Alpha began at Union College, but they rapidly expanded during the late nineteenth century. As more women entered the college ranks, sorority chapters came into being. Pledging, hazing, and initiation became a regular part of college life at many campuses. Intercollegiate sports expanded and football rivalries gave focus to campus loyalties. Mixing between men and women on campuses became more common, and students embraced courtship rituals as part of college tradition. Students also were a more noticeable force in the small communities that hosted the colleges. "Town and gown" came into the language, and students ventured off campus and into the community's streets with parades and festivities, as well as pranks.

Some of the tolerance for youthful high jinks was explained by a new awareness of a special stage of life called "adolescence." Educators considered students to be freely acting out tensions caused by the difficult transition into the sobering responsibilities of adulthood. Colleges recognized social as well as academic needs during this transitional period. Teens had extra "nervous" energy to release because of sexual and social frustrations, and many authorities pointed out that collegians' shenanigans provided natural outlets (see Kett

1977). Social activities, pragmatists argued, provided skills and practical experiences that carried over later into society. More organized festivities—some established by the college, others by the students—thus came into being to meet or control these needs.

During the twentieth century, Americans increased their faith in higher education as a stepping-stone to success for themselves and their children. The traditional elitist image of colleges came into question as immigrants, blacks, and other groups called for the wider availability of colleges to the common person. Whereas colleges in the nineteenth century were expected to be separate from society, twentieth century schools were increasingly called upon to represent and affect society.

Enrollments dramatically increased at several points in the twentieth century. After World War I, colleges enjoyed their rah-rah period, days of raccoon coats and goldfish swallowings, as college enrollments and spirits grew. The class of 1929 was almost double that of 1919. After World War II, some ninety thousand veterans swelled the ranks of colleges and called for more studies in technological, business, and professional areas. Older and generally less tolerant of boisterous fun than traditional students, the veterans influenced the decline of hazing and other initiation traditions at college campuses. In this period, the trend was toward expanding existing colleges rather than adding new ones. By increasing the number of students within a single location, budgets—it was thought—could be stretched further. Many colleges merged or sought university status.

Enrollments leveled by 1953, but thereafter rose steadily toward the student explosion of the 1960s. Another doubling of enrollment occurred between 1960 and 1969. Large public universities especially grew, with campuses of more than twenty thousand students becoming more common. Federal and state programs made possible a rising level of loans and grants to needy students. Activists argued that attending college was a right, and increasingly a necessity, rather than a privilege of affluent citizens. Student unrest over the Vietnam war and civil rights jumped onto national headlines. The role of the college acting *in loco parentis* was actively challenged. Colleges dropped their supervision of visitation in dorms by the opposite sex and pulled back on dress and moral regulations. Colleges increased student governance. In surveys, students answered that seeking "meaning" for their lives was what they wanted out of the college experience. In that search, they signed up in large numbers for social sciences and humanities offerings.

Students during this period assaulted the "ivory tower" image of the university. They demanded the university take a direct role in solving social problems on campus and around the nation. They called for measures to insure an egalitarian, compassionate example on campus. Students complained about the increasing alienation of the lone student in the large bureaucratic university. Reflecting concerns about society at large, students lashed out at the educational giants for constricting, isolating, and depersonalizing them. Some of the resentment was aimed at the "computerization" of students, with its assignment of numbers to individual lives, and its large lecture halls seating five hundred and more. Administrators responded with the establishment of student assistance programs, small residential colleges within the large university structure, and ethnic and religious organizations to provide social support.

By the 1980s, campuses settled down, but new tensions threatened the self-assurance of the colleges. A barrage of reports criticized the education students were receiving. Two of the most notable were *College: The Undergraduate Experience in America,* by Ernest Boyer of the Carnegie Foundation for the Advancement of Teaching (1987), and *The Closing of the American Mind* (with the caustic subtitle, *How Higher Education has Failed Democracy and Impoverished the Souls of Today's Students),* by Allan Bloom of the University of Chicago (1987).

Citing the exodus from humanities and social sciences to narrow vocationalism—in a cafeteria-style curriculum run rampant—the collegiate critics shared the opinion that education had eroded, students were dispirited and ignorant, and colleges had become distended and incoherent. The National Commission on Excellence in Education, adding that general observation as well as standardized tests showed that American students were losing their edge in the world, warned in 1983 that the nation was "at risk" as a result of "a rising tide of mediocrity."

Many colleges responded by restoring general education requirements and re-examining student life issues. In the meantime, students faced more financial pressures as many federal and state aid programs were curtailed. Under the pressure, students continued to seek vocational goals from college and swelled the ranks of business and technical programs. They expected high grades to impress job recruiters and resented the tightening of standards. While finding a meaningful philosophy had been the primary objective for students twenty years earlier, an attitude survey of freshmen in 1988 reported "being very well-off financially" ranked highest.

Enrollments leveled again in the post-baby-boom years as the numbers of students drawn from high schools declined. Yet colleges often made up these losses in a new clientele drawn from minorities, foreign students, and employed adults. Commuting to large urban schools and attending college part-time, became more frequent choices among students feeling the pinch of rising college costs—costs that outpaced inflation.

Meanwhile, other students sought out the intimate liberal-arts college experience. Many of the older coeducational colleges attracted students with claims of tradition and community spirit. Many student groups—fraternities and sororities especially—sought to restore the customs, and with them the school spirit, that had been lost during the 1960s.

The resurgence of tradition and community in the pitches made by colleges was tied to reports of confusion by incoming students. A *Chronicle of Higher Education* report observed that students "are feeling a lot of stress as they face life's choices" and "are worried about how they will survive in a world where they can die from having sex, where roughly fifty percent of marriages end in divorce, and where providing for a family often requires both parents to work full time, even as they try to find time to spend with their children." The report noted that in response "officials at several institutions agree that helping students shape their values has become more important because many of the support systems young people once had at home and on campuses have disintegrated over the last two decades" (Wilson 1990: A1, A28).

To be sure, administrators reclaimed some of their supervisory role over student behavior. Many colleges cracked down on drinking and drug use on campus, even banning smoking in college buildings. While membership in Greek organizations came back strong during the late 1980s, colleges targeted for reform the abuses of fraternity and sorority life, often given to values of exclusion and rowdiness, and many colleges opted for banning the Greek system. Two national fraternities—Zeta Beta Tau and Tau Kappa Epsilon—tried to clean their own houses by eliminating pledging.

Another sore spot, especially for the large universities, was big-time athletics. Intercollegiate sports had become big business in many schools, and the abuses to recruit and retain athletes came out into the open. Reports of payoffs, faked transcripts, and academic dishonesty among athletes and coaching staffs made headlines, and college presidents were forced to intervene.

At the same time, Americans more than ever looked to colleges to insure their future. More than half of all new jobs created between 1984 and 2000 would require post-secondary education, and a third of the jobs would be filled by college graduates, according to the Bureau of Labor Statistics. Americans looked to colleges to do more than preparing students for these new jobs.

Colleges were to provide models for a better society, for basic education, for scientific and technological research, and for the way people lived and interacted on campus. These high expectations pressured colleges to guarantee results in a way they never had before. They were also in a position to explain what they did to the public in a way they never had before. Instruction? Research? Profit? What was higher education about?

Some of this reflection coincided in 1986 with the 350th anniversary of the founding of Harvard, an event that also signaled the founding of higher education in America. The anniversary occasioned discussion of the cultural role of students in the college system. From the historian's point of view came *Campus Life: Undergraduate Cultures from the End of the Eighteenth Century to the Present* (1987) by Helen Lefkowitz Horowitz. From the anthropologist's perspective came *Coming of Age in New Jersey* (1989) by Michael Moffatt. Horowitz described a progression of identities which dominated student life. In the old-time college it was the college men, followed by groups calling for their rightful place at the head, such as the rebels, the organized "frat rats," and the outsiders. The new self-centered outsiders in control today, she says, resist organization and seek achievement defined by money, goods, and status. They combine grade-consciousness and work habits drawn from the old outsiders with a non-intellectualism reminiscent of the old-time college men.

Emulating an anthropological experience among primitive natives, Michael Moffatt narrowed his focus to a small group of students at Rutgers. He found much more joy than Horowitz did in the modern student's life; indeed, he suggested that much of the student's coming of age during a college stay is found in the intentional pursuit of social and bodily pleasures. "At least half of college was what went on outside the classroom, among the students, with no adults around," Moffat wrote, and he asserted that "college was about fun, about unique forms of peer-group fun—before, in student conceptions, the grayer actualities of adult life in the real world began to close in on you" (pp. 28-29).

Folklore, an expression of student life and culture, tells what goes on both inside and outside the classroom among the students. It is a cultural and historical commentary on the classroom and college life. It outlines the responsibility and demeanor expected by students of one another. It maps the dangers that lie ahead and the attitudes left behind in adolescence.

The college experience is considered unique; it lies between the juvenile treatment and parental control of high school and the "real world" of the adult job. To hear students talk about it, college is a strange exotic island on which one is forced to fend for oneself before passage to a continent.

Folklore provides passage from one stage to another through ritual, custom, and object. It defines and describes the subgroupings within the student's world: the "frat rats," the "grinds," the "jocks," the "profs," and all the rest. It is students' unofficial cultural orientation held through the college experience. It offers parables to ponder, rituals to observe, values to honor. Folklore from the nation's colleges opens a legacy of creative expression reflecting student culture, concerns, and roles within an exclusive institutional setting. Most importantly for many students, folklore helps guide them to identities within a new setting often large, mysterious, and imposing. Folklore is a place to begin, and to belong.

This question of identity goes well beyond campus limits. It is an issue in modern society, as individuals wonder about pressures to run their lives as small interchangeable cogs in a massive wheel. Accordingly, some of the return to old collegiate traditions can be seen as an attempt to provide meaning and social support within the mass expanse of the university.

Much of the student culture that once provided such meaning and social support, however, seems elusive or fractured. Some might even say that American colleges have lost the rah-rah culture—and the lore reflecting it—that used to seem so unified (or at least so organized). I would argue that lore still thrives on campus, but that much of its character has changed.

Differing from the communal traditions found in colleges in times past, the folklore of student life today appears to serve more individual needs. It's not as public, not as organized, having been fragmented into the personal realms of students. Replacing many of the old customs are narratives told by one student to another about the contours and dangers of college life. Customs still remain—albeit revised frequently for our complex times—from freshman initiation at Purdue to "senior prank" at Hood, from the "door slams" of the halls to the "line-ups" of the fraternities, and from the "rat line" of VMI to the "running of the rodents" at Spalding.

This book explores the character of traditions found on college campuses today with reference to the changes that have occurred over time. My purpose is, by examining the composition and context of these traditions, to interpret what they reveal about the role of students in American society and culture—and about the nature of tradition itself in complex American society.

For some readers, the very idea that folklore is so common among what passes for America's educated elite is surprising. The formation of folklore, however, is basic to social interaction, and can be especially pronounced in situations where groups are in constant contact or in need of cultural guidance.

Folklore arises from the kind of learning we might call informal, typically outside the formal instruction of the classroom and published text. Passed by word of mouth, custom, and imitation, folklore provides signs of a group's identity. Through special stories, words, and rituals, often known through time, students understand their values and concerns.

Students, especially if they are attending full-time a college away from home, create a distinctive social world. Sharing a similar age for the most part, engrossed in the pursuit of a degree and grades, in frequent contact with one another through classes and residence, separated clearly from faculty and administrators, and often isolated from the support of family and friends found at home, students seek the lore emerging from their common situation. Often carried around day and night, the role of student produces a special brand of anxiety because of the stakes involved and the devotion to task required. Intensive and competitive, college carries with it images of future success and social adjustment.

Other segments of the university have their lore too, but I have chosen to focus on lore expressed by students, for they give life to college. Typically they are the most connected group on campus, and in their lore they reveal much about their society and the future society they will shape. Folklore is indeed especially revealing, because often in the special domain of lore, with its generally longstanding character and allowance for going beyond the limits of formal rules, one finds deep-seated attitudes, fears, desires, and biases that cannot be comfortably expressed in everyday conversation.

"The traditions of a college," Fred L. Pattee, pioneering professor of American literature, explained in 1928, "are those bits of history, mostly unwritten, those events, customs, ideals, men, about which every student and alumnus of the college is supposed to know, but which are next to impossible to find in any book or collection of books" (p. 3). By the nature of their adaptation to a certain college, traditions give each campus a unique character, and by virtue of their similarity in structure and style to those of other campuses, they express a shared culture. As Pattee told alumni, "Atmosphere has been created by the past of the college and this past comes to the student body largely by way of tradition; by a body of information and advice and counsel passed on by word of mouth from college generation to college generation" (p. 3)

The structure of folklore is generally slow to change, but when it does, it is often a sign of dramatic social and cultural shifts. One will find in this book particularly the shift from customs reflecting the communal activities of the old-time college student looking for status and fellowship to the kind of privatized lore stressing the individualistic character of the modern student in search of identity and community. Some student concerns seem timeless—the quest for success, resentment for the "grinds," and the desire to turn the tables on professors—while others reflect the special regional, religious, and ethnic conditions of particular colleges. Both the continuity and variation within tradition are covered in this book.

Since so many folklorists teach college students, one may wonder why such a book-length survey has not been attempted previously. Folklorists have long recognized college traditions, but have generally sought to leave the classroom to find lore among rooted, often isolated communities. A groundbreaking folklorist, Richard Dorson, advised his colleagues in 1949 that "the enterprising folklorist doesn't need to journey into the back hills to scoop up tradition. He can set up his recording machine in the smokeshop on the college grill" (p. 677).

I collected the material in this book in various ways.

• I used my own collections made at various campuses through the 1970s and 1980s.

• I relied on several years of collections and interviews made by students at Penn State from one another.

• I added to this collections from students found in folklore archives at the Library of Congress, University of Delaware, Brigham Young University, University of Pennsylvania, University of Oregon, Utah State University, Wayne State University, West Virginia University, Shippensburg University, Indiana University, University of California at Berkeley, University of California at Davis, and Western Oregon State College, University of Arkansas, Michigan State University, and Western Kentucky University.

• I sent out inquiries for information on traditions to six hundred colleges more than a hundred years old, and received several hundred replies from university archivists and historians, community relations and student activity officers, students, professors, and administrators.

• I prepared a detailed survey on college traditions which I sent to several hundred alumni of different colleges around the country.

• And finally, I scoured the literature—histories of colleges, yearbooks, articles, bulletins, and brochures—for samples of orally collected folklore.

As the material came in, the content of the lore suggested a division first between the academic and social sides of campus life. This is a distinction students themselves point out. Professors would like to think their classes constitute the social basis—and the pleasure—of college life. Students, however, separate the work—what they dub "the grind" of classes and studies—from the pleasure of socializing—the round of idle talk, parties, games, and escapades experienced with other students. (This isn't all that different, by the way, from the general American attitude separating the routine of work from the satisfactions of social life away from the job.) I sorted out a third category for the various scares and distractions from studies—the stories of ghosts in the library and study hall, for example—that lurk about every campus.

To describe the categories, I thought of a traditional verse that characterizes American student life from the early grades on: "Remember the tests, remember the fun, remember the homework that never got done."

Under "Remember the tests," I cover the academic side—the legends and beliefs about exams, grading, cheating, and professors. Under "Remember the fun," I cover the social side—all those class competitions, dorm games, practical jokes, singing events, seasonal festivals, sports rituals, and fraternity and sorority traditions. Then come the scares and distractions under "Remember the homework that never got done." In its scope, the survey takes you from the first to the last day of classes, from "orientation" to the closing chapter of "graduation."

I invite you, as you read, to appreciate the joy and travail of being a student. I ask you to think of colleges as organizations and communities on which cultural expression comments. Reflect, if you will, on colleges as settings for individual development, social and psychological, which folklore signifies. There's much to learn while we're students, and much more to know about the experience as it relates to our individual lives and our society as a whole.

"Remember the Tests"

The first day of class, the professor welcomes the students to the course. He describes his interest in the subject and begins to tell something about himself. Suddenly, a hand shoots up. Taken aback by a questioner at such an early stage in the class, the prof calls upon the anxious student.

"Excuse me, will this be on the final?"

This often-told story reminds students that tests and papers produce the numbers that translate into grades. Although professors would like to think the measure of accomplishment in a course is the learning that occurs, students look to high grades.

With the wide array of courses available to students today, the choice of classes is a great topic of discussion among students. "What should I take?" they ask one another. The reply is typically a rundown of requirements—how many tests, how many papers, how many books to read—and what students have heard about the prof or the class. Sometimes fanciful, often revealing, these stories and beliefs lay out a round of life fragmented into classes where the terrain always seems treacherous. The control students have over the situation is to know what to expect and to master the events that give the numbers.

As if to underscore the primacy of the exams, students tell stories of goldbrickers who miss class and party, only to "ace" (student lingo for receiving an A) the tests. Alfred Rollins, for example, reported in 1961 a story from New York of "the admired giant of the past who had a photographic memory. He could 'party' merrily for thirteen weeks, and then settle down to read the books and write the papers. Quoting verbatim whole pages of the textbook, he would take honors in his exams, despite his enraged professors" (p. 171).

In what sounds like a good Münchausen tale, Walker Wyman tells of the student who didn't show up again in class after the first day—until the final exam. He took it, and got a B. The professor called the student and asked him to explain this incredible feat. "The student said that he thought he could do better than a 'B,' but the professor confused him a little when he attended class the first day" (1979: 82).

To prepare for exams, students talk of "cramming," sometimes taking in weeks worth of material in a single night. A collection from Southern Illinois University in 1966 includes stories of students staying up all night and then unable to stay up any longer, falling asleep and missing the exam. One cautionary tale about drugs as an aid to performance circulated during the 1950s, about a student using benzedrine to take exams. "At last, after several semesters of successful dope jags, he drops to sleep fatefully in mid-examination and has to be carted off to the infirmary" (Rollins 1961: 171).

A variant from the 1970s comes from C.W. Post: "There was this guy who took speed to get him through an exam. He stayed up all night studying and then came into the exam. Most people turned in one blue book, but he handed in four. The trouble was that he was so high that he didn't realize that his pen ran out of ink after the first few paragraphs, so he handed in four blank books and failed anyway." The story persisted through the 1980s, and was even reported in English colleges (Brunvand 1989: 199).

Richard Dorson tells a related story from the 1940s from the University of Minnesota about a student who walks into the final exam having taken a few drinks before to calm her nerves. "She thought the questions looked a little strange, but went at them with a will. Some weeks later she received a grade of B for a course in American political science, in which she was not enrolled, and a statement of incomplete for the course in American literature in which she belonged" (1949: p. 673).

Since students often depend on cramming to get by, the idea of a "pop" or surprise quiz gives them nightmares. Especially at older college halls where doors have transoms, students tell the one about an athletic-looking professor who is asked by students whether he ever gives surprise quizzes. The professor laughs and tells the students that the day he gives a pop quiz is the day he climbs through the transom! A sigh of relief passes through the classroom. Then one day the transom began to creak open and, to the amazement of the students, in climbed their professor, grinning happily and clutching a three-page quiz in his hand.

Some reports attach the story to famed professors who might have had a stint as circus performers before their academic career. In 1979, Oliver Graves collected the story about Professor Menno Spann of the University of North Carolina, and Professor Guy Williams of the University of Oklahoma, who supposedly performed the stunt as early as 1925 (Graves 1979: 142-45;

Brunvand 1986: 192-91). To this list, I now have to add history professor Guy B. Harrison, who was known widely around Baylor University from the 1930s to the 1970s. The story of the transom boast told by "Guy B." still circulates on the Baylor campus, and has a basis in fact, according to an oral history interview with professor Harrison (Keeth 1985: 46). Perhaps existing as a modern take-off on this legend, a story is reported by Jan Brunvand about the journalism professor who promises never to give an unannounced quiz. "When a class protested one day that he was giving a test without announcing it, the professor pointed out that he had run an ad in the local newspaper saying 'Unit Quiz Today in Mr. McDonald's journalism class at 2 p.m.'" (Brunvand 1989: 284).

Looking for luck

Even with cramming, students believe that success on exams involves some luck. Test-takers guess what will be asked, and they think it's not just a matter of knowing the material, but of giving professors "what they want." Surveying 600 students during the 1960s at the universities of Oregon and Utah, Portland State, and Reed College, Barre Toelken found that more than 400 reported engaging in customs during finals typically intended to bring good luck on the exam. The most common had to do with clothing or grooming styles, such as growing beards (or not shaving, or, for coeds, not cutting hair), or wearing "grubby" clothes, especially if these clothes had been worn on "aced" exams. Students sought out "lucky" seats where they had done well on a test. They brought "lucky" pens, again made magical by association with a good exam. Accordingly, students reported as bad luck taking an exam with a new pen. They also clutch traditional lucky charms such as rabbits' feet, found copper pennies, and silver bracelets.

These beliefs are among the most persistent of student folklore. Martha Beckwith, for example, collected the following luck-inducing behaviors from Vassar women in the early 1920s: bringing rose petals to the examination, wearing or using at an examination something that belongs to someone else who is or has been considered a good student in the course, and sitting in the same seat in examination as you did when an examination went well (p. 6). Today's lore of luck is typically more individualized (see Albas 1989). During the late 1980s, Patricia Clawges, a student collector, gathered customs as varied as the fellow from Case Western wearing a baseball cap to exams (a carryover from his hunting days when he turned his bill to the back in order to focus the scope of his rifle) and the student from Dickinson who believed that underlining exams with his lucky ruler insured his high grade.

Some beliefs are tied to locale. At Roanoke College in Salem, Virginia, students kick the post between the administration building and Trout Hall to bring good luck on exams. At Brown, students rub the nose of the statue of John Hay at the John Hay Library. At Wofford College, a plaque devoted to the founder in the Main Building has a misspelling of the word "beneficent." According to legend, the eccentric president refused to have the plaque recast, leaving it instead to warn students about the dangers of sloppy work. Students now rub the misspelled word, seeking good luck and protection from the spelling gremlin lest some prof take points off.

Students also look out for omens. Seeing a dog on the way to an exam is bad luck, probably because "a dog" is considered in folk speech something bad, and the sound of it suggests the grade of D (Baker 1983: 109). Getting a three or a seven in a numbered seat or on a numbered exam is a good omen. Speaking of numbers, some students believe that using a no. 3 pencil insures good luck.

Eating off a green tray is bad luck, green being singled out probably because it suggests the novice, ignorant status of the "greenie." Red trays, in reference to red as a symbol of vitality, bring good luck (Cannon 1984: 42).

Students tell parents and friends not to bother them before an exam; an argument portends misfortune on the test. Stepping over the school seal, as stepping on a sidewalk crack or manhole cover does in children's folklore, brings bad luck. At Eastern Michigan University, for example, students on the way to an exam who step on the school letter "E" painted on the campus grounds will have difficulty passing. From Utah comes the omen that meeting a priest on the way to the test is a sure sign of failure on the exam (Cannon 1984: 43).

Students also call on religious intervention to help them with exams. At Iona College of New Rochelle, a Roman Catholic institution, students write J.M.J. (Jesus, Mary, and Joseph) and S.J.O.C., P.F.M. (Saint Joseph of Cupertino, pray for me) on exams. Saint Joseph (Joseph Desa, 1603-1663) is considered by students to be the patron saint of the stupid, and they can recite a prayer for exams in his name: "Saint Joseph of Cupertino, who while on earth did obtain from God the grace to be asked on your exams only the questions which you knew, obtain for me a like favor in the exam for which I am now preparing or am about to take" (Huguenin 1962: 145-48). Other saints used by students include St. Jude, St. Theresa, and St. Luke. Students attend chapel before exams and sometimes bring rosaries to tests (Clawges 1989: 8).

Roy G. Biv and friends

Students also count on down-to-earth mnemonic devices. Typically passed into students' oral tradition, these devices organize complex lists into sayings or names that help the student commit them to memory. In grade school, students probably met the renowned "Roy G. Biv," a mnemonic device for remembering the order of colors in the spectrum (red, orange, yellow, green, blue, indigo, and violet). Young musicians learn the phrase "every good boy does fine" to remember the lines of the treble clef. In college the devices are often more elaborate, and many take a sexy—or sexist—turn. Electrical engineers learn the color code of resistors by remembering "bad boys rape our young girls but Violet gives willingly" (black, brown, red, orange, yellow, green, blue, violet, gray, white). Geology students learn the Mohs Scale of Hardness as "The girls can flirt and fairly queer things can do" (talc, gypsum, calcite, fluorite, apatite, feldspar, quartz, topaz, corundum, and diamond). Anatomy students might learn the bones of the wrist as "never lower Tillie's pants, Mother might come home" (navicular, lunate, triangular, pisiform, greater multangular, lesser multangular, capitate, and hamate). The Harvard classification for spectral classes of stars—O,B,A,F,G,K,M,R,N,S—is rendered by the sentence "Oh, be a fine girl, kiss me right now, sweetheart." At the Naval Academy, students remember the list of elements to correct the compass as "Can dead men vote twice?" (compass, deviation, magnetic, variation, and true). When going from true to compass, one can recall "timid virgins make dull companions" (Dundes 1961: 139-47).

Crib sheets and blue book scams

Cheating, students believe, might also help in getting good grades. Especially in large lecture classes with tests using multiple-choice and short-answer questions, students hear of traditional ways to cheat from "cheat sheets" or "crib sheets" (small pieces of paper with answers on them) to writing key words or mnemonic devices on one's hand.

There's wide belief among students that teachers try to "trick" or "throw off" students on exams. Such a gaming metaphor suggests that cheating on exams may be seen as part of the game. To students, the exam is apart from "real life," and involves high stakes—the grade (see Mechling 1988: 359). The exam, after all, is a framed activity—like a game—with rules, time and space limits, and restrictions on the resources used within the frame.

To listen to folklore concerning cheating, students feel that professors have an unfair advantage in the game, and cheating is a way students can even things up. Indeed, some of the stories suggest that more effort is put into cheating than into the studying the professor demands. Jay Mechling suggests that cheating may thus be a rewarding form of "deep play." "Cheating," he says, "may offer risks and thrills these adolescents and young adults find in few other places in their lives" (1988: 360). Students typically keep the game to themselves, and may have some guilty feelings about cheating, for they think that other students disapprove on moral grounds. To be sure, more than thirty colleges—including Roanoke, Smith, and Hood—have a tradition in their revered student-enforced honor codes allowing for unproctored exams (Berger 1988: 9).

A whole series of cheating stories uses the intimidating collegiate "blue book" as central symbol. It takes its name from its blue cover; inside it has eight to twenty-four white-paper pages with ruled lines. Blue books go back at least to the mid-nineteenth century, and in those days the whole book, not just the cover, was blue.

The most common blue book cheating story I collected is typically set in a large lecture class of three to five hundred students. Alan Mays of Penn State recalled the story about a student in such a class who was obviously cheating. "The proctor was going to intercept him at the end of the test when he turned in his blue book. The student brought his blue book to the front of the room and shoved it into the middle of the stack of blue books already on the table before the proctor could stop him. He asked the proctor 'Do you know who I am?' Then he turned to face the remaining students still taking the exam to ask them, 'Do you know who I am?' No one responded and he ran out of the room. Since no one could identify him or his blue book, he presumably succeeded in cheating and in getting a good grade on the test" (survey response, 1989). For the teller, the story raised the issue of the temptation to cheat created by a large, impersonal lecture class.

From Berkeley in 1982 comes this story of a stereotypical football player in a classroom of five hundred students: "During the final exam the player got out his notes and began cheating. The teacher saw him and thought he would nail him when he turned the exam in. When this guy went to turn it in and he made sure he was one of the last students working before the teacher came up to grab the exam. Instead of handing it to him he took all the exams on the table, shoved his in between and knocked them on the floor. As he was leaving he said 'find it' and he got away with it." The collector's commentary supports the idea of cheating as part of a collegiate game: "I see it as an another example of students 'beating the system' in the game with the faculty."

In many tellings of the story, the cheater in essence punishes the teacher for his lack of attention in such a large class. In other words, if the teacher deprives the student of a reasonable class, then the student will deprive the teacher of a fairly taken test. In variants, the student keeps on working after the proctor orders the class to stop. The proctor, usually described as being harsh and strict, threatens to punish the student, but the student pulls the trick of shoving the exam into a pile of exams and spreading the exams on the floor (see Brunvand 1986: 198-99). In another variant, the exam-taker is actually a paid substitute for an enrolled student. When the proctor tells the student that he doesn't recognize him, the exam-taker pulls the deception.

Lew Girdler dates his earliest blue book legend to 1937, collected from a Berkeley graduate student: "This student went into his final examination with an A-minus average. There were two essay questions. He knew nothing about the first one, but he was primed on the second. He filled his first blue book with just anything he thought of. Then he labeled his second blue book "II" and began it with what appeared to be the last sentence or two of the answer to the first essay question. Then on the second page of this second blue book he wrote "2" for the second essay question, and a beautiful answer to it. He turned in only the second blue book. A few days later he got a postcard from the instructor saying he got an A in the course and apologizing for having lost the first blue book" (1970: 111).

Another legend raising this issue concerns a two-page exam. The student didn't recognize the material asked for on the first page, so he spent all his time on the second page. When the period ended, he slipped the first page into his notebook and turned in the second page. Once outside the classroom, he hurriedly looked up the answers and filled in the first page. Then he stepped on the page. He gave the page to a friend who had a class in the same room. The friend approached the teacher after class and said he found the page "in the back." The teacher took it, checked through the papers collected in the morning class, and sure enough, found the page was missing. He graded all the papers and gave the student an A (Girdler 1970: 111-12; see also Jeakle and Wyatt 1989: 83).

From San Jose State College in 1967, Girdler reports another blue book legend: "A friend of mine tells this about her brother Jack, a sometime student. Jack found himself sitting in the classroom during an important examination with two blue books, a pen, and a question he couldn't answer. Being naturally bright, if lazy, he thought of the following solution. In one of the blue books he wrote a letter to his mother, telling her that he had finished writing his exam early but was waiting for a friend in the same class and so was taking the opportunity to write to her. He apologized for not writing sooner but said he'd been studying very hard for this instructor, who was a nice guy but had pretty high standards. When the time was up he handed in this blue book and left in a hurry with his unused one. He hurried to his text, wrote an answer, and then put the blue book in an envelope and mailed it to his mother in Boston. When the instructor found the letter he called Jack, who explained that he had written in two blue books and must have got them mixed up and if the instructor had the letter, the answer must be in the mail on the way to Boston. He offered to call his mother in Boston and have her send the envelope back as soon as she got it. He did, she did, and the blue book was sent back, with the inner envelope postmarked the day of the test and the outer envelope postmarked Boston" (1970: 112).

In some legends of a cautionary nature, the cheater is caught. One concerns a student at the University of Alabama who wasn't doing well in chemistry. Then he figured out a foolproof method of passing his final. The room was on the ground floor and his seat was next to the window. The ingenious student arranged a plan with his roommate. The roommate would wait outside the window, be slipped the exam by the student, and take it back to the dorm to answer the questions from the textbook. All went off as planned. The test went out the window, off to the dorm, back through the window, and up to be turned in to the prof within the two-hour test period. The student walked out happy. But when his marks came back, he found that he had failed. It seems that he had answered the questions a little too well. The roommate had used a typewriter.

In another legend that shows professors may not be as dumb as they look, Jan Brunvand reports the story of the University of North Carolina professor who steps out of his office the day before the final exam, leaving the door open and the pile of the next day's tests on the desk. A student comes by to ask a question and, finding the room empty, steals one exam. The professor, though, had counted the exams, and did so again the next morning before going to the classroom. Discovering one missing, he cuts exactly one half-inch from the bottom of all the remaining exams. When the tests come in, the student with the long paper gets a failing grade (1989: 285-86).

Smart answers
Another kind of story honors the noncomformist student who gives clever earthly retorts to lofty-sounding final-exam questions. Probably the most familiar is about the philosophy exam with the single question "Why?" While most of the students write lengthy essays, one student answers "Why not?" (or

"Because") and gets an A (see Toelken 1986: 511; Brunvand 1989: 286; Baker 1983: 109).

Brunvand reports a variant from Harvard concerning a course in freshman metaphysics. "When the students are settled for the final exam, the teacher places a chair on the desk in the front of the room. 'Prove that this chair exists,' he says. 'You have two hours.' As the students begin to chew their pencils and roll their eyes, one student leans back.... He writes, 'What chair?' submits his paper and leaves the room, just as the others begin to scribble furiously" (Brunvand 1989: 286). This student naturally receives an A.

One student who blanked out supposedly wrote on the final fall exam delivered to professor William Lyon Phelps of Westbrook College in Maine, "God only knows the answer to this question. Merry Christmas." The good professor returned the exam with the note "God gets an A; you get an F. Happy New Year" (Healy 1972: 21). The story also appears as a more generalized college jest: "During a Christmas exam, one of the questions was "What causes a depression?" One of the students wrote: 'God knows! I don't. Merry Christmas!' The exam paper came back with the prof's notation: 'God gets 100. You get zero. Happy New Year'" (Copeland 1940: 375).

Feeling that exams often test ability to memorize a narrow range of material rather than awareness of general, pragmatic knowledge, science students may recount the following story. On a physics exam, a student was asked how to determine the height of a tall building using a barometer. His answer: take the barometer to the top of the building, tie a rope to it, lower it to the ground, pull it back up, and measure how much rope was let out. He flunked on the grounds that, though his answer would work, he had not demonstrated any knowledge of physics. When the student protested his grade, his professor agreed to re-examine him. This time the student gave five answers (still resisting the obvious rote response—differential barometric pressures at the top and bottom of the tower): drop the barometer off the roof, time its fall and calculate the height with a particular formula; take the barometer out on a sunny day, hold it upright, measure the length of its shadow, measure the length of the shadow of the tower, and determine the height of the building with a simple proportion; measure the length of the barometer, climb the tower marking off lengths of the barometer on the inside wall, and multiply; tie the barometer to a string, swing it as a pendulum at the street level and at the top of the tower, measure the value of "g" at both points and calculate the height from the difference in the two values; and, the best and easiest way, take the barometer to the superintendent of the building and bargain with him thus: "Mr. Superintendent, here I have a fine barometer. If you tell me the height of this building, I will give you this barometer." For these answers, the student received an A (Moffatt 1989: 22; Dundes and Pagter 1987: 158-59).

The down-to-earth approach to examinations also comes up in the story of a student in a large class who is, as in so many student stories, unknown to the professor. "This student was taking an ornithology class, for which the final exam counted as half the grade. When the professor handed him his exam, the student was shocked to find that the entire exam was just pictures of birds' legs, with the directions 'Identify each species.' (In a variation, the professor sets up a row of stuffed birds with bags over their bodies so that only their feet show.) The student was furious, stormed up to the front of the class, ripped his paper into little pieces, handed them to the professor, and said, 'This is ridiculous!' The professor shouted back, 'You can't do that!' And the student returned, 'I sure as hell can!' The professor screamed, "Then you're going to fail this class. What's your name, anyway?' He pulled out his grade book to note down the offender's fate. The student pulled up his right pants leg to the knee and said, 'you tell me, Prof'" (Brunvand 1989: 277). In the story, the student is outraged at the difficulty of the question. As in many legends told by students, the student confronts the professor, often aggressively as a sign of the tension produced by the situation, and turns the table.

A number of the legends about clever retorts touch on the student nightmare of "blanking out." Richard Dorson reported the story floating around Harvard of "Robert Benchley's feat in handling a question in American diplomatic history on rights to the Newfoundland fisheries. Benchley knew nothing about the matter, so he wrote, 'This question has long been discussed from the American and British points of view, but has anyone ever considered the viewpoint of the fish?' He proceeded to give it, and was awarded, appropriately enough, a C" (1949: 673).

A more recently collected story from Stanford with a commentary on the special treatment of athletes concerns an exam in comparative religion. According to the student collector, "Comparative religion was the snap course football players traditionally took to restore sagging point averages at Stanford. The professor who taught the course...gave the same final exam year after year, and every fraternity had the exam in its files. One heroic quarterback taking the class during a hectic football season was thoroughly primed by his cohorts for the final, so that he could answer the prof's expected essay question.... The question was, 'explain the significance of and list in chronological order five kings of Israel.' Exam time arrived, and the confident gridder sat down to write his blue book. He was horrified when he saw the only exam question, one about which he knew absolutely nothing. The professor had finally wised up and changed his examination tactics by asking his students to 'compare the significant aspects of Shintoism and Buddhism.' Not to be so easily struck down, the gridiron stalwart gave it the old college try, and handed in an exam paper which began as follows: 'Far be it for me to intrude my humble intelligence upon so delicate a subject. Instead I will explain the significance of and list in chronological order five kings of Israel'" (Ligotti 1987: 6).

The story is similar to one reported by a student at a Cambridge, Massachusetts, seminary in the 1950s. "A certain Old Testament professor," he says, "always included on his final exam the question 'List the kings of Israel and Judah in parallel columns.' One year, however, he substituted the question 'List the names of the major and minor prophets in parallel columns.' One student alone passed the course when he began his answer by writing, 'Far be it for me to discriminate among such worthy men, but the kings of Israel and Judah in parallel columns are...'" (Brunvand 1989: 290). Apparently the teller from Stanford used the core of the story to express a parable for the special treatment of athletes within the university.

Finals, and other screams

Some legends suggest that the only way a student can turn in everything a professor demands on a final exam is to be out of this world. From Southern Illinois in 1966, for example, comes this testimony: "Everyone knows about the ghost exam. Prof. Adams of the History Dept. had it happen to him and it is one of the mysteries of campus. It seems that Prof. Adams gave one of his finals a few years back and this one girl turned in a nearly perfect paper. Now comes the truly weird part. It seems that Adams gave the exam on a Thursday but the girl had died in an accident, I think it was a car accident, the preceding Wednesday night. It is really strange but it is supposed to be true" (Procter 1966: 26). You hear these kinds of stories still around finals, especially during the dark days of winter.

The custom of the "primal scream" or "door slams" on campuses indicates the kind of tension that finals produce among students. A report from Franklin and Marshall states, "a 'primal scream' at midnight from one senior—'I can't take it anymore'—soon was supported by every student within chanting distance" (Brubaker 1987:46). At Southwestern University, the faculty cook a midnight breakfast the night before finals, and then during finals the students bellow out their annual scream. The tension from finals released by the scream is clear, but the connection of the scream to the quality of the meal is left somewhat ambiguous.

At Stephens, students prefer to take out their frustrations by slamming doors en masse, which then signals the start of twenty-four quiet hours in preparation for finals. At the University of California at Berkeley, a cry around finals has taken on the name of "Pedro" usually drawn out to "Peeeeeeeeedroooooh" which reverberates over the campus on a late evening. Alan Dundes explains the connection of Pedro with final examinations: "Typically, the president of the University (Wheeler, Sproul) or perhaps a dean or professor loses his pet dog. The sad owner announces that he will cancel finals if someone finds the dog. From that time on, students during the period of final examinations have called for Pedro in the hope of finding the lost dog and thus avoiding finals" (1968: 30; see also Hankey 1944: 29-35).

Papers...

Next to finals, term papers worry students most. Because students expect high grades for their trouble, they are at a loss to explain the varying grading techniques of professors. Folklore offers the kinds of explanations to which students can nod and smile knowingly. One story is that professors grade papers by throwing them down the stairs: those that land on the bottom get an A, those on the next step up get a B, and so on. Among the most widespread and persistent samples of folklore, the story carries an underlying belief that when it comes to papers, weight, not content, is what counts.

Variants of the story suggest that that professors really don't treat students as individuals, or that they make up their minds beforehand about the student's success. William Tillson recounted that "at Purdue, with its scientific bent, the students knew that blue books were thrown *up*stairs in order that the grade distribution more nearly approximate the bell-shaped curve" (1962: 56). Richard Dorson in 1949 told a story about his chemistry professor at Harvard who distributed his papers to his family: "he gave the Es himself, his son-in-law the Ds, and so on up to the baby, who, being the slowest, marked the As" (p. 673). Then there's the tale of "the professor who customarily placed his papers in two heaps, representing the good and the bad students. When he came across an error by a good student he disregarded it, saying, 'He knows better than that.' When he saw a correct answer by a poor student he marked it wrong saying, 'He couldn't have meant that'" (p. 673).

Professors arbitrarily piling papers in anal-retentive style frequently appear in student stories. Here's one I heard about a Duquesne professor in 1989: "He shuffled the exams and blindly separated the one pile into several. The first pile he designated the As, the second pile the Bs and so on." The story was also reportedly told in the nineteenth century about famed Harvard professor Nathaniel Shaler (1841-1906) who piled bluebooks in a mountainous heap on his sofa. After they had aged a week, he plunged both hands deep into the heap and carried all he could to a chair on the opposite side of the room. A second week went by and he carried another armload to another chair, and he made a similar move after the third and fourth week. Those in the first chair he gave As, those in the second got Bs, and so on. All those that slipped onto the floor flunked (Cowley and Reed 1977: 35). At Hope College, the Reverend Mr. Dykstra supposedly received grades for students directly from God (survey response, 1989).

Another belief questions whether professors really even take the time to look at papers, especially those of very large classes. If reading great quantities of written material is difficult for students, how could it be reasonably done by professors? Students thus tell about a paper handed in with a title page, a first page, and a bibliography. In the middle was a bunch of blank pages. The student received an A.

...and recycled papers

If a paper receives an A, however mysteriously, student stories ask "why not give it another go?" Jan Brunvand reports the story from California about an instructor famous for his low grading scale. "After years of giving only D's and F's, one year he finally gave a paper a B-minus—his highest grade ever. Word got around campus about the grade. Then the paper itself started to get around. The lucky student sold the term paper to the highest bidder, who then turned in to the same professor. This time he gave it a B. The paper was re-recycled again the next year, and it received a B plus. Just as the students were beginning to lose respect for the professor, the roving term paper was turned in a fourth time. This time it got an A. The teacher's written comment was, 'I've read this paper four times now, and I like it better each time" (Brunvand 1989: 286-87).

From campuses where fraternities keep files of successful papers comes the story of the student who pulls a paper from the file to hand in to a professor. The professor writes on it, "A—When I wrote this theme when I was a freshman, it only received a C and I always thought it worth an A" (Fitton 1942: 41; see also Brunvand 1989: 287; Baker 1983: 108). Jan Brunvand reports a story from a marine-biology course in which a student hands in an A paper with a slick illustration of a whale. The paper is recycled, but the third time around a student handed it in without the illustration. The written comment from the professor was "I liked it better with the whale."

To add to this cycle, Hope Coulter sent me her memory from Harvard of a course called "The Great Age of Discovery, 1400-1520," nicknamed "Boats." "A guy who had artistic leanings took the course one year and for the paper turned in a not-very-impressive piece of prose, triple-spaced, with big margins, but with an intricate line drawing of a ship included. He made an A. The next year his roommate took the course and turned in the exact same paper, with the drawing. He made an A, too. The third year another roommate of theirs took the course and turned in the by now two-year-old paper, but he thought it was too risky to include the line-drawing again, so he tore it out. The paper came back to him marked "C—where's the picture?"

Unwritten rules

Fitting in with student beliefs about the arbitrary nature of grading is the one about the "suicide rule." Students say that if your roommate commits suicide during the semester, especially late in the semester, you are entitled to an automatic "4.0" (an A in every course) for the semester. Although I have yet to find a college with such a rule, folklorists have found the belief at campuses from one coast to another. In a report from the University of California at Berkeley from 1982, a freshman offered the belief as an unwritten rule of the university; she heard it from someone on her floor who heard it from someone else during summer orientation. To these impressionable freshmen wondering about the grind lying ahead, the story confirmed the stresses of academic work and the importance placed on grades. A 4.0 for the semester, in other words, will make it all better, even the trauma of death close by. Reporting on Tufts, for example, Lisa Birnbach wrote, "People work for grades and the tension can get relentless," and then she quoted a student, "A lot of students think they'll die if they don't get an A in economics. You get a 4.0 for the semester if your roommate commits suicide" (p. 177; see also Brunvand 1989: 295-98; Moffatt 1989: 88; Cowan 1989).

On a related note, the bells of the Campanile at Berkeley play "Danny Deever" the last day before finals; students feel "close kinship with Danny Deever," Alan Dundes explains, because he "is executed by hanging" (1968: 30). In these stories, life is traded for the grade; in getting a 4.0 the student does not grieve, but rather takes the deceased student's place in line. The belief is so widespread that it has also entered into the grim humor heard around finals.

The student collector from the University of California reported that if someone would say in anguish, "I can't take this anymore!" someone else would humorously tease, "straight As for your roommate." She commented, "This kidding around usually eased the tension by assuring people that everyone else was feeling the same pressure."

The other famous unwritten rule known by almost every student is the one about waiting in class for a late professor. Professors get the most time, up to twenty minutes, while associate professors get perhaps fifteen, assistant professors five or ten, and lowly instructors no time at all. Although it's been reported by many generations of students, I have yet to find this rule in any college policy book (see Cannon 1984: 43; Toelken 1986: 518; Levine 1987: 28). As folklore, the rule serves notice of university hierarchy—among professors and among students—and of the structured campus existence, governed, as it so often seems, by a bewildering assortment of rules. This bit of folklore has one certain benefit: as undergraduate Michelle Blau from the University of California at Berkeley told a student collector, it "takes the responsibility off the students for deciding how long to wait."

Slang, from toadies to brownnoses

Students have a vocabulary they are sure is part of some official lexicon, but which rather is part of the collegian's folk speech. Among the most extensive lists are those for classes and types of students. Students identify easy courses as guts, cakes, puds, puddings, cinches, snaps, skates, and breezes; hard courses are bitches, screamers, grinds, and ball-breakers. During the nineteenth century, zealous students were called digs, fags, grubs, polers, or blues. Today, they are grinds, grunts, gunners, geeks, gweeps, dweebs, and throats. Students who gained teachers' approval were bootlicks, fishers, piscatorians, toadies, and coaxers. Now they're brownnoses and ass-lickers. The special derision in folk speech held for the grind comes from beliefs held by students regarding grading. Students believe that professors grade according to a standard set by the leading student. To hear professors tell it, there is a standard of work to be followed regardless of who is in the class. But "average" students think that they can do better if the grinds, marked as class traitors, would hold back.

Other forms of folk speech identify campus characters, especially those with privilege or specialty, knocked down a peg. Athletes are jocks, beef, and bulletheads. Those with aristocratic airs might be dubbed preppies, frat boys, or razor-necks. Popular students, or those that would like to be, are B.M.O.C. (big men on campus) or campus queens. It's worth noting that the slang for

unpopular students—the drudges, nerds, and geeks—matches closely the argot
for diligent students. Religious students are Bible bangers and Bible beaters;
students of agriculture are aggies, grangers, or sod-busters; and geology students are rock hounds, mud smellers, and pebble pups. Those in the Greek
system, or Greekdom, are frat rats and sorority bitches; at some campuses with
large fraternity populations, those not in the frats are called 'siders or outsiders,
hallmen, barbs or barbarians. Some fraternities and sororities have nicknames
such as Sig Pigs for Sigma Pi, Yak-Yaks for Acacia, Sammies for Sigma Alpha Mu,
and Gumbies for Sigma Tau to go along with the kinder names of Tri Delts for
Delta Delta Delta, Phi Psi for Phi Kappa Psi, and Delts for Delta Tau Delta.
Students also have plenty of expressive verbs. Miss a class and you're cutting it,
bagging it, or blowing it off; finally get to studying and you're cramming, boning
up, pounding or cracking (the books). Fail a course and you flunk it, or among
some black students, you punch it; get an A on it and you ace it.

Among the most frequently encountered collegiate nicknames are those
told in jest for schools, buildings, courses, and faculty. Some of these nicknames
reach well back in collegiate history. A source from 1856 lists Brick Mill being
used for the University of Vermont (Hall: 38); today, "mill" is more often
attached to large public universities dubbed "diploma mills." Other common
ones heard today are Zoo Mass for the University of Massachusetts, Suitcase U.
for Kent State, Silo Tech for Iowa State, and Moo-U for Michigan State. These
often change over time. Franklin and Marshall was known as Fast and Mushy in
the 1920s and Fumble and Mumble in the 1960s.

Music students at the University of North Texas refer to the Music Recital
Hall as the Purple Palace; at Millersville when you go to study at the Helen A.
Ganser Library, you're going to visit the Hag.

If some of these folk names are localized, others cross campus lines. Many
science buildings are known as bughouses, chemistry buildings are chem halls,
and student centers as unions or stud buildings. In colleges with examination
rooms, the name "sweatboxes" is commonly applied.

Nicknames for faculty appear to be especially strong in smaller colleges
with a unified community. At Setrales College, a school of around a thousand
men in 1969, students called faculty everything from Fuddy-Duddy for a fussy
professor to Leather Lungs for a loud faculty member. The largest percentage of
nicknames, almost twenty-eight percent, were attached to personality traits,
especially those displayed in class (McGeachy 1978).

Morsels from the curricular menu

Sometimes students lampoon the whole curriculum. During the 1960s, a time of student unrest, a sheet went around about the course offerings at the University of California (sometimes Columbia or another school was substituted). It listed freshmen courses as Riot 101, Insurrection 121, Russian 101, Lab (Riot Technique), and Political Science 101, Dirty Books 101, Russian 102, Insurrection 122, Lab (Mob Rule), Arson Techniques 101, and Arson Lab. By the time the student gets to the senior year the courses are Introduction to Free Love, Beard Growing 311, Sandal Mending 302, and Rules and Regulations for Understanding Welfare and Unemployment Collection (Dundes and Pagter 1978: 138-40).

Much has changed in student attitudes during the materialistic 1980s. The most common lampoons of course offerings now list Money Can Make You Rich, Talking Good: How You Can Improve Your Speech and Get a Better Job, Overcoming Peace of Mind, The Repair and Maintenance of Your Virginity, and High Fiber Sex (see Dundes and Pagter 1987: 266-67).

Many students across the country call an introductory geology course Rocks for Jocks, a western history course Cowboys and Indians, and a children's literature course Kiddy Lit. Sociology courses on deviant behavior often become Nuts and Sluts, modern art turns into Spots and Dots, and introductory music into Tunes for Goons (see Sykes 1988).

In their courses, students have to "hit the books," and they hurl some of their sharpest barbs at academic book titles. Commenting on their reading load, and showing considerable creativity, students of literature at the University of Delaware came up with a technique to cut in half the number of pages to be read. They proposed combining at least two major works of literature into a single work. Some results were *Catch-22,000 Leagues Under the Sea* by Verne Heller, *As I Les Miserables* by Hugo Faulkner, *Dr. Faustus and Mr. Hyde* by Thomas Lewis Stevenmann, and *The Stranger in the Rye* by Camus D. Salinger.

Other titles are bawdier and are reminiscent of parodies found in children's folklore, although they often relate to problems in college such as *The Worried Maiden* by Pastor Period, *The V.D. Symptom Book* by Urine Trouble, and *Wasted to the Max* by Iona Syringe (see Dundes and Georges 1962: 224; Doyle 1973: 52-54; Clerval 1986-87: 139-41; Aman 1986-87: 141-42).

Studying and other games

Humor about the grind of student life plays a great role in releasing tension and revealing, by both affirmation and denial, some gut attitudes. In 1986, I recorded Penn State students jokingly telling me why they don't study. Senior Chris Detweiler made the pronouncement, "The more you study, the more you know, the more you forget. The less you study, the less you know, the less you forget. So why study!" The lines have been around at least since 1940 when they appeared in a collection by Lewis and Faye Copeland (p.375).

The role of studying appears in a jest that also suggests sexual tension between students and professors. A young attractive coed visits her male professor's office and announces that she will do anything for a good grade in the class. "Anything?" the professor asks with a smile. "Yes, anything," she replies. The professor leans closer and startles her, saying, "Try studying then!" (see Toelken 1986: 505; Carey 1988: 7; Mr. "J" 1981: 92).

Although students sometimes claim to disdain anything resembling studies and tests, they have folk versions of their own in the form of mental games played back at the dorm. In "Dictionary," for example, one person chooses a word from the dictionary at random. This word should be one the others don't know. The dictionary holder pronounces the word out loud and spells it for the group. The other players write down their guess at what the word means. The dictionary holder meanwhile writes down the real definition. The holder then collects all the pieces of paper and reads each one. They are read randomly, so that the other players do not know which person wrote which definition. Each player tries to guess which one is right. After each person has voiced a guess, the dictionary holder tells the correct definition. Players get points if someone else voted for their definition or they guess the correct definition; the dictionary holder gets a point if no one guesses the correct definition.

Another "test" students give one another takes the form of deductive riddles. Once given, the oral exam is commonly turned into a riddle contest. Also going by the name of "logic puzzles" or "thought games," the texts are apparently illogical or unusual situations, especially involving death, which have shaggy-dog twists; most often, they appear to be mini-murder mysteries (Dorson 1959: 267; Moore 1974: 119-25). The riddler may state the following: "A man is found hanging from the ceiling in a locked, empty room. There is a puddle of water. How did he die?" The answer is that he stood on a block of ice (Penn State Folklore Archives, 1978). In a variation, the riddler says that the man had burns on the bottom of his feet rather than giving the information about the puddle (Moore 1974: 119). The test-taker may respond with this one: "There is a man playing ping pong in a room locked from the inside. There is a spider web in the corner. The man dies. How?" The answer is that "The web caught the ping pong ball, and the man thought someone was in the room with him and had a heart attack because he was blind" (Penn State Folklore Archives, 1978). There are scores of these kind of riddles, and a contest can last quite a while (see Sentman 1972).

Another intellectual folk test that is popular with students can also go on and on. Going by the name of Botticelli, the "game" is elaborate because participants are simultaneously test-takers and test-givers. The game involves guessing the identity of a famous personality, fictional or real, in history, art, music, or literature. A leader gives only the initials of the celebrity, and the group guesses by listing credentials that fit such figures with the same initials. Each time the leader cannot figure out the name that another player has in mind, he or she must answer truthfully a direct "yes or no" question about the original celebrity (Brunvand 1986: 385). I was introduced to this game in graduate school in New York and I've heard it from students since from one coast to the other. I still remember it as the main time-killer when we students pooled together to drive to some distant conference. A simpler variation of this game is Twenty Questions, in which a group guesses a historical or literary figure. The group gets twenty questions to come up with the identity of the figure.

Absent-minded professors...
The person on campus with the answers is supposed to be the professor, but anecdotes freely question this authority. Student folklore portrays professors as absentminded, arrogant, dull, impractical or lacking common sense, singlemindedly devoted to their subjects, and always in danger of going "over the edge." The most commonly heard absent-minded professor anecdote in my collection is about the particular professor on campus who walks around in a haze.

Here's one, turned in by a student collector in 1969, about a philosophy professor from Calvin College. "Professor Runner is a brilliant philosopher, but very absent-minded. He walks around in a trance most of the time. In fact, a friend went up to Professor Runner one day on campus to ask him a question. When he was through answering the question, Runner asked if he had been coming out or going into the cafeteria. 'Out,' said the friend. 'Thank you,' the professor replied, 'then I must have already had lunch'" (Berkeley Folklore Archives; see Toelken 1986: 507; Wilgus 1972: 25; Jackson 1972: 5).

In one variation, the student asks the professor the way to his office. The professor replies "If it is that way, then I've had my lunch; if the other way, then I must be on my way to it" (Wyman 1979: 85). According to George Carey, the story as it is told at the University of Massachusetts has the vague professor answering a student's invitation to lunch with "Which way was I headed when you stopped me?" "Toward Bartlett Hall," says the student. "Sorry, then," says the professor, "I can't join you. I've already eaten" (1988: 8)

Students also report the story about philosopher Irwin Edman of Columbia and mathematician Norbert Wiener of MIT (Cowley and Reed 1977: 37; Jackson 1972: 5; Wilgus 1972: 25). Indicating that this anecdote goes back well before those esteemed figures were around, a related story is told about Isaac Newton, the great English physicist who taught at Cambridge during the late seventeenth century. A friend paid the great scientist a visit one evening. The servant announced that his master was in his study and not to be disturbed. The visitor decided to wait since it was approaching Sir Isaac's dining hour. The table was set and in a short time a boiled chicken under cover was brought in. Time passed. The fowl was growing cold, but Sir Isaac did not appear. Finally, being hungry, the visitor devoured the fowl and covered up the empty dish. At the same time he asked the servant to have another chicken boiled for Sir Isaac. But before the second bird was ready, the great man came down. He apologized to his visitor for his delay and added, "Give me leave to take my short dinner, and I shall be at your service; I am fatigued and faint." He then took the cover off the dish, and finding the plate empty, turned to the visitor with a wan smile. "You see what we studious people are; I forgot that I had dined" (Cowley and Reed 1977: 36).

The professor stories are mostly about men, dominant yet apparently helpless men. From Purdue and Illinois comes the story of the professor asked by his wife to change clothes for dinner. Finding himself in the bedroom undressed, he could think of only one reason to be there, and put on his pajamas and went to bed at 6:30 p.m. (Tillson 1962: 55-56; Dorson 1949: 672). From Gettysburg College in 1974 I heard about the professor who drove his car to Philadelphia to do research. Forgetting he had driven, he took the train back (see also Jackson 1972: 6). Richard Dorson offered a version in 1949, with the additional detail that the professor "bawled out his wife for not meeting him at the station with the auto" (p. 672). He also gave the related story of the Harvard professor who drops his wife at a mailbox (sometimes it's a gas station rest room) and then continues on his journey. Some time later he notices her absence and informs the police.

In addition to showing that professors are more mindful of their studies than of their loved ones, some of these stories also suggest that professors are used to having things done for them. Consider the story from Cornell of the professor who had announcements appear almost simultaneously of his new book and his wife's new baby. The professor, when congratulated by a friend about the "proud event in your family," naturally thought of that achievement which had cost him the greater effort. He modestly replied, "Well, I couldn't have done it without the help of two graduate students" (Keseling and Kinney 1956: 148).

Some of folklore's surest demonstrations of absent-mindedness occur during the classroom lecture. For example: A biology professor comes into the class with a paper bag stuffed with something and announces that today the dissection of the frog will be demonstrated. He reaches into the bag to get the frog, but finds a ham sandwich instead. He scratches his head and says to the class, "Hmm. I wonder what I ate for lunch" (Jones 1977: 11-12).

In a variation commenting on female professors, the young English professor reaches behind her ear for her pencil. Instead she finds a tampon. Startled, she asks, "What did I do for my period this morning then?" A carryover from jokes in adolescent folklore, this story uses the symbolic tampon to show the vulnerability of women as they enter into professions (Bronner 1985: 39-49).

Several professor stories resemble old numskull tales like those in international circulation about the man who searches for an axe which he carries on his shoulder, or who doesn't recognize his own horse (motifs J2025.1, J2023, from Thompson 1966:169). From Berkeley in 1964, comes this story told by Carolina Clare, who learned it, she said, from another student at Arizona State. "A professor came into class one day, took his wrist watch off, and placed it on the desk in front of him so he could watch it as he lectured. He began his lecture, stopped, looked at the watch, picked it up, and said, 'I find someone's wrist watch here on my desk. Did anyone lose it?' A student raised his hand and suggested that the professor take the watch to lost-and-found after class. The next day the professor came to class and announced that he had lost his wrist watch. He asked if anyone had found it.

Mac Barrick, a Dickinson alum, told me of the history professor in the 1940s who wrote a list of things he had to do when he got home, walked to the post office, and mailed it to himself "special delivery." He hurried home so he would be there when it arrived. This reminds me of the numskull tale about the fool who writes himself a letter. When someone asks what the letter says, he replies that he doesn't know because he won't get it until the next day (motif J2242.3, Baughman 1966: 326).

From Cornell comes the story of the professor who eased back to his office after class. He found a long line of students waiting in front of the door, so he took his place at the end of the line (Cowley and Reed 1977: 36). This numskull story bears some resemblance to the one reported in 1940 about the professor who rings his housebell and is answered by a new housekeeper. "Um-ah—is Professor Thompson at home?" he asks, naming himself. "No, sir," she replies, "but he is expected any moment now." The professor turns away and the housekeeper closes the door. Then he sits down on the steps to wait for himself (Copeland: 386). Or there's the absentminded professor who jabbers well into the night about theories with his guests. Finally, one guest says, "I hate to put you out, but I have to meet a nine o'clock class in the morning." It seems the professor thought he was at his own house (Cowley and Reed 1977: 37).

Sometimes forgetfulness is blamed on singleminded devotion to one's subject, often displacing connection to people. Richard Dorson, for example, gives the story of a University of Texas professor of ichthyology, walking across the campus with a colleague. A student greeted the professor, who answered impersonally. "Don't you know the name of that friendly student?" the colleague asks. "I have made it a point," replied the ichthyologist, "never to learn the names of my students. Whenever I remember a student, I forget a fish" (1949: 672). The story apparently dates from much earlier, for it is reportedly told about David Starr Jordan, who came to Stanford as president in 1891 after establishing an international reputation for his encyclopedic knowledge of fish and their classification. In this story, however, the professor is less arrogant, for he "determined that he would also come to know each student by name." Several years later he was asked how he was progressing. Jordan sadly said he had given up. "I found that every time I learned the name of a student, I forgot the name of a fish" (Cowley and Reed 1977: 36).

...and arrogant ones

The arrogance of professors is nowhere better shown than in the migratory legend about renowned teacher-scholars who do not hold the Ph.D. When asked why he never pursued the degree, the professor haughtily snaps back "Who would examine me?" The story is frequently attached to famed professors George Lyman Kittredge and Bernard De Voto, who taught at Harvard from 1888 to 1936 and 1929 to 1936, respectively (see Reuss 1974: 306; Emrich 1972: 324). Yet the story is updated in our day to describe any distinguished professor without the doctorate. For instance, the story is told about the noble-sounding Richebourg Gaillard McWilliams of Birmingham-Southern College who presided over forty-two years of literature and composition classes (Raines 1986: 46), and about R.L. "Beowulf" Brown of Middlebury College (Carey 1988: 7).

Professors who have the Ph.D. and appear enthralled with themselves might have the story told about them of a car ride shared with a younger associate. For five hours the great one reminisces about himself, his writings, and his friends in the field. Finally at the end of this time, he looks at his junior companion and says, "Well, I've talked enough about me. Now you talk about me for a while!" (Reuss 1974: 313).

Professors can do no wrong, or so they think, anyway. There's the college professor instructing a military economics class on technical terms. The professor explains the terms with the aid of diagrams on a chalkboard. When a student remarks that he had misspelled a word, he quickly answers, "Like I always said, I consider a person dumb if he can't think of more than one way to spell a word" (Mitchell 1976: 563).

In some stories, students fight back. One such story is frequently attached to the United States Military Academy at West Point, but can be heard about a number of demanding institutions. Here's one version from the late 1970s: A young cadet was preparing a physics paper to prove that if all the toilets at West Point were flushed simultaneously, the water pressure would be sufficient to burst pipes throughout the plumbing system on campus. His professor returned his paper saying the idea was nice, but the figures and calculations used for the computations were in error and it would not work. In a furtive attempt to prove his theory, the cadet arranged for the "West Point Flush." Plumbing burst all over campus, and supported his theory. He was still given a failing grade on the paper, but no one challenged it for credibility.

Students, aware of the "publish or perish" motto in academe, believe that professors treat them as secondary to their writing tasks. One story circulates about prolific Harold Bloom of Yale who was called at his home in New Haven by a graduate student. Bloom's wife answered, "I'm sorry, he's writing a book." "That's all right," the student replied, "I'll wait" (Parini 1989: 1, 24).

Sometimes students show their resentment of the famed professor who is everywhere but in class. From Sarah Lawrence College comes the story of the professor who becomes so fond of giving outside lectures that he decides to tape his weekly remarks to his seminar group. He sends an assistant to lead the group in his place. When he unexpectedly returns early because of a canceled engagement, he goes right to his classroom to see how his students are getting along. As he opens the door, he hears his own voice coming out of the tape recorder—and in the students' places are twelve other tape recorders ("Campus" 1963: 217-18; see also Toelken 1986: 505).

What contributes to these sometimes outlandish stories about their professors? For starters there's the fact that at many campuses, faculty—involved in research, with offices far from student hangouts, or maintaining a professorial image—keep their personal distance from students. The distance allows for student speculation in story. At the same time, students feel they need to "scope out" their professors, to know what they're like so as to know what to expect from them in class, on exams, and particularly at grading time. Students, in the best American anti-authoritarian tradition, recognize the authority of professors over them and use folklore to bring the faculty down a notch or students up a few. Many of the stories humanize professors, reducing their authority and showcasing their fallibility. As people priding themselves on intellect, professors are often shown to be lacking in sense, and especially lacking in personality.

Students typically judge harshly the performance of professors in class. It's not just that a professor can be dull, but that he or she is in control, right or wrong. From Wisconsin comes the story of the geography professor lecturing from faded notes, droning along about the Mississippi River dumping each year 9,980,000 tons. He turned the page and started another topic. A brave student asked, "The Mississippi River dumps each year 9,989,000 tons of what?" The professor turned the yellowed page back, and again intoned, "The Mississippi River each year dumps 9,989,000 tons," paused, turned the page, and said, "It don't say" (Wyman 1979: 85).

At Ohio State, the story gets around about the lecturer who began reading in a wheezy, cracked voice. At the bottom of page one, he turned the leaf and continued reading. What he read repeated the first page, and the third was the same. The typist had delivered the notes to him in triplicate (Cowley and Reed 1977: 36; see also Carey 1988: 7). In a variation I received from Harvard, the story is about a famed philosophy professor who lectured on logic. Previous to the class, some graduate student sneaked into his office and disarranged his lecture notes. When the professor read through his notes, however, he didn't notice the difference (survey response, 1989).

Science students like to tell about the faulty logic of their instructors, or even fellow students, with the story of the frog-jumping experiment. The scientist put the frog on the floor, told it to jump, and it jumped. He measured the distance and wrote down in his book, "Frog jumps 12 feet with both legs." Then he cut off one of the frog's legs, put the frog on the floor, and told it to jump again. It did, and the scientist measured the distance and wrote in his book, "Frog jumps 6 feet with one leg." Then he cut off the frog's other leg, put the frog on the floor, and told it to jump. The frog just sat there. After about five futile minutes of telling the frog to jump, the scientist wrote in his book, "Frog can't hear with both legs cut off" (Baker 1986: 101). Variations exist with fleas, flies, and grasshoppers (see Beezley 1981: 117; Mitchell 1976: 449-50). During the 1960s and 1970s, the story was frequently reported as a "Polack" joke, an ethnic version of the moron or numskull jest (Motif E6.8, Clements 1969: 21; Mitchell 1976: 334, 622-23).

A related story appears much earlier, in the 1840s, this one from Yale. "A young physician, commencing practice, determined to keep an account of each case he had to do with, stating the mode of treatment and the result. His first patient was a blacksmith, sick of a fever. After the crisis of the disease had passed, the man expressed a hankering for pork and cabbage. The doctor humored him in this, and it seemed to do him good; which was duly noted in the record. Next a tailor sent for him, whom he found suffering from some malady. To him he *prescribed* pork and cabbage; and the patient died. Whereupon, he wrote it down as a general law in such cases, that pork and cabbage will cure a blacksmith, but will kill a tailor'" (Hall 1968: 433).

If a professor's thinking can be faulty, sometimes in lore it can appear downright deranged. The ultimate sign of going over the edge, especially in the worst dreams of students, is the failure to hand in grades. From Sul Ross State College (now University) comes the story of a man who was no longer on the faculty. "The man had gone to pieces. His wife had left him; and although he was reputed to be a good teacher, well liked by students, he had become troubled and embittered to the point of incompetence. On the last day of finals he started hitting the bottle with abandon. The three-day period for turning in grade reports elapsed. The dean, unable to locate the man at his home, finally reached him at a disreputable bar across the tracks. Since the drunk professor had no grades prepared, the dean attempted to read his class rolls to him and secure the grades in that manner. The effort proved useless, however, and the dean had to make some disposition of the grades himself, since the best response he could get to his calling off of the names was comments of the order, "That bitch? Give her a D!" or, "Hell, flunk ol' Gibson, the bastard!" (Bratcher 1972: 121). Sometimes the story reflects on a professor who goes over the edge because of a divorce. The professor can't recall any names until Mr. Smith comes along. "I remember him now," he says, "Give him an A—poor devil, he's married" (Bratcher 1972: 122).

Again there's a nineteenth-century precedent, this one from Cambridge in 1896. Describing elderly tutor Walter Pater, the author offers that "his temperament, it is true, sometimes made it difficult to work with him. On one occasion, at the examination for scholarships, he undertook to look over the English essays; when the examiners met to compare marks, Pater had none. He explained, with languor, 'They did not much impress me.' As something had to be done, he was asked to endeavour to recall such impressions as he had formed; to stimulate his memory, the names were read out in alphabetical order. Pater shook his head mournfully as each was pronounced, murmuring dreamily, 'I do not recall him,' 'He did not strike me,' and so on. At last the reader came to the name of Sanctuary, on which Pater's face lit up, and he said, 'Yes; I remember; I liked his name'" (Bratcher 1972: 122-23.)

Legendary characters

As the last story shows, many collegiate stories are attached to specific legendary characters. A strong cycle of stories, for example, revolved around the great Harvard professor of literature George Lyman Kittredge (1860-1941), often referred to as "Kitty" by his many students of ballad, folklore, and English literature. Characterized as a distinguished, imposing figure, possessed of a stern New England morality, Kittredge once encountered several undergraduates raucously singing "The Bastard King of England." He rapped his cane sharply on the brick sidewalk and ordered them to stop singing. He told them that it was ungentlemanly to abuse the night in such a way. "Behind those open windows," he said, "are ladies in bed who cannot help but hear the words you are singing." The students apologized profusely. As he left, he tapped his cane, turned and told them, "By the way, the words you were singing to that last stanza were not quite correct. They should go like this..." (Emrich 1972: 323). When a brash character supposedly asked Kittredge how much time he spent preparing for his class, he cut in, with authority and dignity, "A lifetime!" (Rollins 1961: 168-69). This sounds like the story about literature professor Frank O'Malley of Notre Dame. At a reception honoring a pretentious visiting professor of psychology, the pedant condescendingly asks what O'Malley's field of specialization might be. Eyeing the man coldly, O'Malley replies, "What field? Why, my dear man, the entire world" (Leary 1978: 134-35).

Kittredge supposedly expected traffic to stop when he crossed the street. Also in line with his lofty status, the story is told about his working in his office and startling the cleaning woman with his presence. She jumps and exclaims "Jesus Christ!" "Not quite Madam," Kitty grandiosely replies, "merely his loyal and humble servant, G.L. Kittredge." Sporting a beard, but almost no hair on the top of his head, Kittredge is the subject of an off-color joke about the coed who approaches him one day to ask his definition of a eunuch. "A eunuch," he answers pompously and a bit obscurely, "is a one-balled man." "But aren't you a eunuch then?" asked the confused girl, noticing his hairless pate. "No, my dear," said Kittredge, a gleam in his eye, "I am a two-balled man" (Reuss 1974: 314).

Stories also abound about the great mathematician, cybernetics pioneer, and MIT professor Norbert Wiener (1894-1964). In the stories, he appears absentminded, myopic, brilliant, savagely moral, egotistical and at the same time insecure. Although absentminded he is capable of prodigious feats of mind and memory. Wiener supposedly was able to tell students exactly where books, even the most obscure, were located in the library, but he couldn't find his own house. It seems that Wiener and his family bought a new house. They had been living in the old place for years and years and they needed a place with more room for the growing family, so they moved out of their house. Knowing of his absentmindedness, his wife gave him a slip of paper with the new address. She even put it in his coat pocket. Wiener took the train from their home to spend the day at MIT, and when he came home, just as his wife expected, he went straight for the old house. He remembers then that he moved and that his wife wrote out the new address for him. He begins to look through his pockets, but then remembers that the new address is in his raincoat, which he left at his office. A little girl passes by on a bicycle, and Wiener is sure she lives in the neighborhood, so he stops her and says, "Little girl, little girl, I'm professor Wiener. I used to live here, but we moved today and I don't know where the new house is. Do you know where my family moved?" She replies, "Mommy thought you'd forget, Daddy" (Jackson 1972: 4; Wilgus 1972: 25).

Wiener's work and the lore about it epitomizes the bridging of science and the human condition. In one anecdote, a Naval computer problem has all the experts stumped. He had designed the sophisticated, top-secret computer for a ship out in the middle of the ocean. When the Navy bigwigs approached Wiener for help, he folded his arms behind his head and leaned back in his chair. Then he thought for a minute and told the baffled officers to remove a panel in the computer, behind which they would find a mouse that had eaten through one of the wires (Jennings 1986: 16). Yet this is the same professor who walked into a freshman calculus class and started writing difficult equations on the board. A freshman raised his hand and after a while, Wiener noticed him. "Yes?" "Ah excuse me, sir, but, I, um, think you're in the wrong classroom. This is freshman calculus. "Oh," Wiener said and walked out the door. Five minutes later, still waiting for their instructor to come in, the freshman notice that Wiener had come in the back door and begun writing differential equations on the back board (Jackson 1972: 6).

Migratory legends about asking someone the direction he was headed so he can figure out whether he had lunch or not, and the one about driving to a destination and taking the train back, forgetting that he took the car, are commonly attached to Wiener. Beyond his absentmindedness, however, are stories bringing out his poor eyesight, a trait often attached to professors in folklore. Supposedly Wiener had moldings put in so he could find his way from his office to his classroom. According to a legend collected from an MIT alum in 1982, Wiener liked to read while walking around the room feeling for the moldings. But one day a class was in session inside an open door off the hall and Wiener walked right around the door jam and circumnavigated the classroom, before heading back out (see also Jackson 1972: 12-13). He also went blindly around the room when he wrote on the board. He finished at the blackboard and kept on going writing on the walls and the doors and everything that came into his way. He got into such a habit with this behavior that the school supposedly built a room for him with blackboards on four walls (Wilgus 1972: 24).

Also of legendary stature is Notre Dame professor Frank "Big O" O'Malley (1909-1974). One story is about his extended lecture on James Joyce. The lecture is stunning in both its clarity and complexity. An admiring student offers congratulations as the professor fumbles to put away his notes, only to observe that these notes are blank sheets of paper (Leary 1978: 134-35; see also Woodward 1984).

Another literature professor, Fred L. Pattee (1863-1950) of Penn State (in whose honor the library was named), has a similar story told about him. Pattee handled the devotional part of the college's morning chapel services. One morning he opened the big chapel Bible and proceeded to read, or so it seemed, one of the longer psalms. Admiring his delivery but suspecting some variation from the text, a student took a look at the Bible. Pattee later explained to the student's amazement, "I forgot my glasses and had to read from memory" (Pattee 1953: 342-43).

Students looking for their comeuppance over these imposing figures often find it in jests about exam situations. There's the one about a logic professor from Ohio State who wants to give his classes a difficult question. He determinedly asks the class "The United States is bounded on the north by Canada, on the south by the Gulf of Mexico, on the east by the Atlantic Ocean and on the west by the Pacific Ocean. How old am I?" A student blurts out "You're forty-four." The professor is amazed. "Right, but how did you reason it out so quickly?" "Well," the student explains, "I have a cousin who's twenty-two and he's only half crazy" (Keseling and Kinney 1956: 120). In a variation, the math professor addresses the question to a freshman: "If there are 48 states in the Union, and superheated steam equals the distance from Bombay to Paris, what is my age?" (Copeland 1940: 380).

In a commonly heard anecdote that reveals student stereotypes of professors, the instructor comes into the class for the first time. Standing at the podium, he condescendingly addresses the students. "If there are any dumbbells in the room, please stand up." A long pause ensued and then a lone freshman stood up. "What, do you consider yourself a dumbbell?" asked the professor. "Well, not exactly sir, but I do hate to see you standing up by yourself," said the freshman (Keseling and Kinney 1956: 116; Copeland 1940: 375).

Another story in which the professor is embarrassed concerns the professor lecturing on the Magna Carta. "You in the back," he calls out, "What was the date of the signing?" "I don't know that," comes the relaxed reply. "You don't! I assigned this stuff last Friday. What were you doing last night?" "I was out drinking beer with some friends," comes the reply. The professor puffs, "You were! What audacity to stand there and tell me a thing like that! How do you ever expect to pass this course?" "Wal, I don't know. Ya see, I just come in to fix the radiator," comes the cool response as the professor turns red (Copeland 1940: 376).

Another puffy professor neared the close of a history lecture and was indulging in a rhetorical climax when the hour struck. The students immediately began to slam down the movable arms of their lecture chairs and prepared to leave. The professor, annoyed at the interruption of his eloquence, held up his hand: "Wait just one minute, gentlemen. I have a few more pearls to cast" (Copeland 1940: 383). Sometimes the closing line is "casting imitation pearls before real or genuine swine" (Toelken 1986: 505; Dundes 1968: 28-29).

As for the legendary pedantry and dullness of professors, a story is told about the religious lecture at Hobart. The lecturer used the six letters forming the name of the institution for the headings of the subdivisions of his extended address. "H" stood for holiness, "O" for obedience, "B" for beneficence, "A" for adoration, "R" for righteousness, "T" for triumph. He gave fifteen or twenty minutes to every subject. As the students made their way for the exit, one student said to another, "Damned good thing we aren't attending the Massachusetts Institute of Technology!" (Copeland 1940: 382). A related story concerns one Professor Brown explaining himself on the telephone. "No—not Bond—

Brown. B as in Brontosaurus, R as in Rhizophoracae, O as in Ophisthotelae, W as in Willingbalya, and N in Nucifraga. Do you comprehend?" (Copeland 1940: 383).

Reflecting the dramatic increase in the numbers of immigrants' children entering colleges during the twentieth century are a few dialect jokes in student repertoires. I recall often hearing one such joke at story-swapping sessions while I attended Harpur College (part of SUNY at Binghamton) during the early 1970s. Harpur drew many children and grandchildren of East European Jews from New York City. The story was told of the parents who sent their boy upstate to the fancy-shmancy college (sometimes the school is Harvard or Yale), so that he could talk like an highfalutin educated American. They go with the boy to the school to ask the aristocratic English prof to give him special attention. "Oy, von't you tich ar' boy so he can spik vonderful?" "Harumph," the prof says in his best Brahmin English, "I shall see what I can do with this savage tongue to improve his diction." They return at the end of the year to find out how the boy is doing. They come into the prof's office and ask him his opinion. The illustrious prof tells them "Oy da boy spiks poifect" (Leacock 1935: 181-82; Cottom 1989: 8).

Sex in the classroom

A great deal of student humor about the classroom involves sexual themes. In these stories, the young student who has sex on the brain is contrasted to the crusty professor who conveys the innocence, or self-denial, of intellectual pursuit. There's the joke about the professor discussing the question of human and divine origins. The graybeard prof asks the young coed, "Who made you, little girl?" She answers, "Originally or recently?" (Legman 1968: 75). There's also the tough prof who gives students painful quizzes, which he irritatingly calls his "little quizzies." After the third or so ordeal with these "quizzies," a coed tells her classmate, "If those are his quizzies, I hate to see his testies!" (Brunvand 1962: 62).

Probably the most common off-color story concerns the prof who instructs the class to write an essay including four subjects: religion, royalty, sex, and mystery. The prof coldly announces, "It'll take quite some time to write an essay of this nature and smoothly incorporate all subjects, so please begin." About fifteen minutes later, a boy raised his hand and announced that he was finished. The startled prof says, "I don't see how you can be finished with an essay of that nature in that short a time." "Well, I have," said the smiling student. "If you think so, read it aloud." The student read, "'My God,' said the queen, 'I'm pregnant. I wonder whose it is?'" (Baker 1986: 194-95; see also Legman 1975: 90). In a collection from the University of Arkansas at Fayetteville Folklore Archives, the responding student is an Aggie transfer student who turns in, "'Good God,' said the homecoming queen, 'I'm pregnant. Who did it?'" (1973). In a variation from USC, the prof demands brevity, religion, royalty, and modesty. The student finishes quickly and reads the result, "'My God,' said the countess, 'take your hand off my knee'" (Carlinsky 1971: 117). Gershon Legman records a version of this variation as early as 1935 from the University of Michigan (1975: 90).

Another frequently reported joke is about the college professor of anatomy who asks, "What organ of the body enlarges to six times its natural size?" No one answers. The professor redirects the question to Miss Smith. She responds, "Well, I, um, I don't see why I should be called on to answer such a question!" The professor then announces, "Everybody gets zero for not studying today's lesson. The only organ of the body that can enlarge to six times its natural size is the pupil of the eye." In some versions the professor looks at the embarrassed student and says, "And as for you, you're due for a terrible disappointment" (Legman 1968: 140). In a variation, the question is "What portion of the body becomes harder than steel?" and the answer is "the fingernails. And as for you, you're nothing but an idle dreamer." Sometimes the student flees from the embarrassment, and the professor innocently asks the class, "What's so bad about the pupil of the eye?" (Toelken 1986: 507).

Anthropology professors soberly delivering their graphic descriptions of exotic rituals are the subject of a widely circulating joke, sometimes told as a legend. The professor describes a tribe in Asia, South America, or Africa that is known to have a penis fifteen inches and longer when in the state of excitation. At this point two or three coeds get up and start to leave the room, either because they are offended or need to go to another class. He shouts at them, "It's no use being in a hurry to get there, girls. The boat probably won't leave for another week" (Brunvand 1960: 250-51; Tillson 1962: 55; see also Brunvand 1962: 62). In a twist that bears a resemblance to the plots of some international tale types, the professor, this time of anatomy or biology, purposely describes the tribe's parts to shock coeds right out of his class. All but three leave when he cites the measurement, and the rest walk out when he delivers the punch line (Brunvand 1960: 251; see Aarne-Thompson Tale Type 1828 about the parson who preaches so that half the congregation weeps and other half laughs. It turns out he preached without breeches.).

The story about the wisecracking professor has been collected in America since the 1940s at Columbia, Michigan, Purdue, Detroit, and Indiana, and it's still getting around. A possible precedent is in a story attached to English anthropologist A.C. Haddon (1855-1940) who taught at Cambridge. "He was discussing Sociology," according to an account, "and, as happened so often when he was talking about his Torres Straits Islanders, had exceeded his hour. He was describing how in some islands the women, not the men, make the proposals of marriage, when the women students from Girton College, knowing that their cab would be waiting impatiently outside, unostentatiously slipped out at the back. The temptation was too great. He called out, 'No hurry, there won't be a boat for some weeks'" (Brunvand 1960: 250).

Coeds take much of the sexual heat in these jokes, partly as a contrast to the stereotype of the cold male professor, and a general pattern in society to target young women for humorous sexual derision (see Legman 1968, 1975). A story comes from Northwest Missouri State College in the 1960s, for example, about the geography professor who explains that the term "backward" is no longer used when describing the economy of a primitive state. To avoid hurting the pride of such countries, the term "underdeveloped" is considered preferable. Looking around the lecture hall, he saw one student who didn't seem to understand the psychological implications of the two words. "Well, Miss Turner," he asked, "Which would you rather be—underdeveloped or backward?" Her quick reply was "Backward, sir!" ("Campus" 1966: 56).

Another joke comes from campuses as far flung as Harvard, Indiana, Antioch, and Michigan State. A psychology professor bans knitting in his class because, as he states, "You know, knitting is a form of socially acceptable masturbation." In the next class session, one coed is knitting. The professor says, "Young lady! Did you hear my last lecture?" The coed replies, "When I knits I knits and when I masturbates I masturbates" (Brunvand 1962: 62). Related is the story about the guest professor at an eastern university who is aghast when several coeds calmly take out knitting bags and begin to ply their needles. He could hardly finish the hour. By the time the class met again, however, he was ready with a solution. "I have an important announcement to make," he says. "It is simply this—only those young ladies will be permitted to knit in class who are pregnant." There was no more knitting in his classes ("Campus" 1962: 180I; see also Brunvand 1960: 251).

Women also take heat in many of the old stories because they symbolically intrude into a formerly male preserve. They are accused of distracting the men and upsetting the intellectual focus of the college. A Milton professor, for example, is supposed to have walked into his classroom on the first day and asked all the young women in the front row to cross their legs. "Now that the gates of Hell are safely closed," he says, "we may begin our discussion of *Paradise Lost*" (Toelken 1986: 505). The Dean of Women according to legend meanwhile advises women never to wear patent leather shoes on a date, for they reflect underwear. "Never wear a red dress, it inflames," she adds, and "don't eat olives, they're passion pills" (Hunter 1977: 12). Many of the jokes appear to emphasize the importance placed on the appearance and submission of the coeds. College humor typically emphasizes the submission of students generally, but with jokes on coeds, the sexual theme becomes more pronounced.

One exemplary anecdote with medieval roots is told about the young looker who proposes marriage to Professor Einstein. She explains to the famous teacher that with her looks and his brains they could have wonderful children. The professor responds, "But my dear, what if they had *my* looks and *your* brains" (Johnson 1960: 248-49). It is as if the sexuality of coeds, not their intellect, is their main asset to be developed.

When they're not claiming merely to be having a laugh at the expense of the unusual college situation, students, both male and female, may use the jokes as weapons in the battle of the sexes played out on the campus battlefield. In some mixed settings, students use jokes for sexual teasing, especially at their age of sexual awakening, although college men's risqué humor tends to be more obscene and hostile (Mitchell 1985: 163-86). In some of the more recent stories, the question is raised whether coeds come to college for a degree or a husband. Maybe, as some students like to tease, there are women who come for a MRS. degree. Yet I have no equivalent joke for college men looking for a wife. Men in the jokes value work, aggression, and dominance.

Evidence of humor responding to women as student workers is in this joke currently making the rounds of the campuses. "This man was sitting in a bar one night and an attractive young woman came in alone and sat down beside the man at the bar. After a few minutes the man attempted to start a conversation by asking her for a match, but to his surprise she said in a loud voice, 'What kind of girl do you take me for?' Now the man was very embarrassed because everyone in the bar glared at him so he turned away and went back to his drink. After a few minutes the woman was still sitting beside him and he began to think that possibly he had been a little forward and might have offended her somehow. So he said, 'I'm sorry if I appeared forward when I asked for a match. I was only trying to be pleasant.' The woman answered in a loud voice, 'How dare you make such insinuations? If you don't leave me alone I'll have the police called!' The guy still couldn't figure out what he was doing wrong, but he realized that he had better just leave and avoid any real trouble. He finished his drink and quickly headed for the door, but before he could leave the young woman had caught up with him and said, 'I think I owe you an explanation. I'm a graduate student in sociology and I'm studying people's reactions to an embarrassing situation. You were a good subject and I'm sorry if I upset you.' To which the man replied, 'Fifty Dollars?!'" (Mitchell 1976: 512-13).

Some of the jokes are signs of change, for they draw attention to out-of-favor attitudes. Others in this era of change are showing up with women in tough academic roles. "How many feminists does it take to change a light bulb?" students ask. "One to screw it in and five to teach courses (or write books) about it." An alternative answer is "That's not funny!" (Dundes 1987: 145-46). From Pennsylvania and Oklahoma, and probably elsewhere, comes the story of a feminist professor, a Spenser scholar, who supposedly had the name of the alley where she lived changed from Jenkins' Rear to Faerie Queene Lane (collected 1989).

Fun with photocopiers

Much of the student humor is now being passed with the help of the photocopier. An important academic tool on campus, the photocopier also can serve students' social ends by spreading folk expressions put into a form with which they instantly associate—paper. A well known piece of photocopied humor is a letter home from a young coed. Like the oral humor I have been surveying, the photocopied pieces repeat and vary, and are often anonymous in origin. One version, circulating around Oklahoma in 1988, catalogs students' views of parents' worst fears (see Dandes & Pagter 1978:40-41).

Dear Mother and Dad,

It has been three months now since I left for college. I have been remiss in writing and I am very sorry for my thoughtlessness in not writing before. I will bring you up to date now, but before you read on, please sit down. You are not to read further unless you are sitting down, okay?

Well, then, I'm getting along pretty well now. The skull fracture and the concussion I got when I jumped out of the window of my dormitory when it caught fire shortly after my arrival here is pretty well healed. I only spent two weeks in the hospital and now I can see almost normally and only get those sick headaches once a day.

Fortunately, the fire in the dormitory and my jump was witnessed by an attendant at the gas station near the dorm, and he was the one who called the fire department and the ambulance. He also visited me in the hospital and since I have nowhere to live because of the burnt-out dormitory, he was kind enough to invite me to share his apartment. It's really a basement room, and it's kind of cute. He is a very fine boy and we have fallen deeply in love and are planning to get married. We haven't set the exact date yet, but it will be before my pregnancy begins to show.

I know how much you are looking forward to being grandparents and I know you will welcome the baby and give it the same love and devotion and tender care you gave me when I was a child. The reason for the delay in our marriage is that my boyfriend has a minor infection which prevents us from passing our premarital blood tests and I carelessly caught it from him. This will soon clear up with the penicillin injections I am taking daily.

I know that you will welcome him into our family with open arms. He is kind and although not well-educated, he is ambitious. Although he is of a different race and religion than ours, I know your oft-expressed tolerance will not permit you to be bothered by this fact.

Now that I have brought you up to date, I want to tell you that there was no dormitory fire, I did not have a concussion, or a skull fracture, I was not in the hospital, I am not pregnant, I am not engaged, I do not have a disease, and there is no miscegenation in my life. However, I am getting a "D" in history and an "F" in science, and I wanted you to see those marks in the proper perspective.

Your loving daughter

Many examples of photocopied folklore, like the body of oral folklore, concern exams. In the photocopied folklore students can parody the form of the exam as well as its content. Appropriate to a technological form with an emphasis on appearance and a modern service role that emphasizes the bland formal front or performance, much of the photocopied humor is understated, mimicking therefore the style as well as the form of technological service products. A photocopied sheet circulating with "Student Death Tag" at the top is an example.

This tag is to be attached to a student only after death has been established using the following procedure.

If, after several hours, it is noticed that the student has not moved or changed position, the professor will investigate. Because of the highly sensitive nature of our students and the close resemblance between death and their natural classroom attitude, the investigation will be made as quickly as possible in case the student is asleep. If some doubt exists as to the true condition, extend a copy of an exam as a final test. If the student does not recoil, it may be assumed that death has occurred.*

*Note: In some cases the instinct is so strongly developed that a spasmodic shuddering and shirking reflex may occur after death. Don't let this fool you.

This bit of student folklore appears to be an adaptation of photocopied humor circulating around corporate offices since the 1960s (Dundes and Pagter 1978: 86). Sent from "Your Big Brother," the parodied memo is entitled "Instructions on Death of Employees." It notes that "a close resemblance exists between death and the normal working attitude of employees," and a pay check is used as the final test. Whoever adapted this text to the college scene must have associated the conditions of mass corporate bureaucracy with their own in the large university.

Students ridicule university entrance exams, especially for a rival university. One common example floating from photocopier to dorm room usually has twenty questions. Q: Where do they bury people living west of the Mississippi? A: Please do not bury living people! Q. What is Smokey the Bear's middle name. A: The. Q: What can you fill a bucket full of to make it lighter? A: Holes (*Seventh* 1988: 10-11).

Other parodied entrance exams use the ancient rebus form, such as this one from Texas A&M (*Tenth* 1988: 14-15; see also Dundes and Pagter 1987: 139-41; Preston 1982: 104-121).

r/e/a/d/i/n/g   Reading between the lines.

stand
I   I understand.

0
M.D.
Ph.D.   Two degrees below zero.

ii   ii
o   o   Circles under the eyes.

dice dice   Paradise.

he's/himself   He's beside himself.

ecnalg   Backward glance.

r
road   Crossroad.
a
d

t
o
u   Touchdown.
c
h

death/life   Life after death.

Another popular piece of photocopy humor highlights what students feel is the unreasonableness of college exam questions, especially in the normal time given. Like other forms of photocopied occupational lore, this humor emphasizes the extraordinary demands on laborers to perform animatedly, to do everything and do it well (see Dundes and Pagter 1978, 1987; Bronner 1984). This particular example has been collected since the 1970s from California to England (see Dundes and Pagter 1987: 160-61). This version came to me from Oklahoma in 1988.

Instructions: Read each question carefully. Answer all question. Time limit-4 hours. Begin immediately.

HISTORY: Describe the history of the papacy from its origin to the present day, concentrating especially but not exclusively on its social, political, economic, religious and philosophical impact on Europe, Asia, America, and Africa. Be brief, concise and specific.

MEDICINE: You have been provided with a razor blade, a piece of gauze and a bottle of Scotch. Remove your appendix. Do not suture until your work has been inspected. You have fifteen minutes.

PUBLIC SPEAKING: 2,500 riot-crazed aborigines are storming the classroom. Calm them. You may use any ancient language except Latin or Greek.

BIOLOGY: Create life. Estimate the differences in subsequent human culture if this form of life had developed 500 million years earlier, with special attention to its probable effect on the English parliamentary system. Prove your thesis.

MUSIC: Write a piano concerto. Orchestrate and perform it with flute and drum. You will find a piano under your seat.

PSYCHOLOGY: Based on your knowledge of their works, evaluate the emotional stability, degree of adjustment and repressed frustrations of each of the following: Alexander of Aphrodisias, Ramses II, Gregory of Nicea, Hammurabi. Support your evaluations with quotations from each man's work, making appropriate references. It is not necessary to translate.

SOCIOLOGY: Estimate the sociological problems which might accompany the end of the world. Construct an experiment to test your theory.

MANAGEMENT SCIENCE: Define management. Define science. How do they relate? Why? Create a generalized algorithm to optimize all managerial decisions. Assuming an 1130 CPU supporting 50 terminals, each terminal to activate your algorithm, design the communications interface and all necessary control programs.

ENGINEERING: The disassembled parts of a high-powered rifle have been placed in a box on your desk. You will also find an instruction manual printed in Swahili. In ten minutes a hungry Bengal tiger will be admitted to the room. Take whatever action you feel appropriate. Be prepared to justify your decision.

ECONOMICS: Develop a realistic plan for refinancing the national debt. Trace the possible effects of your plan in the following areas: Cubism, the Donatist controversy, the wave theory of light. Outline a method of preventing these effects. Criticize this method from all possible points of view. Point out the deficiencies in your point of view, as demonstrated in your answer to the last question.

POLITICAL SCIENCE: There is a red telephone on the desk beside you. Start World War III. Report at length on its socio-political effects, if any.

EPISTEMOLOGY: Take a position for or against truth. Prove the validity of your position.

PHYSICS: Explain the nature of matter. Include in your answer an evaluation of the impact of the development of mathematics on science.

PHILOSOPHY: Sketch the development of human thought; estimate its significance. Compare with the development of any other kind of thought.

GENERAL KNOWLEDGE: Describe in detail. Be objective and specific.

EXTRA CREDIT: Define the Universe. Give three examples.

Also for extra credit you can answer the Shakespeare question (see Mitchell 1976: 223-24). This version comes from a coed at Berkeley, 1978, who got it from some English majors at the school.

Identify each block in the diagram with one Shakespeare play.

miscarriage		
wet	dry	
3 "	6 "	9 "

Moving left to right and down from the top, the answers are *Love's Labour Lost, A Midsummer's Night Dream, Twelfth Night, Much Ado About Nothing, As You Like It,* and *The Tempest.* In some versions the last block is *The Taming of the Shrew.*

For English 101, you might see a parody of the rules of grammar—otherwise known as the "rools of grammore" or "grammer as wrote." Here are some highlights from the list (*Ninth* 1982; see also Dundes and Pagter 1978: 39-40; Dundes and Pagter 1987: 121-22).

1. Don't use no double negatives.
2. Verbs has to agree with their subject.
3. Try not to over split infinitives.
4. Just between you and I, case is important to.
5. Proofread your theme to see is any words out.

The photocopier has circulated around campuses many parodies of songs held sacred. The "Battle Hymn of the Republic" has long been a target for students since elementary school when they sang, "Mine eyes have seen the glory of the burning of the school, We have tortured every teacher and we've broken every rule" (Bronner 1989: 97-99). Here's a collegiate version, where the "final" battle between teacher and student occurs in thermodynamics (see also Pankake 1988: 101). This often-copied songsheet came from Wayne State by way of the University of Maryland where it reportedly came from MIT, or was it Ohio State?

Free energy and entropy were whirling in his brain
With partial differentials and Greek letters in their train
With Delta, sigma, gamma, theta, epsilon and pi
Were driving him distracted as they danced before his eyes

Chorus:
Glory Glory dear old Thermo
Glory Glory dear old Thermo
Glory Glory dear old Thermo
We'll pass you by and by

Heat content and fugacity revolved within his brain
Like molecules and atoms that you never have to name
And logarithmic functions doing cakewalks in his dreams
And partial molal quantities devouring chocolate creams

They asked him on this final if a mole of any gas
In a vessel with a membrane through which hydrogen could pass
Were compressed to half its volume what the entropy would be
If two thirds of delta sigma equalled half of delta pi

He said he guessed the entropy would have to equal four
Unless the second law would bring it up a couple more
But then, it might be seven if the Carnot law applied
Or it almost might be zero if the delta T should slide

The professor read his paper with a corrugated brow
For he knew he'd have to grade it, he didn't quite know how
Till an inspiration in his cerebellum suddenly smote
As he seized his trusty fountain pen, and this is what he wrote

Just as you guessed the entropy, I'll have to guess your grade
But the second law won't raise it to the mark you might have made
For it might have been a hundred, if your guesses were all good
But I think it must be zero 'til they're rightly understood

Final Chorus:
Glory Glory dear old Thermo

Glory Glory dear old Thermo
Glory Glory dear old Thermo
We'll try again next year.

Parodying all the scientific laws students must memorize as well as the ubiquity of rules on campus, students frequently circulate the "Laws of Applied Terror." This one comes from Penn State Harrisburg in 1981. I first saw it hanging in a student club lounge, and it spread quickly from there.

1. When reviewing your notes before an exam, the most important ones will be illegible.
2. The more studying you did for the exam, the less sure you are as to which answer they want.
3. Eighty percent of the final exam will be based on the one lecture you missed about the one book you didn't read.
4. Every instructor assumes that you have nothing else to do except study for that instructor's course.
5. If you are given an open-book exam, you will forget the book. Corollary: If you are given a take-home exam, you will forget where you live.
6. At the end of the semester you will recall having enrolled in a course at the beginning of the semester—and never attending.

These laws resemble "Murphy's Laws," sometimes known as "Finagle's Laws," circulating in many offices and labs around the country. So as not to expect success all the time, or so as not to be disappointed when things don't go the way you want, Murphy's Laws boil down to "If anything can go wrong, it will" (see Dundes and Pagter 1978: 69-75).

Besides laws, other revered texts such as prayers and scripture commonly receive parody in student life. Parodies of this sort are known generally in American culture, but some have been designed specifically for the student's lament (see Monteiro 1964, 1976). Here's a parody of the twenty-third psalm circulating in photocopies from Oklahoma.

The professor is my quizmaster, I shall not flunk. He maketh me to enter the examination room; He leadeth me to an alternative seat; He restoreth my fears. Yea, though I know not the answers to those questions, the class average comforts me. I prepare my answers before me in the sight of my proctors. I anoint my exam papers with figures. My time runneth out. Surely grades and examinations will follow all the days of my life, and I will dwell in this class forever.

It's fitting to close this chapter with a scriptural parody floating around Indiana universities about the last days of finals, just before the time of judgment.

And it came to pass early in the morning of the last day of the semester, there arose a multitude smiting their books and waiting. And there was much weeping, and gnashing of teeth, for the day of judgment was at hand and they were so afraid. For they ought to have done, and there was no help for it.

And there were many abiding in the dorm who had kept watch over their books all night, but it naught availeth. But some there were who arose peacefully for they had prepared for themselves the way, and had made straight the path of knowledge. And these wise ones were known to some as the burners of the midnight oil, and by others they were called curve lousers.

And the multitudes arose and ate a hearty breakfast, and they came to the appointed place and their hearts were heavy within them. And they had come to pass, but some they were to pass out.

And some of them repented of their riotous living and bemoaned their fate, but they had not a prayer. And at the last hour there came among them one known as the instructor, he of the diabolical smile, and passed papers among them and went upon his way.

And many and varied were the answers which were given, for some of his teachings had fallen among fertile minds, others still had fallen flat. And some there were who wrote for one hour, others for two, but some turned away sorrowful. And many of these offered up a little bull in hopes of pacifying the instructor, for these were the ones who had no prayer. And when they had finished, they gathered up their belongings and went away quietly, each in his own direction, and each one vowing to himself in this manner—"I shall not pass this way again, but it is a long road that hath no turning."

No, life need not end with finals. The release, the amusement, the fantasy, the truth, the perception, the connection, the collective wisdom of folk story and belief keep many a student alert. Also enlivening student spirits on the turn in the road that is college are some fun and games away from class. It is this festive, social side of the college experience that I survey next.

Sophomores hamming it up at Penn State, 1908. (Penn State Room, Pattee Library)

"Remember the Fun"

The college experience is one of transition. It's a bridge between aspiration and occupation, freedom and responsibility, parents and community, dependence and independence, adolescence and adulthood. With its dormitories and distractions, it's a place without much comparison in the child or adult world. Away from home, away from family and friends, in competitive pursuit of learning, students are set out on their own—and naturally seek other young, lost souls. A host of games, rituals, festivals, pranks, songs, and other traditions help provide social bonding, cultural growth, and individual transition. In the old-time college, the school often took much of the responsibility for attending to the festive needs of students, but now students mostly fend for themselves.

Greenies in dinks

The first adjustment comes when students arrive as freshmen on campus. In the old-time college, frosh wore identifying coverings on their heads ("beanies," "pots," or "dinks"), or ribbons, often colored green to signify the novice state, on their clothes. In addition, they might have worn name tags to identify themselves, but lettermen nonetheless called them "rats," "greenies," "plebes," "fish," "scrubs," "slimers," "babes," and "booloos" to underscore their lowly biological status in the college niche. The sophomores posted signs around campus warning the freshmen to "Tremble and Obey," as one read at Berkeley (Dundes 1968: 21). Even more colorful were signs advising the frosh to know the Alma Mater, to divest of all high school articles, to avoid stepping on grass, to wear green ties and dinks, and to attend all events, among other demands and prohibitions. At different campuses, the signs carried headlines with similar blustery rhetoric, as these two attest:

> Suckling Frosh Beware! Ye mewling, pewking Babes, ye green and spineless
> Gonionemi, Taeniae Solia, Ascares Lumbricoides, Fasciolae Hepaticae of 1929,

hearken to the edicts of the supremely ILLUSTRIOUS CLASS OF 1928. Grovel then, ye infants, before the thunderous reverberations of our ultimatum.

(Franklin and Marshall)

Proletarians of ye measly, slimy, despicable, uncultured class of 1916 PROSTRATE yourselves to the most illustrious and omnipotent class of 1915. Now that you have absorbed sufficient knowledge into your sterile brains, to warrant your entrance into the sacred portals of RUTGERS COLLEGE the class of 1915 has condescended to become supervisor of your future conduct HARKEN ye boobs and obey these '15' commandments, bi-laws, and instructions which the honorable class of 1915 has deemed it proper to promulgate for your conscientious perusal and absolute assimilation."

(Rutgers)

To learn the hierarchy of the campus, frosh sometimes paid respect to seniors with a bow, performed stunts, and ran errands for upperclassmen. Here's a graphic description from the diary of one Penn Stater in the 1880s. "Soon after our arrival in town the visits from the sophomores began. They were usually dressed in black sateen shirts and corduroy trousers, and a slouch hat or a cap bearing the class numerals. Each carried a huge paddle which was sometimes used to induce cooperation on the part of the freshman. At those times the hazing took the nature of digging for water in the unpaved dusty road, praying for rain, barking at the moon or possibly delivering an impromptu speech. A favorite request was to deliver a three minute speech on Hereditary Barrenness. If the freshmen dared to resist the sophomore's tauntings they could very well find themselves in a molasses feed. The erring freshmen were required to take off their clothes and cover themselves with molasses. The sophomores provided them with a few coats of feathers until the humiliated freshmen looked something like a walking pile of leaves" (Bronson 1968: 1,4).

The frosh could get the better of the sophomores in a roughhouse competition. Preparation for these competitions built class unity and instilled male values of competition, toughness, and perseverance thought to be necessary for success in college and in the professions that awaited them after college.

Many old-time colleges condoned these activities because they were thought to release the "animal spirits" of the men and redirect them at one another. (The colleges preferred this to the violence directed at the faculty and administration during the early nineteenth century.) The severe—if playful—indoctrination, schoolmasters thought, quickly made college men out of high

Freshmen feathered by sophomores for violating initiation rules, 1910.
(Penn State Room, Pattee Library)

school boys. It gave them no time to dwell on home, quickly forged friendships among the classmates, and replaced old family or community loyalties with ones focused on the class and college. As with other primitive rites of passage, freshmen initiation moved from a ritual separation of the new recruits to a transitional stage, where challenges and tasks are put before the initiates, to an incorporation stage, in which they are united into the community (see Van Gennep 1960; Young 1962; Vizedom 1976; Raphael 1988). Initiation ridiculed the freshmen's past and set their minds on the future, specifically on achieving the privilege of upperclassmen. At the same time, upperclassmen learned to maintain their advantage, and protect (somewhat imperially) their campus status over the lowly elements of society.

Another justification for freshmen hazing was that once past the manageable, playful traumas of initiation, students were more capable of withstanding the stresses (mild by comparison they thought) of studies and examinations. Finally, as a preparation for the adult world of work and family, students were reminded of the hierarchical order of society. Especially when social evolutionary thought was in its heyday in the late nineteenth century, the idea of climbing from the lowly, despicable depths of freshman ignorance to the privileged pinnacle of senior enlightenment was akin to the struggle up the theorized social ladder from savagery to civilization. It led, some college officials thought, to a natural selection of the fittest in the academic evolution of students.

Freshman hazing and class competition are not completely a thing of the past. At Howard Payne University in Brownwood, Texas, a small Southern Baptist school founded in 1889, freshmen initiation today lasts two weeks and still involves hazing reminiscent of the old-time college. On the first or second Friday of the fall semester, freshmen attend "Round Up" in a campus auditorium. They sit on the bottom floor of the auditorium, and the upperclassmen in the balcony throw toilet paper and other objects, while shouting "poooor freshmen" or "fresh meat." Then the upperclassmen line up outside while the freshmen, dubbed "fish," receive their beanies. As the frosh leave they are pelted with shaving cream, eggs, flour, and water. Each frosh is assigned a big brother or sister for the two weeks. During initiation, the "fish" scrub the cement pond with toothbrushes, and serve the upperclassmen by answering requests to fry like bacon, look for an imaginary contact lens, recite poems, and sing songs, or perform "mini ha-ha's." (In this latter ritual, a group of freshmen lie on one another's stomachs and laugh, each one adding another "ha.") The initiation has its share of special days. On "dress-up day," the upperclassmen get to dress the fish in any kind of costume they want, and finally, on switch-out day, the frosh get even with their big brother or sister.

Rushes and scraps

From the eighteenth century to the early twentieth century, colleges allowed, even encouraged, class "scraps" and "rushes." As early as 1794, a mass sophomore-freshmen wrestling match was reported at Harvard, later superseded by a no-holds-barred football game (Hall 1968: 500). Through the nineteenth century, a favorite, if hazardous, "scrap" at many campuses involved the whole freshman and sophomore classes in a contest to push a giant ball to one end of a field. Many injuries and a few deaths occurred in these donnybrooks, leading to the tradition's demise.

Class "scrap" between freshmen and sophomores, 1916.
(Penn State Room, Pattee Library)

In the "cane rush," the frosh and sophs vied to get the most hands on each other's canes—class badges and symbols of adult maturity. The "cider rush" at Penn State involved deception as well as brawn. Freshmen sneaked a barrel of cider on campus, and claimed victory if they could deliver it to the juniors. The sophomores sought to foil the plot by spilling or capturing the barrel. In a few years, after reports of broken bones and lacerations, the rush was held with an empty padded barrel.

Penn State also featured a "picture rush." The freshmen had to make arrangements for a class picture, while the sophomores tried to break it up. In 1908, the rush disrupted six class sessions in two weeks when rumors spread among the sophomores of an impending freshmen picture (Dunn 1973: 8-9). The "flag rush" was a military-style event in which the freshmen put their flag to wave atop Old Main. These rushes became marathons, with reports of injury-ridden rushes commonly lasting as long as five days. At Tufts, the tradition ended in 1900 after a freshman drew a pistol on a roommate (Miller 1966: 397).

A milder version of the rush still is the highlight of the first week at small Juniata College. In the "storming of the Arch," freshmen assert themselves by annually attacking the sophomores and wresting control of the symbolically named Cloister Dorm from them. The men hurl eggs and tomatoes, and try to humiliate each other by stripping opponents.

As classes became larger and contained more women, and as some colleges encouraged a more egalitarian or relativistic view of society, many class competitions went by the wayside. According to Penn State's Fred Pattee in 1928, "as the number of students increased and classes began to approach the thousand mark, as in all growing universities, the scraps assumed dangerous proportions and some were abolished by Student Government action" (p. 5).

The manly battle between the classes continued in many colleges with the biggest and strongest chosen to represent the class in tug of war and tie-up scraps during the first week. In the tie-up scrap, fifty men entered on each side for six five-minute periods. Contestants had a length of rope with which they tried to bind the hands and feet of opposing classmen. The class with the most claims of binding the enemy won. In variations, tie-ups meant kidnapping officers of the opposing class and holding them until the opposing class relented. At Emporia State in Kansas until the 1950s freshmen normally removed their beanies at the homecoming football game, where they threw them up in the air at halftime, but they could remove them earlier by challenging the sophomores in a tug of war across a lake (Maxwell 1987: 11).

Today, probably the most celebrated class battle occurs at Hope College in Holland, Michigan. Beginning in 1897, the "Pull," as it is known there, involves two teams of eighteen men tugging a six hundred foot, twelve hundred pound hawser rope. Both have student coaches who work their teams across opposite sides of the muddy Black River. One modern addition has been the "morale girls," who cheer and comfort the contestants. As the contest begins, the morale girls provide drink and food, shout encouragement, tape wounds, and give blankets. No longer a contest over the right to remove beanies, it is now a matter of pride and spirit at the small liberal arts college. The event also has a way of bringing men and women together in embrace. In 1977, the Pull lasted a record three hours and fifty-one minutes, in contrast to the two and one-half minutes

The ''Pull,'' Hope College, 1988.

Victory for the Freshmen! Hope College, 1988.

Tug of War between freshmen and sophomores at Penn State, 1919.
(Penn State Room, Pattee Library)

of 1956. In 1988, the 92nd Pull was won after a three-hour struggle, appropriately enough, by the class of '92. If you're keeping score, the sophomores have won thirty-four times, the frosh eighteen.

The women's way

Women in colleges developed often separate initiation rituals serving to instill some different values. Artistry and creativity, rather than brawn, typically are the order of the day. At Hope College, freshmen and sophomore women compete for the coveted Nykerk Cup established in 1936. "Song women" sit properly unbent with gloved hands on their laps; "morale guys" offer support with booming cheers and thoughtful gifts. Several hundred women present a play and an oration, and participate in the chorus. Although judges determine a winner, the women—in the spirit of cooperation—have a ritual "meeting in the middle," a chaotic conglomeration of all the happy participants in which losers can't be separated from winners.

Vassar upperclasswomen welcome the frosh the first week of school by serenading them in their dorms with class songs. Amidst beer and Vassar Devils (ice cream with chocolate cake and sauce), the frosh kneel to the seniors and respond with a song composed for the occasion. The event climaxes when each house sings for administrators, and the senior class officers and the president of the college select a winner.

At Chatham College, a small women's college in Pittsburgh, Pennsylvania, the song contest began in 1921, but died during the turbulent 1970s. In 1985, the tradition was revived with the encouragement of alumni. The victorious class wins a cup for singing the traditional Chatham song and a song of their own making. The original song offers the students a chance to lampoon themselves. The winning entry for 1986 was "Our Favorite Things" set to the tune of the same name:

> U of Pitt doctors and CMU hackers
> Tartans and Panthers and Steeler linebackers
> Duquesne musicians they all come to call
> We've mixers and parties and dates with them all.
> Fall Fling and Egg Nog and Thanksgiving Dinner,
> Cookies and turkey won't help us get thinner,
> Candlelight Service the joy that it brings,
> These are a few of our favorite things.

Sometimes called "songfests," or "stepsings" when they are traditionally held on the steps of a college hall, the contests often coincide with parents and alumni weekends early in the fall semester. At Hood College, a women's college in Frederick, Maryland, each class prepares two songs—one on a theme for the competition and another for the big sisters of the class. Each class enters the chapel in a different way. The frosh, for example, run in with one hand on their dink-adorned heads and the other at their sides, and at the signal of the "song leader," the line stops and sits down. The sophomores, in class skirt and blouse, jog in with their hands behind their backs; the juniors, decked out in class blazers, saunter in snapping their fingers; and the seniors, befitting their lofty status, walk in slowly wearing black robes. Since 1923, a similar tradition has thrived at Cedar Crest College, a small women's college in Allentown, Pennsylvania, where, according to a school publication, "Song Contest is to Cedar Crest what football is to Ohio State—the tie that binds."

Many women's colleges also have "lantern nights" early in the first semester. At Bryn Mawr near Philadelphia, a lantern-giving tradition begun in 1896 celebrates Athena, the goddess of wisdom. Representatives of the three upper classes present wrought-iron lanterns to new students at a solemn ceremony in October. Dressed in black academic gowns, participants assemble at dusk in a cloistered garden at the heart of the campus. Upperclasswomen sing a Greek hymn as they present the lanterns, and the new students respond with one of their own after they receive the gifts (Briscoe 1981: 119-50). Since 1921 alumnae at the University of Pittsburgh's "Lantern Night" have offered the gift to incoming women to light their way in the search for truth over the following four years. In a variation at Cedar Crest, students use candles to symbolize carrying on the spirit and tradition of the college. During the first vespers service in September, each "big sister" lights a candle from the flame at the altar and would then turn to brighten the unlighted candle of her frosh "little sister."

The big sister, little sister (and less frequently, big brother, little brother), tradition is a longstanding institution, especially at women's colleges. Big sisters help underclasswomen get set up at the college. They throw parties for them, show them the ropes, and generally look after them. At schools such as Agnes Scott and Hood, the student body is organized by sister classes. Juniors are sisters to freshwomen and seniors are sisters to sophomores. The sisters are often bound in a mock wedding ceremony.

At Cedar Crest, little sisters present big sisters, dressed in black, with long-stemmed yellow roses at a candlelight dinner. After the meal the little sisters form an arch through which the juniors walk to a ring ceremony. Each junior is called to the stage and a ring is put on her finger.

At Wells College in Aurora, New York, a school of approximately five hundred women, every frosh is assigned a "sister" from each of the three upper classes. Introductions are made in surprise summer letters with unknown addresses. This nurturing relationship develops a family tie on campus. At Wilson College, freshwomen receive an "Aunt Sarah," a graduate of the college who corresponds with the student once each month.

At Keuka College, about the same size as Wells, each sophomore chooses a "Little Bud," who is not aware of the Big Bud's identity until a ceremonial breakfast. If a Big Bud has two or more Little Buds they are commonly known to each other as Budsters. A Big Bud's Big Bud is known as Grandbud and her Big Bud is a Great-Grandbud. Juniors select freshwomen to be their "Little Sister" and seniors select freshwomen to whom they will be a "Senior Pal." In a special ritual called the "Pow Wow," juniors leave campus and leave clues to their whereabouts. Their Little Buds have to find the juniors before breakfast at 6 a.m.

Of rats and men

Men at various colleges still have their initiation traditions, although they tend to be more intrusive. At Purdue, an initiation tradition in a men's dormitory in Cary Quadrangle dates back to 1929. Serving to promote unity among these "hallmen" not aligned with the fraternities, the event begins between five and six in the morning the day before classes start. Upperclassmen in the dorm wake the freshmen by banging on their doors with baseball bats and other noise-making implements. After being rousted from their beds, the freshmen are herded into the basement where they learn risqué folk chants and songs relating to life at Purdue. They are then led by a Cary "executive" to serenade various halls on campus. The vilest cheers are saved for fraternity houses on campus. "Drink beer! Drink beer!," they shout, "Drink beer, goddammit, drink beer! I won't drink beer with any man, Who won't drink beer with a Cary Man!" The walk home takes on the look of a rabble, as the group shouts and gestures in a gang (Salmon 1983).

Other male traditions tested one's mettle with vomit-inducing trials. Cal Tech for many years had what they called the "blowhard contest" for freshmen. Students stuffed oysters, juice and all, into a six-foot long plastic tube. One frosh was put on each end of the tube, and at a signal each would blow as hard as possible into the tube. The loser would end up either swallowing or inhaling the oysters, usually leading to involuntary puking (Dodge, et al, 1982: 45).

From Harpur College come reports of "chunking" contests after the consumption of alcohol. After a violent vomit, a student had "loser" written on his arm during the night; but a student who seemed more adept at "tossing his cookies," "driving the porcelain bus," "praying to the porcelain goddess," or letting out a "technicolor yawn," was rewarded with a six-pack of beer. Students noted incidents and wrote commentaries on such performances on a "chunk list" posted in the underclass dorm (Raftery 1989). One also encounters descriptions of fraternity initiations where pledges vomit after chewing tobacco, another manly symbol (Raphael 1988: 87-88).

Football teams and marching bands, groups demanding cohesiveness, also carry on initiations. Two weeks before the football season, freshmen players at Michigan State, to give an example, go through some rites. "We had to stand up in the cafeteria during this thing called the Booger Show and sing 'I'm a booger snot,'" a new football player reported. "Some guys would tell us to go to the back of the cafeteria and do situps and pushups." MSU's marching band meanwhile takes its freshmen out on a midnight march or "hayride" and shows them what it takes to be a member of the team. "Freshmen are treated like any rookies would be on a sports team," a band member remarked, and added that nothing more strenuous occurs than what happens on the day of a game (Boettcher 1980: 1-2).

Military schools have some of the most active initiation ceremonies. At Virginia Military Institute, initiation lasts a year. Called a "rat line," the initiation calls for upperclassmen to order freshmen to perform rigorous physical exercises. Classmates thus refer to one another as "Brother Rats," and work toward incorporation at "Breakout," the proud day when upperclassmen recognize the rats as a class worthy of the VMI name. On this day, the cadet is symbolically reborn, for students refer to the day as the class birthday. Many even engrave the date on their VMI class rings. According to one sophomore who made it, "It's a bonding experience. You learn quickly to respect the older cadets and the history of traditions of V.M.I." ("V.M.I.'s" 1989: 47).

At Texas A&M, the Corps of Cadets, some two thousand cadets out of thirty-six thousand students, vigorously maintain the "Aggie Spirit" in a tradition of initiation. The freshmen work from being lowly fish to their version of a "Breakout" at the "Final Review" nine months after entering the corps. They trade a cap with no braid for a cap with black braid; they remove the black cotton belt with a small buckle and replace it with a black nylon belt with a large buckle; they remove the flat brass, which they have found so hard to keep looking good, and replace it with curved brass, which they have customized. Before the Final Review, however, upperclassmen order fish to "hit a brace" or "pop to"—stand at stiff attention and introduce himself as a fish. If the performance is not satisfactory to the upperclassmen, the freshman cadet may have to perform push-ups or "sit on a pink stool," taking a position as if sitting on a stool, with his back against the wall and his legs bent at the knees at a ninety-degree angle with no support for his bottom (Graham 1985).

Freshmen with beanies, bowties, and name plates obediently singing for sophomore "hatmen," 1950s. (Penn State Room, Pattee Library)

Making status visible

A strong feature of freshmen initiations is the recognition of material emblems of the campus and its hierarchy of privilege. The wearing of freshmen beanies established rank associated with dress. Sophomores were often "hatmen," identified by their fuller soft hats, while seniors got to wear stiff hats. At Arkansas seniors wore derbies, at Franklin and Marshall they wore high silk hats and straw hats, and at Berkeley they wore sombreros. Decorated canes and pipes, associated with aging and idleness, were other popular senior accessories forbidden to freshmen (see Brubaker 1987: 28; Miller 1966: 397; Boney 1984: 207). Corduroy pants were another sign of upperclass status. At Purdue, students decorated what they called the yellow "senior cords" with designs showing school spirit (Mohler 1977: 8). At Hood, sophomores wear blazers and juniors receive rings.

Letters, colors, names, and numerals all take on symbolic importance in the college class hierarchy. Freshmen were commonly prohibited from displaying their graduation year or school letter. At Georgia Tech, and many other schools, each class had its own color to honor and protect, and graduating seniors bequeathed their colors to incoming freshmen (Newchurch 1985: 14).

This use of class colors evolved into the selection of school colors so common today; the most popular combination is blue and white, followed by blue or purple with gold (Snyder 1949: 257-59).

Some schools elaborate on the color scheme to form "Odd-Even" alliances among its classes. At Wells, women who will graduate in odd-numbered years join the "Odd Line" against women in the "Even Line" who will graduate in even-numbered years. The teams compete in singing, skits, and basketball games. The Odd's traditional colors are purple and yellow; the Even's colors are blue and green. Each class gives its color a special name and constructs a banner proclaiming itself; some examples are Imperial Purple, Blueberry Blue, and Blazing Yellow. In addition to having a color, classes at Keuka in upstate New York take names of tribes in the Iroquois Confederacy.

Besides colors, the inscription of letters and names for all to see can take on significance in a college social world where one's class and the people in it leave after a short four-year stint. Especially at western colleges, it became customary for the freshmen to show their moxie by painting the school letter on a hillside while the sophomores tried to stop them (Dundes 1968: 24-25). The battle evolved into a joint pep effort before football Saturdays (Parsons 1988: 15-23). At the College of Puget Sound (now University), a four-sided post, eight feet long became ceremonially important for incoming freshmen. On each side was a record of the graduating classes. Incoming freshmen would be marched in through the gate enclosing the post and pause at the monument in contemplation. Four years later, this same class upon graduation would march past the color post in the opposite direction (Earley 1987: 36).

An old inscribed sidewalk is at the University of Arkansas. Begun in 1905, the walk, according to legend, was a unifying response to freshmen-sophomore scraps at the turn of the century. Students inscribed their names and class year in the early years, but as class sizes grew the job was taken over by physical plant employees (see Wylie 1933: 168-72; Parler 1984: 26). At Western Oregon State since 1962 it's the freshmen who have annually left their mark in the cement. The location is a sidewalk at the college's football stadium; in 1988, nearly seven hundred names and doodles were left for posterity.

A sign of status on campuses is the right to roost. Campuses often had "senior fences" and "senior benches" kept off limits to freshmen. The University of Idaho had a cement seat traditionally reserved for seniors in front of the administration building. Underclassmen were told that they had no time to relax on this bench. Violators of the restriction were tossed into the nearby lily pond. At Berkeley early in the twentieth century, use of the senior bench as

Freshmen signing walk at Western Oregon State College, 1950s.

well as some exclusive staircases was also kept from women as well as freshmen (Dundes 1968: 27). Sophomores at Pomona College claimed an arch in front of a college building and excluded freshmen from walking through it.

At the University of Georgia, freshmen were forbidden to walk under an arch separating campus and downtown Athens. According to F.N. Boney, the tradition "persisted until the university grew so large that it was no longer possible to tell who the freshmen were" (1984: 165).

Despite this early semester friction, unity often came by the start of classes or later at homecoming. To stress this "incorporation" stage of rites of passage, many colleges have ceremonies at the end of freshmen week that bring together the whole college community. Hood students attend a "pergola party." Upperclasswomen wake freshwomen at one or two in the morning and force them down to the pergola, an arbor-like passageway with a roof on which climbing plants grow. First the freshwomen run around the pergola; then the freshwomen and upperclasswomen all join hands around the structure. Dressed in ceremonial black robes and carrying candles, student leaders then walk down the center path to the pergola. In a spirit of unity, they sing the Alma Mater and lead everyone in song. After the ceremony, everyone goes to the dining hall to break bread together.

Called the "pumphandle" at Knox College and the "handshake" at Union College, students in an annual event shake hands with administration and faculty and then fall in line themselves, so that everyone has shaken hands with everyone else before all is said and done. At Knox, the last person through the line ends up shaking hands with about twelve hundred others.

The majority of today's freshmen undergo "orientation" rather than initiation. The orientation has more of a therapeutic style; it seems more psychological rather than cultural. Rather than displacing uncomfortable feelings of homesickness and transition through rites of passage, students are encouraged to discuss their feelings with one another. They "get in touch" with their emotions and with one another in encounter groups. To discourage privileged cliques and competitions for dominance, students are encouraged to assert their individuality and from there to make their own connections based on common interests, regardless of class standing. Discarding an evolutionary model in favor of relativism, students learn that each position, each group, is relative in worth. One is not better than another, but rather different, and sensitivities are developed toward those differences in a plural society. Students recognize the ideals expressed in this approach, but still yearn for an exclusive cultural identity to give them a place to belong, a tradition and loyalty to claim, in the transition that college life brings. In the last decade, especially, many commentators have lamented the loss of cultural rites of passage—rites which undergirded transition in age, status, and responsibility—and criticized the self-indulgence of therapeutic approaches (Raphael 1988; Lears 1981).

Homecoming

Usually the first big event on campus after classes start in fall is Homecoming. Homecoming extends the family and community metaphor at many colleges. Like Thanksgiving, which brings family members in this mobile society home to share in festivity, homecoming brings alumni back to campus to share their common bond with one another and with students. Spreading quickly during the mobile 1920s, the activities of homecoming were designed to heighten the "spirit" of the college and remind one of the values of the college haven. For students, homecoming is an extension of rituals begun before classes started; for alumni, it is a renewal of old ties.

At the old-time college, homecoming often featured a bonfire into which freshmen flung their beanies and thus attained full-fledged student status. At Earlham, students liked to burn privies along with their beanies. At the University of Florida's homecoming, called the Gator Growl, freshmen had to bring their weight in wood to the bonfire. (Local disfavor with the practice may have had to do with the frequent appearance in the pile of restaurant and city limits signs.)

At most homecomings today, students put on festivities—often around the central event of an intercollegiate football game—for the benefit of returning alumni and parents. Students decorate the halls and Greek houses on campus, sometimes adding the extra touch of toilet paper streamers in the tree-tops. They prepare floats for an elaborate parade. Georgia Tech has its "Ramblin' Wreck" parade and Auburn annually answers with their "Wreck Tech" parade. Onlookers at Auburn taunt sorority and fraternity pledges who must walk the parade route in their pajamas. At Tech, the parade features vintage automobiles creatively hacked, chopped, and sawed into mechanical sculptures. The battered cars serve as pre-game symbols of anticipated victory on the playing field, appropriate to aggressive engineers showing mastery over their mechanical icons (Weales 1957; Rountree 1985).

Fraternity brothers at Delta Chi House working together on Homecoming decorations, 1980. (Penn State Room, Pattee Library)

The parade showcases student creativity and humor. Freshmen, especially, parade in outlandish costumes, and provide self-mocking floats. At Western Oregon State, the homecoming parade becomes a "noise parade;" students make a riotous din with the help of car horns, fire engine sirens, whistles, and school bells. At the University of Arkansas, the big hit for many years in the parade was the "Freshman Story" float, a portrayal of the freshmen as untamed savages (Wylie 1933: 187). At the University of Alabama, in a well-established tradition, law students don formal attire for homecoming and, accompanied by dates, continue their celebration on flatbed trucks (Wolfe 1983: 214).

In the spirit of incorporation, the taunting in floats and house decoration is usually directed at the day's opponent, thus uniting the campus against a common enemy. Students construct environments such as the one directed against the Vanderbilt Commodore football team that showed gravestones and coffins. A huge sign in front blared the message "Commodores Will Be Coughin'" (Egan 1985: 112). At Lawrence, students built a large railroad engine and the sign "It's No Loco-Motive To Want To Run Over Carleton" (Lawrence 1988: 32).

Homecoming decoration, Lawrence University, 1975.

Bringing some dignity to the homecoming procession, a Homecoming Queen accompanied by her court of maids rides majestically in the parade. Southwestern University, however, has a parody of this tradition. Not having a football team, Southwestern has homecoming nonetheless and parades a homecoming queen who is a man dressed as a woman. Students dress in costumes based on a theme; in 1988 the hit of the parade was a fraternity who led a "briefcase" brigade.

Chatham College in Pittsburgh, a women's college, puts on a tag football game and "cheap floats" led by a kazoo marching band made up of students from other schools. There are cheerleaders shaking pompons in the parades— never mind that they're not in the school colors. As for the floats, each "cheap float" committee gets 4,000 white paper napkins, three cans of spray paint, and a large wedge of plywood with which to work.

Many small colleges have another version of homecoming in Parents and

Alumni Weekends. Often a highlight of these events is a formal ring ceremony for the juniors, at which they ritually receive upperclass status. Usually the ceremonies are conducted in black robes, and, given our associations with receiving rings, often take on the character of a wedding—in this case a marriage to school and classmates. At Saint Mary of the Woods College, a women's college, the "Woods' Wedding March" is played. One junior expressed its meaning this way: "It links us to members of our class and every other class," and another added "There's just a special bond, a certain kind of friendship there when you meet someone wearing a ring." At Mary Baldwin, another women's college, students receive their rings in November in a weekend devoted to the women's fathers, "Junior Dads' Weekend."

At Virginia Military Institute, a men's institution, cadets consider the "Ring Figure" the most important event next to graduation. In this event, the rings are received twice—once from the superintendent of VMI and later at a ballroom ceremony from dates. Each year's class designs its own ring, and it becomes a source of pride because, they claim, at thirty-three pennyweight it is the biggest ring in the country. A sign of machismo, if the ring were "any heavier...it would be considered a weapon" (Birnbach 1984: 414). In a variation, Wells women in Aurora, New York, receive "Junior Mugs" and celebrate their arrival with a rowdy party called the "Junior Blast." The freshwomen celebrate by tampering with the juniors' rooms—moving their beds and leaving clues to their location—while the upperclasswomen are breaking in their mugs.

All Hallows' Eve

Hallowe'en on many campuses brings out student high jinks. It was a time of costume parades and pranks (Walden 1987; Dick 1967), tolerated because the holiday marked not only the time when nights get longer and colder, but also when the harsh realities of exams and studies set in. At Stetson, memorable events at Hallowe'en included toilet-papering the campus and moving wagons up onto the tower of Elizabeth Hall (Lycan 1983: 151).

At Butler University, a long procession of men in white bedsheets enters the dormitory courtyard behind a leader carrying a pumpkin. The hooded figures form a circle around the leader, who murmurs eerie incantations. The crowd is hushed. The leader ceremoniously pulls a baseball bat from beneath his sheet and smashes the pumpkin to a pulp while the crowd goes wild with cheers (survey response, 1990).

At Transylvania, appropriately, students for many years ghoulishly celebrated Rafinesque Day around Hallowe'en. The day is named for Constantine Samuel Rafinesque (1783-1840), a professor of natural history and botany known for eccentricities and unceremoniously storming out of town for good in 1826 after a tiff with the college president. Supposedly this foreigner left a curse on the college, and the story is told that shortly thereafter, the president died and the college burned. Transylvania students came up with a "tomb" for Rafinesque (actually he was cremated and the remains there are someone else's) in Old Morrison hall, a place for tellings of spooky stories about the irascible prof. On Rafinesque Day students built a bonfire, and dressed as undertakers solemnly carried a black coffin around the fire, against a background chorus of blood-curdling screams from classmates (Boewe 1987).

Christmas

The old college calendar typically started later than today's popular early semester system, so students were still in school up to, and sometimes after, Christmas. Denominational schools, especially, came up with communal festivities for the event. Typically these festivities involve special meals and lighting ceremonies for trees and Yule logs. At Oglethorpe University, trumpets sound in each quadrangle as a summons to Christmas dinner. A roasted boar's head, borne on a silver tray, is accompanied by a procession and singers into the college hall. The provost presents the chief singer with the orange from the boar's mouth, and then distributes among the company the bay leaves, rosemary, and holly springs from the tray. The school explains this tradition with a reference to a medieval legend about a English student attacked by a wild boar. The student was reading Aristotle and rammed his book down the throat of the animal, thus using wisdom to conquer "even the treacherous beast." Victorious over the boar, the student brought the animal, Aristotle and all, to the college cook for Christmas dinner. It was observed that the diners grew wiser with every bite. Today, the dinner at the small school of about a thousand students reaffirms that the college is "a close-knit community" (letter from Patsy Dickey, 27 March 1989).

At Findlay and at Juniata, what made the Christmas banquet special for many years was that faculty members served students. At Hollins, faculty come unannounced to student residences and sing Christmas songs. Several Christmas festivities including a dinner for students are annually held at Mary Baldwin College in Staunton, Virginia. Prior to the dinner, seniors dedicate the Christmas tree to a Mary Baldwin family in need of the college's support. Reaching out to the community, students also sponsor "Christmas Cheer," consisting of carol singing and a reception on the candlelit campus. A similar event occurs at Stetson every year. Called by the chimes in Hulley Tower, nearly five hundred students sing carols by candlelight and let a Yule Log burn away the troubles of the past year. Out West such things are done big, and Western Oregon State for twenty-two years held a ceremony claiming to light the nation's largest Christmas tree, a 122-and-a-half foot giant sequoia—until a storm in 1972 took away the top nine feet.

Back at the dorms before Christmas, one is likely to run across "Secret Santa" customs. Students in a hall draw names of residents for whom they will serve as a Secret Santa. They do good deeds for them or bestow small gifts on them, but the identity of the do-gooder is kept secret until a party just before Christmas.

In a common variation in coed dorms, men and women challenge each other to perform embarrassing stunts. As one might expect in this situation, many of the stunts involve sexual teasing. Michael Moffatt observed this at Rutgers, and commented that "it was widely felt to be 'fun,' and it was widely considered to enhance floor sociability at a time when the beginning-of-year friendliness had petered out" (Moffatt 1986: 171). A shy young man was challenged to take a shower in the womens' room while singing "I'm a Virgin"; a freshwoman jock was required to give a weight-lifting demonstration in a skimpy bikini (Moffatt 1989: 106-11). What's the connection, then, if as Moffatt observed, many of the stunts seemed demeaning? The answer, according to Moffatt, is "the American cultural rule, You should be willing to make an idiot of yourself in front of your friends. If, under the ritual circumstances of Secret Santa, you make an idiot of yourself in front of your coresidents on a dorm floor, you are then reenacting all of them *as* friends. You are making them all back into friends—or at least into friendly acquaintances, whatever tensions and conflicts you may have had with one another over the previous three months" (Moffatt 1989: 134-35).

Women's colleges have a particularly strong tradition of Secret Santa, and they tend to play up the theme of benevolence. Students leave cheery notes and small gifts, and arrange for kind favors for the "Santee." When it's not called Secret Santa, it might be called Spider and Fly, as it is sometimes at Wellesley; Elfing, as it is at Mount Holyoke; and Peanut Pals, as it is at Cedar Crest. In Peanut Pals, the do-gooder is the "shell," protecting her "peanut." The practice is also adapted to other holidays. At Occidental College, students engage in Secret Sweeties for Valentine's Day, and at Millersville, they have Bashful Bunnies for Easter and Secret Pumpkins (or Haunted Honeys) for Hallowe'en.

Who started this?

Founder's Day or Charter Day is often the occasion for building community spirit. Founder's Day at Hollins College, a women's college, occurs in mid-February and honors Charles Lewis Cocke. At noon, members of the senior class and one female member of the community chosen by that class walk to the Cocke family cemetery and place a wreath on his grave. Founder's Day at Sweet Briar College involves the big sister-little sister tradition. Seniors pass their academic robes down to the juniors, and the juniors' little sisters "sew pockets filled with goodies into their big sisters' robes" (Birnbach 1984: 408). Pomona College has a "Ceremony of the Flame" at its Founder's Day on October 14; accompanied by singing, students light one another's candles in a darkened hall.

Students have been given to parody of solemn founder's day activities. At many campuses faculty and administrators control the festivity, which typically features a convocation with an address by a distinguished visitor. At Berkeley, students once controlled Charter Day, but when faculty took the event over, the students responded by an interclass fight the night before Charter Day to paint the class year in bold white numerals on Charter Hill (Dundes 1968: 23). Today at Berkeley, students honor a patron saint of college parties, John Ergman. According to legend, Ergman was sent from Bowles Hall to get a twelve-gallon keg after the beer supply ran out, but he never returned. Days later, students say, his dead body was found leaning against a tree with an empty keg beside him. Now students hold a J.P. Ergman Memorial Festival.

At the University of Nebraska at Lincoln, Charter Day, February 15, became Ivy Day to plant eastern collegiate foliage out on the dry plains. Seniors marched to the steps of the library, planted ivy, and affirmed their loyalty to the university. Now the university has grown tremendously and has many colleges, each looking for its sense of self, under its wing. Architecture college students came up with Hinsdale Day, a special event commemorating two urinals in the ground floor bathroom of Architecture Hall. Traditionally observed November 1, the celebration includes a 21-flush salute to the urinals, once a (forgive me) fixture on campus, made by university faculty member Winfield E. Hinsdale in 1910. Explaining the event, a student said that "since Hinsdale Day is a tradition unique to the Architecture College, it helps give the college an identity."

To hear students tell it, they die on exams and live for parties. Party weekends with jovial themes are cherished traditions at campuses all across the country. At the University of the South, three party weekends—fall, winter, and spring—have a formal charm. Various social organizations host parties, including the Wellingtons, who wear British-looking gowns and collars and the Highlanders who wear Scottish kilts and capes. The University of Texas at Austin parties in the name of Eeyore, the great grey donkey in A.A. Milne's books. Held since 1964, the annual spring event invites guests to dress in costume, and features a Maypole and birthday cake. Since 1980, students at SUNY Fredonia welcomed spring with Fredonia Fest, an annual homage to the Marx Brothers. The Marx Brothers connection goes back to the 1933 film "Duck Soup," a comedy set in a mythical kingdom called "Freedonia." It's now quite a party when a thousand students gather with Marx Brothers masks on.

Students show off Marx Brothers look at Fredonia Fest, 1987 (SUNY Fredonia)

The rites of spring

Spring seems to bring out the most hilarity in students. Spring festivals, known as "riots," "rites," "flings," "fevers," and "storms," serve notice that the school year is almost over, the days are longer, and the sun is shining once again. Typically, the festivities are meant to release tension shortly before finals.

There's pattern to this release recognizable in folklore. One source is ancient: the connection of spring with birth and renewal. People come out of their womb-like homes and emerge outside to flourish. Spring is also a time when the ground becomes fertile, and many college festivities respond with tree and flower planting ceremonies. Spring to the ancients was also a time of reversal. The light replaces the dark, the green replaces the brown, the warmth replaces the cold. In keeping with this idea, many spring festivities feature comical reversals. Men dress as women, students act as faculty, adults act as children.

Soon time and life will be theirs, students think, but not before the last repressive hurdle of finals. In the student's spring, parody and antithesis are particularly evident. Parody serves to take control of collegiate icons, lessons and institutions drummed into the heads of students as part of sober everyday existence. Antithesis turns things on their heads to defy adult or administrative norms of control and maturity. Especially appealing to students is turning the intellectually rational into the socially absurd.

Student riots of fun have precedents in the old-time college. From 1853 to 1859 at Harvard, students bellowed "Heads out!" from their windows during the spring. The cry called students out into a raucous crowd which swept through the grounds and into Cambridge. After 1900, the cry became "Oh Rinehart!" The real Rinehart, John Bryce Gordon Rinehart, apparently was a teetotaling, studious Harvard Law School student, whose classmates continually called for him to go out on a spree (Baum 1958: 292).

Since the nineteenth century the rallying cry to mischief at Penn during the vernal equinox has been "Oh, Rowbottom!" The facts are less sure here, but according to legend, "Rowbottom or Rowbotham had a roommate who kept late hours. The stay-out was often locked out and could be heard in the wee hours calling for Rowbottom to let him in. Somehow, Rowbottom's name became connected with campus carousing" (Baum 1958: 293).

In the 1920s at Illinois, students held the "Spring Riot." As one alum remembers, "It occurred on no particular date, but broke out spontaneously on one of the first warm evenings in spring. It was heralded by students throwing open their windows and yelling 'Yahoo'" (Hankey 1944: 34). These "riots" often involved storming theaters, throwing rocks and water balloons, breaking furniture, and raiding dorms for undergarments.

Partly to channel these outbursts into manageable festivities, colleges allowed organized spring rites on the campuses. In the Spring Fever at Saint Louis University, students sponsor a triathlon consisting of an egg toss, White Castle hamburger-eating contests (replacing goldfish eating), and jello wrestling. Viterbo College holds the Courtyard Carni in the campus courtyard. There are kegs of beer, mattress races, egg tosses, and water-bucket brigades. The college president submits to the dunk tank; students who hit a target drop the proud prez into the water. Students collect cash to sign arrest warrants on faculty who are confined in a mock jail.

The University of Nevada at Reno has Mackay Days, named for a benefactor of the mining school. Held since 1914, the annual spring festival now includes contests in beard-growing (celebrating fertile growth) and pie-eating (celebrating excess), drilling and mucking contests out of the mining tradition, and dances that invite students to move freely once again.

Notre Dame has an annual three-day spring extravaganza called *An Toastal* (Gaelic for "festival"). A good bit of drinking occurs and a competition is held for the tallest stack of beer cans. One can also witness dubious achievements in jello tossing contests and kissing marathons. In a kind of parody display, students hold events designed to humiliate and defile contestants, events such as egg tossings, mud volleyball games, and "flour blowing contests," in which contestants blow at flour in pie pans until a coin at the bottom is revealed. The festival also has three other features commonly found at other campuses: a bizarre animal race, a parody of a beauty pageant, and parodied theatricals or follies (Leary 1978: 140-41).

At Notre Dame's bizarre animal race, students bring their pet beasts—turtles, cockroaches, flies, snakes, and ducks—to the main quad for exhibitions of speed, such as they are (Leary 1978: 141). At Oregon State, sororities enter turtles into races at Gill Coliseum; each turtle comes with a rooting section. Earlham College, located in the state which gives us the Indianapolis 500, has a racing tradition of its own in the Bundy 500. Bundy is an old dorm on campus, which by reputation has a problem with cockroaches. Bundyites annually have a contest to see who can catch and raise the biggest and fastest cockroach.

In the state that gives us the Kentucky Derby, we have Spalding University's annual Running of the Rodents, "the most exciting two seconds in sport." Held the week before finals, the event is run on the faculty parking lot, transformed for the day into Spalding Downs. The starting gun goes off at high noon, and entrants run for the winner's bowl and a custom-made garland of Froot Loops. Along with the event, the festivities include a Rat Ball featuring the election of a Rat King and Queen, a Rattus Parade full of frivolity, and (oh, yes), a Human Race.

Other starting guns on college campuses during these crazy spring days mark bed, tricycle, raft, and more human races. After the bedpan and wheelchair races and pie-eating contests are done at Hahnemann University's annual spring event, the highlight is the hospital bed race. Six-person teams push decorated beds which vie for prizes honoring creativity and humor as well as speed. In 1987, the Fleet Enema Team's chocolate-pudding-covered bed lost out to the balloon-bedecked Happy Birthday Team's bed for funniest entry. Best Overall was Oral's Angels, a bed satirizing television evangelist Oral Roberts. Four "angels" and dollar bills surrounded a nursing student.

Going back further in tradition are various raft races and mock regattas honoring the thawing of the rivers at springtime around campuses. At the annual Harvard Raft Race, students construct makeshift rafts and race them a short distance down the Charles. Most of the rafts, such as a cardboard replica of a pink Cadillac with a poster of Elvis at the front, sink, and it doesn't help that spectators pelt the contestants with eggs and other food projectiles. The challenge at Trenton State's Annual Lake Crossing is to build a craft costing ten dollars or less. At Swarthmore's Crum Creek Regatta students construct makeshift boats out of innertubes.

Students of Indiana University at Bloomington are quite serious about their spring tradition of Little 500, a bicycle race held at a distinguished outdoor stadium where fraternities seek bragging rights by entering the winning team. The event was made famous by the 1979 movie "Breaking Away." Sometimes as many as thirty thousand onlookers turn out for Penn State's annual Phi Psi 500, held since 1968. This human race winds through the streets of State College and stops at six bars for refreshment. Along with this race is the "Anything Goes" competition, which parades contestants in thematic costumes down the street. Hare Krishnas pray to a keg, three dancers dressed as a popular snack entertain as Big Fig and the Newtones, and seven runners bedecked in bulbous black costumes with fuses atop their heads spell out "BOMBED."

Events such as the Phi Psi 500, where drinking is conspicuous and crowds are unwieldy, are changing or ending. This turn reflects less tolerant societal attitudes toward the excesses of alcohol consumption. At the Phi Psi 500, for example, bars now serve runners non-alcoholic beer and costumes are more closely monitored to prevent offensive messages. The Beaux Arts Costume Ball, formerly featuring themes such as "The Court of Charlemagne" and "An Evening on Mars," held at Carnegie-Mellon University in Pittsburgh since 1915 was canceled in 1989 after college officials barred it from campus. Especially since Pennsylvania enacted legislation making universities liable for drinking incidents on campuses, college officials were naturally wary of the spring blow-out sometimes attracting more than twelve hundred students and causing as much as $50,000 in alcohol-related damages. In 1987, college officials at the University of California at Chico canceled Pioneer Days after two thousand mostly drunken students smashed windows, pelted police, and damaged cars when parties in preparation for the festival spilled out into the street. At

Colorado State University, police resorted to tear gas canisters to disperse thirty-five hundred students, many throwing rocks and bottles, gathered for the school's annual College Days. College officials threatened cancelation of College Days, a festive tradition going back to the turn of the century.

Follies, flings, and frolics

At northern colleges, where the coming of sunshine and warmth follow endless months of gray and cold, students also hold sober rituals, even if done tongue-in-cheek. At the State University of New York (SUNY) at Binghamton, students observe the "Stepping on the Coat Ceremony" to mark the end of winter, and the start of the all-too-brief warm season. A proclamation is read: "We are here today to celebrate an occasion of great importance to you all. It is a time of rebirth, a time of new awakening, when flowers emerge from the dead soil and bodies emerge from beneath the heavy layers of winter clothing. A miracle has occurred and we are in the midst of it. Look around you, you can see that it is true—once again after the winter of our discontent there is, once more, grass on the campus." Attendants remove a coat from a well-bundled student and help him to ritually stomp the symbol of cold discontent in this ceremony held for more than twenty years near the center of campus.

At SUNY Albany, thousands of students celebrate a related spring ritual known as Fountain Day. As the university president throws out the first Frisbee, streams of sobering cool water rise in an enormous fountain on campus and students wade in. The ritual is a symbolic reawakening of life. As one junior professed, "So many people are dormant the rest of the year, that an event like this, people resurface and show their faces." Another commented, "It's a big university, but today makes everyone feel a lot closer" ("Everybody" 1989: 54).

In the spirit of reversal, many campuses during the spring host theatrical "follies" and "frolics," satirical musical skits by students poking fun at student leaders, faculty, and administrators. Often the freshmen, such as those at Mary Baldwin, take up the follies as a chance to give the school back some hazing. Students commonly take as their models satirical skits put on earlier in their lives at summer camps and high schools. Besides liberal-arts colleges, professional schools of business such as the University of Pennsylvania's Wharton School have their follies. The plot of the production in 1989 targeted Wharton's dean as the "Silver CPA" (he has white hair and formerly headed a big accounting firm) who "buys" faculty from other schools ("It's" 1989: 1). In a skit about business ethics, the cast sang the following to the tune of Michael Jackson's "Beat It":

I cheated, cheated
And I probably sound conceited
You're probably angry
I'm overjoyed
I work on Wall Street
You're unemployed.

Law students nearing the end of their academic trials participate in the University of Virginia's "Libel Show" and Duke's "Flaw Day." Professors may be portrayed as lecturers inducing snoring or fiendish monsters enjoying the suffering of captive students (Clawges 1989: 11). In the stressful atmosphere of the medical school, follies are intended—often through dark humor—to break tensions associated with a caregiving profession. As Anne Burson observed of one teaching hospital in Philadelphia, "An anesthesiologist may be portrayed as a Samurai who obtains blood samples by making a screaming lunge with a sword at his patient (many anesthesiologists in large city hospitals are Oriental). A pharmacist may sing a Gilbert and Sullivanesque patter song listing the drugs supposedly unavailable in the hospital. A skit about those doctors who treat the genitourinary tract may be entitled 'Pomp and Circumcision' and contain a song such as 'To Pee the Impossible Stream'" (1982: 29; see also Burson 1980).

Male May Day, Western Oregon State College, 1935.

These are "inside jokes" meant for a specific audience to laugh at itself; they contain not-so-veiled complaints about the student's education within the playful context (see Hufford 1989: 136-37). But such skits can verge on the cruel, and often they deal in offensive stereotypes. For this reason, the curtain closed on follies at Cedar Crest College, the University of Arkansas, and the University of Northern Colorado. Franklin and Marshall's answer was for administrators and faculty to join students in its "Fum Follies." The college president came out as smiling, lying, television pitchman Joe Isuzu and told the throng that his college tuition is only $5.95, and he showed a photograph of the new residence hall—the Taj Mahal.

Other dramatic reversals common at college campuses involve men playing women's roles. Oregon State claims the "Junior Follies," an all-male musical show, and a men's theatrical group holds a similar event every spring at Penn. The Oregon State extravaganza includes a singing chorus and dance line in drag. At Shorter College in Georgia, college men held a womanless wedding (Gardner 1972: 329), and at Juniata men uproariously served women breakfast on May Day (survey response, 1989). In the 1930s, students at Western Oregon State held a male May Day pageant, a ritual usually reserved for women. Since 1976, men from Butler Hall at the college have been holding the Butler Beauty Pageant. In a parody of the Miss America pageant, contestants taking fake names such as "Ima Fox" dress in women's evening gowns and swimsuits, perform stunts in a talent competition, and answer questions. Looking at the event critically, however, more than a reversal in the name of spring is apparent. Such ritual displays reinforce male dominance, especially in tense situations or ones where threatening signs of change are about, by directing attention to the absurdity of men taking women's roles (see Spradley and Mann 1975: 134-35).

Comical displays in collegiate ritual reversals by women are infrequent. Influenced by changes in social dating patterns, reversal events for women such as Sadie Hawkins Day at Houghton College and Dutch Treat Week at North Texas State met their demise. At these events, popular during the 1950s, women approached men for dates and paid the bills. At Brigham Young University, proud of its conservative family values, Sadie Hawkins continued through the 1980s.

For more than seventy years women at Milwaukee-Downer College (now part of Lawrence University in Appleton, Wisconsin) fought over a man's top hat in the "Hat Hunt," held in the spring. According to legend, the hunt dates to 1894 when one Parson Ames wearing a tall silk hat visited Downer College to address a chapel audience or visit a faculty member. Some say that mischievous freshwomen took off with the headgear, while others claim that seniors swiped it for their theatrical production. The interclass rivalry became the heart of the event years later. Upperclasswomen hide the hat and freshwomen look for it, often having to wade through streams, chisel through rocks, and dig in the earth. One year it was found inside a stuffed seal in the college museum and another it was suspended from a register in the chapel. The hunt began by tradition on April 29 and the freshwomen were given until May 29 to come up with the prized possession. If they didn't find it, they had to entertain the sophomores; if they did, the upperclasswomen gave the frosh a banquet. The freshwoman who finds the hat is carried by her classmates on a huge wooden tray used in the dining hall. For the next twenty-four hours, students carry her to classes. The finder also receives the honored title of First Hat Girl, and she,

"First Hat Girl" carried to class, Hat Hunt, Milwaukee-Downer College, 1940s.
(Lawrence University)

the president of the freshwomen class, and another student selected by these two hide the hat for the hunt the following year. The significance of the find is indicated by the remark made to a reporter in 1944, "I would rather find the hat than be class valedictorian." But the disruption the hat hunt brought to campus for a month disturbed some college officials who for years threatened to put an end to it. The president of the college during the 1920s protected the event, saying "You must understand that it is with young women as with young men, in the spring their blood gets a little warm and Hat Hunt helps to take out a little of the ginger" (Peterson 1964: 31-36).

At Brenau Women's College, a similar tradition exists today with the Spade Hunt. Two shovels, one small and one large, adorned in ribbons of the class color, are hidden somewhere on campus by the seniors, and juniors have three days to find the prized item. Women go out in search of the shovels in military or hunting camouflage outfits (Andrews 1988).

Students now often represent their major rather than their class in the spring events. A rite of spring held around St. Patrick's Day at Cornell, in often chilly Ithaca, New York, calls for freshmen in the College of Architecture to design and build a paper dragon thirty to forty feet high and then parade their creation around the Ivy League campus. Architecture students in costume follow their creation. Onlookers have been known to throw eggs and oranges at the "dragon of winter." The festivities end when the students, showing their rivalry with the future engineers, set the dragon afire on the engineering quad. As the construction burns, the "dragon of winter" has been slain. (In 1988, the engineers added their own contribution to the rite of spring, a twenty-foot-high dragon-slaying knight on a horse.)

Engineers at many campuses take special interest in spring events around St. Patrick's Day because St. Patrick was by legend an engineer. At the University of Missouri at Columbia, engineers added to traditional St. Patrick's Day events with a parade, snake killing, a mass "kowtow" to St. Patrick, the collecting of shillelaghs from the woods, bringing St. Patrick into town on a manure spreader, and performing drill-team figures with lawn mowers.

At the University of California at Davis, Aggies have their spring event called Picnic Day. The festivities kick off with a cow milking contest, usually won by the campus chancellor, and usually eliciting sexual wordplay. Headlines proclaim "Chancellor Puts Squeeze on Big Teats." Related to this theme, tee-shirts and bumper stickers read "UC Davis...The Best Dairy-Air for 75 Years." The highlight of Picnic Day, however, is a parade with floats. Several mock drill teams, such as Alpha Falfa Oink, the Animal Science department's precision shovel drill team, add levity, but much of the parade admiringly showcases horses. (The campus's mascot is the mustang.) Other attractions include a rodeo, sheep dog trials, dachshund races, dog frisbee contest, and a polo match—events showing the athletic abilities of dogs and horses often working in conjunction with humans. Cows, pigs, and goats—less a human extension than dogs and horses—tend to be ridiculed during the events, and as the tee-shirt slogan suggests, the animals are associated with the scientific aspects of Aggie work. Aggies proudly bring out their humanistic work with nature by giving reverence to horses and dogs, but the other animals, given to non-pet status and much potentially disturbing animal experimentation at the university, attract derisive humor. According to Davis faculty members Jay Mechling and David Scofield Wilson, this festival thus serves to deal with cultural ambivalence caused by the nature of work on campus; the event orders categories for participants in this college culture who both admire and abuse animals (1988: 303-17).

Tree fêtes

Nature also enters heavily into college culture in ritual tree plantings. They get special attention during spring events for many symbolic reasons. Plantings fit the theme of growth presented by both spring and the college experience. Further, the pastoral campus with large shady trees and flower beds has historically been the ideal image of campuses because it embodies the peace and contemplation evoked by nature. In addition, trees planted by a class preserve the presence of that class long after its members have left.

Beginning in 1903 and for seventeen successive years, Baylor senior classes garbed for the first time in their caps and gowns solemnly paraded in pairs to a

The 1906 class tree, a proud sycamore, is the backdrop for this class at Vassar.
(Vassar College)

central quadrangle. They were followed by the junior class, who joined them in forming a circle around the site. The presidents of the two classes saluted each other in carefully worded speeches of jocular challenge. A tree was placed in the ground, and each of the seniors scooped a spadeful of dirt around its roots. The senior class then ceremoniously handed the spade over to the juniors for use the following year (Keeth 1985: 10).

At Vassar today each class chooses a tree on campus or plants a new one to become its class tree. Tree planting as part of an elaborate spring ceremony—complete with a Tree Day Mistress—was a regular part of Tree Day held during the spring at Wellesley for almost ninety years. It fell victim to the lack of patience during the 1960s for formal programs and the redirection of attention away from campus (McCarthy 1975: 236-40).

At Simpson College, a special campus day devoted to cleaning the grounds developed out of Tree Day. It may not sound like fun, but in an assuring spirit of community on a surprise day, usually in April, the chapel bell rings in the morning to announce that all classes are cancelled. Students, faculty, and administrators work side by side to clean the campus. At noon the campus community joins together in a picnic and games (see also "College" 1856: 378-80; Kern 1984: 144). The 1920 yearbook of the University of Puget Sound claimed that "more college spirit and enthusiasm prevails on this day than on most any other occasion" (Earley 1987: 37).

Surprise vacations

The idea of a surprise vacation day, sans clean-up chores, exists at many campuses. At Keuka College, it's called the "Senior Scourge" and held during the spring. Seniors plan a picnic and party for the juniors and then surprise them with the location. At Mary Baldwin, it's called "Apple Day," happens in the fall, and is secretively organized by the sophomore class. Each spring at Coe College in Iowa, the retiring student body president is honored with the task of calling the day when no classes will be held. The chosen day remains a secret, but usually occurs ten days before finals. The victory bell sounds at six in the morning and the student body president and crew run through the dorm halls yelling "It's Flunk Day!" and delivering the Flunk Day newspaper lampooning members of the college community. The whole community heads to a nearby park for an all-day picnic.

Knox College in Galesburg, Illinois, also has its Flunk Day at which students are roused early in the morning by Old Main's bell. They are then treated to a carnival atmosphere on the grounds with pie-throwing free-for-alls, tugs of war with the Fire Department, and fireworks. According to tradition, it's a day "when no one cares how many 'flunks' you receive."

This kind of surprise vacation day most popularly goes by the name of "Mountain Day" (Juniata College, Elmira College, Smith College, Mount Holyoke College), but it is also known as "Stop Day" (Stephens College), "Spree Day" (Clark University), "Tinker Day" (Hollins College), "GIG Day" ("Get into Goucher," at Goucher College), "Fox Day" (Rollins College), and "Toe-Dipping Day" (Chatham College).

Special privilege is given seniors on a special day at several campuses. At Houghton and Mary Baldwin colleges, seniors are excused from class for a day usually associated with revelry. At the University of Nebraska at Lincoln in 1898, the senior class staged the first "Seniors' Day" or "Sneak Day." Seniors entered the chapel and sounded horns, tin whistles, squeaking dolls (Manley 1969: 264-65). Today at St. John's College in Annapolis, Maryland, seniors without warning hold "Senior Prank"; they signal the closing down of campus by decorating campus and performing a comical skit. The class of 1988 rolled a 300-pound Trojan horse made of papier-mâché onto campus. Seniors interrupted Monday night philosophy seminars wearing Greek dress and presented a parody of *The Odyssey*. The next day, the class threw a feast that drew 450 students, faculty, and staff—a nice turnout considering that the school's entire enrollment is under 500.

Since the 1930s, senior pranks have also highlighted Cal Tech's Ditch Day. Seniors devise elaborate mechanical defenses on their doors, and leave campus for nine hours. Underclassmen, through ingenuity rather than brawn, try to get past the defenses and get to the booze and sweets left as rewards for their efforts. Underclassmen, for example, successfully talked their way past a computer with a voice synthesizer. Prompted by a keyboard outside the door, the computer sentry dispensed a series of clues and plaints as the underclassmen got closer to the password which would open the door (Ellis 1987: 102-4).

Senior women frequently get special treatment during May Day celebrations. At Bryn Mawr, sophomores wake up early May 1 to pick flowers and put them in baskets for the seniors. Baskets in hand, the sophomores proceed in a group through the dormitory at dawn. They approach a senior's room, knock on the door and wait for signs of life. Then they sing a traditional song such as "The Hunt is Up," which carries the lines "Awake! all men, I say again, Be merry while ye may! For Harry, our king, is gone a-hunting, To bring his deer to bay" (Briscoe 1976: 221). The sophomores hand the risen senior her basket and she usually jokes appreciatively with the crowd before going back into her room and

May Day Court, Milwaukee-Downer College, 1914. (Lawrence University)

May Day Queen crowned at Penn State, 1959. (Penn State Room, Pattee Library)

Freshmen jesters tying ribbons to Maypole, 1928. (Penn State Room, Pattee Library)

Wrapping the Maypole, 1957. (Penn State Room, Pattee Library)

preparing for the day's activities.

The day lets underclasswomen say goodbye to the seniors. The seniors are given adoration before being symbolically excluded from the student community. The seniors, for their part, perform dances and dramas that stress their refinement and maturity, their achievement and vitality. Some of this emerges especially clearly in ceremonies with more than a hint of sexual awakening—from the presentation of flowers to the dance around the Maypole. With the fertility of the merry month of May comes feminine rebirth into a new stage of life.

It's still early morning at Bryn Mawr when the seniors come down to be the sophomores' guests of honor in a champagne and doughnut toast. Then it's the seniors' turn to wake the college president, and the college bell rings in the May. In a connection to the medieval tradition at Oxford, seniors sing the Magdalen "Hymn to the Sun" from a tower on campus (see Judge 1986: 15-40). Breakfast includes the special treat of strawberries and cream. After awards and a procession of heralds, dancers, and the May Queen, students dance around Maypoles. The May Queen is crowned, Morris dancers complete their figures on the green, and the audience then gathers for the annual springtime drama in which the feminist-heroine slays the decidedly masculine dragon of winter. Picnic lunch follows, with wandering minstrels, jugglers, and fencers. Theatricals and art exhibitions, often on an Elizabethan or medieval theme, fill the afternoon. In a farewell gesture of fertility, the seniors plant a tree and bring ribbons, coins, and trinkets to hang on it.

After a medieval banquet and renaissance choir concert, the last step-sing of the year occurs under cover of darkness. (Coffin and Cohen 1987: 165-66). It concludes with the "Good Night" song, during which the seniors file away from the steps. Their chorus is distant indeed by the time the song ends. In a "moving up" ritual, the juniors occupy the positions held by the seniors on the steps, and the other classes move up in turn. After a moment of contemplative silence, the students give two cheers, one for the seniors and one for the college, and then complete the evening with an English country dance (Briscoe 1976: 240-41).

Features of the Bryn Mawr May Day, held since 1900, occurred at many campuses, particularly from the early 1900s to the 1960s. The inspiration for the event is the English folk celebration, connected often to Elizabethan tradition. In it, flowers and greenery are gathered at dawn; a youthful May Queen is crowned with flowers and surrounded by a court of maids and children thus making the link between femininity and the fertility of the season; and girls costumed gaily in virginal white, ribbons in hand, dancing around the Maypole (Long 1977: 66-75). The athletic, artistic, and feminine components of the festival appealed to many women's colleges when they took it up during the late nineteenth century, a time when medieval rituals of many sorts, swept through society (see Lears 1981: 141-82). To the Elizabethan motif of May Day, schools frequently added Greek dances, hymns, hoop races, and exhibitions invoking classical symbols of higher civilization. At colleges such as Oregon Normal (now Western Oregon State), May Day was considered "the biggest and most colorful event of the year" ("Tradition" 1935: 1), and at Hampton it was "the prettiest and most attractive of our social gatherings" (Kenwill 1886: 70).

Various changes did May Day in, however, by the 1960s. Alterations to the semester calendar meant that May Day came perilously close to finals, and students were unwilling to devote time to the preparation required for the event. Students were less inclined to focus their social energies on campus, since they were doing more things as individuals away from the college. The pomp of the event meant less to iconoclastic students of the 1960s, and they sensed that the ceremony conveyed stereotypes of women as dainty and dramatic. Women wanted to be less associated with nature and more with modern reality, especially in the workplace. Women no longer displayed their athletic and artistic prowess through May Day activities as they once did; they sought outlets more integrated into the mainstream. Colleges during the 1960s commonly replaced May Day with parents' weekends, spring weekends, singing competitions, tree days, and spring homecomings, or eliminated it altogether.

Some colleges have revived or revised the event in recognition of the need for re-establishing traditions. At Wells College, May Day was celebrated from 1922 until the early 1960s, and then it began anew in 1979. According to the senior student coordinating the event in 1979, "The idea appeals to present students because it welcomes spring in a symbolic and nostalgic way" (Miller 1979). Freshwomen kick off the festivities with a "Freshwomen Dance Around the Maypole," accompanied by English medieval music. Two May Queens, members of the junior and senior classes, are crowned, but in better accord with modern sentiment, the crowned students are picked by drawing lots.

Formerly the queen's spot was reserved for a senior who represented "the highest tribute which could be paid to beauty." Against the background of a Grecian temple, a pageant of women and children made an invocation to a tree, and after the coronation wound ribbons around the Maypole.

May Day at Earlham College, celebrated since 1875, has probably been the college's longest continuous social tradition, and now is bigger than ever in its revised form. Today the Olde English theme is played up more than the feminine display, and works to build an intimate sense of community for the college. "Through the day a spirit of rural festivity will pervade the campus-village and bring pleasure to thousands," according to an announcement. Queen Elizabeth leads a procession to the green, children frolic, and students raise a Maypole and then sing and dance around it. Performances of St. George and the Dragon, and scenes from *A Midsummer Night's Dream, Pyramus and Thisbe,* and *The Mad-Cap Marriage of Beatrice and Benedick* enliven the festivities.

As the themes of the latter three plays suggest, love and marriage is normally a strong motif in May Day activities. Coming before the traditional wedding month of June, May Day celebrations at some schools looked like wedding ceremonies. The women proceeded in formal white dress with train-bearers, attendant maids, and flower girls—in front of parents and friends. At Mount Mary College, May Day called for the crowning of the Virgin Mary's statue before the Queen of May, "dressed as a bride while her attendants…wear long pastel shaded tones" ("May" 1939: 1). Hoop exhibitions and races, with all their vaginal symbolism, were regularly part of May Day celebrations, and the races regularly rewarded winners with portents of marriage. The winner was, by tradition, the first from the class to be married, and Bryn Mawr students add that the *runner-up* will be the first to get the Ph.D. (McCarthy 1975: 247; Briscoe 1976: 235; Betterton 1988: 170).

Greek Hoop exhibition, May Day, 1914. (Penn State Room, Pattee Library)

At Wellesley, the winner was presented with a wedding bouquet and sometimes wreathed with flowers. If the winner was by chance engaged, her fiance was asked to pose with her in the magic circle. Formerly, seniors raised their hoops to make a picturesque archway for women proceeding into chapel (McCarthy 1975: 247).

Hoop races today are often part of other occasions besides May Day. At Barnard, they are part of Greek Games, at Cedar Crest part of Soph-Frosh Day. In this new day, Wellesley women give the hoop race, now held in April, a new interpretation. They say that the winner will become a corporate chief executive officer.

At Brenau Women's College, juniors still use the occasion of May Day to honor departing seniors. Juniors wrap the Maypole, make ivy chains and crowns, and offer the seniors an entertaining skit (Andrews 1988). Wells juniors and seniors make up the court of the majestic May Queen, complete with jesters, while freshwomen dance around the Maypole.

A particularly elaborate celebration occurs at Keuka College. It begins with "Freshman Stunt," in which students spoof the college and honor their Big Sisters, Big Buds, and Senior Pals. On Saturday, classes gather in chapel for "Moving-Up Ceremony," in which classes officially advance in rank. Interclass crew races follow. The May Day Court at Keuka recognizes women chosen from each class who have been active in the college for the past year. Finally, a festive dinner dance caps the May Day celebration.

The spectacle of sport

May Day may have celebrated femininity, but the main spectacle of masculine competition, and by extension of college spirit, was found at most campuses in the sports stadium. Since 1869, when Rutgers met Princeton in something of a grudge match, football has caught on as the event bringing out the most people from the college community (Moffatt 1985: 5; Rudolph 1962: 373-92; Rader 1983; McCallum and Pearson 1971).

In contrast to women's associations with the blossoming spring, men looked to the cool brown fall as the setting for football battles in the dirt. A common exhibition of men at football pep rallies at many colleges was the noisy pajama or nightshirt parade, either before the big game or after a victory. At the University of Kansas, well into the 1950s, male students "participated in the Nightshirt Parade, an event held the night before the first home football game. The men assembled on campus dressed in nightshirts or pajamas, marched to Massachusetts Street downtown, and snake-danced to a bonfire and a rally at the bridge, followed by free movies" (Nichols 1983: 8). A pajama parade dating back to Stanford-California football games around the turn of the century at Berkeley evolved into a "Pajamarino," featuring costumes emphasizing the elaborate and fantastic (Dundes 1968: 30).

Spectators at college football games have a variety of traditions to guide them. Texas A&M fans, for example, are known for their Twelfth Man tradition. According to legend, after the Aggie football players were put out of commission by numerous injuries, the coach called a student-athlete out of the stands to suit up. Since 1922 the Aggie student body stands to indicate their readiness to serve as the twelfth man for the team (Adams 1979: 118). Aggies may also give the "Gig 'em" sign by clenching their right hand as if calling someone out in baseball. Probably the best known gesture in college football is the "Hook 'Em Horns" sign introduced to University of Texas Longhorn fans in 1955 (Berry 1983: 18). Made by extending the index and little fingers and tucking the middle and ring fingers beneath the thumb, the signal is sometimes jokingly turned upside down by Oklahoma fans at Oklahoma-Texas games creating the sign of the horns hitting someone in the rear end.

Kansas Jayhawk fans "wave the wheat" by stretching their hands over their heads and moving them back and forth. They have also been well known for their haunting "Rock Chalk, Jayhawk, KU!" chant since the late nineteenth century. (The Jayhawk rhyme referred to the chalk rock on Mt. Oread, the university's campus.) At Penn State, the massive football stadium traditionally reverberates with the sound of one side yelling "WE ARE!" and the answer "PENN STATE" coming from the other. This is the same crowd which has a tradition of irreverently singing "We don't know the goddamn words" over and over when the school song is called for, and during the game throwing marshmallows dyed in the school colors at one another.

Cheerleaders spur on the fans. The familiar "Rah, Rah, Rah" of college cheers comes from the "Hip, Hip, Hurrah" of British yells. Many American cheers spring from the old cheers of the Ivy League (Spectorsky 1958: 220-22). Here are two from Yale and Princeton:

> Brekekekex, ko-ax, ko-ax,
> Brekekekex, ko-ax, ko-ax,
> O-op, O-op, parabalou,
> Yale, Yale, Yale,
> Rah, rah, rah, rah, rah, rah, rah, rah, rah,
> Yale! Yale! Yalc!

> H'ray, h'ray, h'ray,
> Tiger, tiger, tiger,
> Siss, siss, siss,
> Boom, boom, boom,
> Ah, ah, ah,
> Princeton, Princeton, Princeton!

And here's a 1930s variation from Roanoke College:

Brackety-ackety-ack
Brackety-ackety-ack!
Hullabaloo! Hullabaloo!
How-do-you-do?
How-do-you-do?
Roanoke!

Cheers today often urge on the warriors on the field. Roanoke cheers today, for example,include "We're tough, we're mean, That's why we call it the Maroon Machine!" and "Give 'em the axe, axe, axe! Where? In the neck, neck, neck!" (Traditions Cluster 1981: 43-45).

College football lights towers, sets off cannons, and rings bells. At Texas for many years, a thirty-story light tower emblazoned the night sky with orange when the team won. The lighting tradition has been expanded to signal victories in basketball as well (Berry 1983: 43-45). At the University of North Texas, a green light shines from the bell tower of the Administration Building. Texas students are in the habit of lighting red candles before a game to give their team good luck (Berry 1983: 50). At Texas, cannons boomed for years when the Longhorns scored a touchdown, until the Southwest Conference, fearing an accident, outlawed cannons for conference games (Berry 1983: 62). The Oklahoma Sooners still have their covered wagon and horse team which runs onto the field after a score.

Bell-ringing at many campuses signals a football victory. (At women's colleges it signifies a student's marriage.) At Franklin and Marshall, bell ringing for a football victory was a regular tradition from 1890 until 1958, when the college president put a stop to the racket. When the team beat regional rival Gettysburg College, students regularly went to the president's house to call for the celebratory cancellation of Monday's classes (Brubaker 1987: 69). Virginia Hooper wrote me to recount the time Georgia beat Georgia Tech in the 1940s, and the bells rang all night (letter, October 9, 1989). At Brown, the bell on University Hall still calls students to classes and signals football victories. Celebrations of victory often spill out into the street. At one of Auburn's oldest intersections, Magnolia Avenue and College Street, students gather after football victories with rolls of toilet paper in hand and decorate what they call "Toomer's Corner."

Colleges traditionally leave their fiercest regional rivals for the last game of the season, and, just to heighten the stakes, play for a named trophy. This game also brings out the most revelry from students, complete with pranks, songs, jokes, parties, and public displays. Purdue and Indiana battle for the "Old Oaken Bucket," Michigan and Minnesota vie for the "Little Brown Jug," and Stanford and California battle for the "Axe." Some others you might not know about are the "Bronze Turkey" fought over by Monmouth and Knox colleges, the "Goat" signifying victory for Carleton or St. Olaf colleges, the "Hickory Stick," a prize for the winner of the Northeast Missouri State-Northwest Missouri State game, and the "Victory Bell," the stakes at the Cincinnati-Miami of Ohio game.

Since the 1960s, college basketball has taken on the feel of spectacle as well. With some arenas holding as many as twenty thousand fans, the indoor setting can give rise to some carrying on. At Notre Dame, the first basket by the Fighting Irish is rewarded by a storm of confetti from the student section. Students also are known to dress outrageously, wearing a basketball shell, sometimes complete with a small hoop, over the head. Students paint themselves in school colors and wave handkerchiefs. Fans in the student section also try to distract opposing players, waving and shouting when a foul shot is taken, and pointing and chanting "You, you, you" when a foul is called. Fans also mimic the "high-five" hand slaps used by the players on the court. Basketball referees have an especially hard time of it from students as well as from coaches. When I attended St. Peter's College games during the 1960s, fans threw a large inflated fish down onto the court to show that a call "stunk"; a student at courtside would pick it up and throw it back into the stands. Adding to basketball's appeal in college is the emergence of women's teams with avid followings and some of the zaniness once thought reserved for men's teams (see Beezley and Hobbs 1988).

Of the popular sports pranks of the past, the most common to pull on a collegiate rival was to kidnap the mascot. A North Carolina State alum recalled the following pranks pulled on rival North Carolina: "I think it was 1941 or 1942 when the football games with UNC featured a freshman team game one week and the varsity game the next. A group of State students kidnapped the UNC ram. The UNC administration threatened to cancel the varsity game if the Ram was not returned. He was sheared and dyed with good textile dye—red on the head end and blue on the other" (Beezley 1981: 114). When security on mascots tightened, students bought paint to get their message across. In a legendary incident after the Franklin and Marshall-Lehigh game in 1948, students whitewashed "F&M" over walkways and awakened the Lehigh student body in the middle of the night (Brubaker 1987: 131). Students might also go after an opposing school's statuary. At USC, the statue of the USC Trojan is wrapped in plastic before the UCLA-USC game to protect it from cross-town raiders.

Tormenting the faculty

Most student pranks are pulled within the safer confines of the home campus. Farm animals figure prominently in pranks pulled on faculty. Typically, animals with non-pet status are used to victimize instructors. A report of a cow smuggled into the second-story classroom of an unpopular instructor occurs as early as 1876 (Dundes 1968: 22; see also Rollins 1961: 165; Turrell 1961: 162; Mook 1961: 243; Manley 1969: 258; Mechling and Wilson 1988: 312). According to an account from Brown, a cow was "led up the stairs of University Hall, to the roof, where her tail was tied to the bell, which she rang with determination. It seems to be a characteristic of cows that they will sometimes go up stairs, but they are reluctant to descend" (Worthington 1965: 53).

It is also characteristic that they can make a mess. At the University of Florida during the summer of 1986, veterinary students released a pig into a packed auditorium, and freed a sixty-pound porker into a faculty member's office. There they dramatically defied the boundaries between the formal, "unnatural" institution and informal nature.

Students derive a great deal of mirth from the incongruity of animals in buildings or atop towers, and they defy authority under the protection of a playful frame. They also point out with this incongruity that the power relationship between faculty and students is "unnatural" and can be easily disrupted. This disruption, comes most frequently in late spring when students anticipate graduation, or under cover of Hallowe'en darkness.

Students also show their power by performing improbable feats. Students regularly disassembled wagons and reconstructed them on top of towers or inside college rooms; later automobiles served just as well to astound the college community (Dodge, et al, 1982: 10-11; Utt 1968: 96; Worthington 1965: 53). The point of the stunt is to turn heads, to shake up the order of things; routine is broken by those without the power of dictating routine. Sometimes college icons, usually heavy and large, are moved. Just a few years ago at Hamilton College, students lifted the half-ton statue of Alexander Hamilton off its base and transported it to a distant farm field.

Today, some of the most outrageous pranks, sometimes called "hacks," come at the hands of engineering students. Before Hallowe'en in 1985, a telephone booth appeared atop a 148-foot dome overlooking MIT. Maintenance workers prepared to bring the booth down when the phone rang for them! The following year, the dome sported a small house complete with mailbox and welcome mat (see Theroux 1986: 60-65; Dodge, et al, 1982: 35-38).

Penn State students tweaked their professors for forty years before the Great Depression by constructing a mock faculty graveyard. It was the culmination of a long year and a reversal of the feeling students had of being "buried" by work. One headstone was a podium complete with book and notes on top. Mock memorials such as drinking jugs, coffins with students' nicknames for profs on them, and epitaphs proclaiming professors' fates dotted the grounds. One epitaph was in the form of a Western Union telegram to the students from the devil assuring them that one professor burned with lots of smoke and a pungent odor (Bronson, May 10, 1968: 1).

Into the 1950s, the idea of mock graveyards was picked up by freshmen who left verses in the ground for sophomores who hazed them. Some of them read "Here lies a Hatman who thought himself wise. He tried to make a 'frosh' wear two bow ties" and "Black Hatmen take heed! Here lies one who didn't. He rests in pieces." The mock cemetery still surfaces occasionally on fraternity

Mock memorials at the "Penn State Cemetery," 1920s. (Penn State Room, Pattee Library)

"Sophomore Cemetery," 1950s. (Penn State Room, Pattee Library)

front yards during homecoming when they help to "bury" football rivals.

Students traditionally tormented faculty and administrators by stealing bells or clappers, placing privies (and now portable johns) in the middle of quadrangles, painting various college cannons and statues odd colors, and rolling cannonballs (now bowling balls) down steps to make a terrible racket. In another statement of incongruity, huge commercial statues of animated figures and animals from fast-food restaurants and convenience stores find their way to college courtyards (see Dodge, et al, 1982: 31). Revered statues are incongruously decorated with sunglasses, hats, and even lingerie. At Harvard, the statue of John Harvard is frequently dressed up; at Penn State it's, Coach Paterno's bust.

College lawns and quadrangles, long the sacred grounds of the campuses, are frequent targets of pranksters. Earlham College has landscaped a heart right in, well, the heart of the campus. In 1971, students removed all the tables and chairs from the dining hall and set them out on the heart. In 1986, a group of students swiped four hundred knives and stuck them in the heart.

One student prank in particular comments on the computer age and its impersonalization of the campus community. Students plant the name of a fictitious student and regale one another with stories of the success of this student slipping undetected through the electronic collegiate system. The stunt has precedents, however, in pre-computer days. As the story normally goes, the fictitious student is enrolled in a course and receives a grade from the absentminded professor (see Dodge, et al, 1982: 15; Stec 1985: 2). At Georgia Tech, a fictitious student named George P. Burdell emerged when Ed Smith, class of 1931, received two admissions applications by mistake. Working together with other students, Smith saw the mythical Burdell through to a Bachelor of Science degree, and legends circulated about the stunt yearly after that (Newchurch 1985: 12-13; Betterton 1988: 179; see also Shulman 1955: 93-104). But as Mary Louise Fitton said in 1942, "Every campus has a tale about an imaginary student whose name turned up through some mistake on a class roll and whose existence was prolonged as long as possible by his gleeful colleagues" (p. 40).

Here's how Walker Wyman ran into the variations of this legendary prank from Massachusetts to Minnesota: "The story told when I was in college was that of the old horse that graduated from Harvard. The students enrolled an old milkwagon horse named Bill, paid his fees each semester, and took his exams. Classes being so large, no professor ever had any occasion to know Bill.... The same story is told about the U.W.–Madison, and perhaps elsewhere in Wisconsin, about the enrollment of a student by name. But in the computer age, names are unimportant, only numbers count. Students took this non-existent student's exams and finally graduated a *number* with an 'A' average. Students at St. Olaf in Minnesota tell about graduating a dog" (1979: 89).

...and each other

Many pranks by students are played on other students, especially in the dorms. Like other restrictive institutions that throw strangers together, including summer camps and military bases, college dorms often socialize residents through pranking (cf. Posen 1974: 299-309; Graham 1985: 105-21). As with freshmen initiations, groups, especially male groups, bring a fresh recruit into the fold by what they perceive as comical pranks.

The pranks are usually not randomly chosen; they follow a pattern of extending fears associated with living in an institutional setting. Under the protective frame of play, pranks there focus on the fear of being alone, of entrapment and confusion. Typical approaches are ritually polluting another's clean space, bringing disorder to the order of things, and disrupting routine. The fear is ridiculed, and one is expected to rely on or respect the group rather than oneself for adjustment.

Common examples of pranks that bring confusion and disorder are moving furniture from a room to another spot, short-sheeting the bed, tilting cans of water against a door so that it spills in when the door is opened, and blowing talc into the room. During the nineteenth century, students "smoked" freshmen by blowing smoke into their rooms, and in the twentieth century "stinked" them (Hall 1856: 434; Simmons 1967: 230). A favorite prank today is "pennying in" doors. Pennies are jammed between the door frame and door so that the person inside can't get out. A nineteenth-century precedent for this practice is "screwing up," or fastening the door shut with nails and screws during the night. During the 1960s students also "coked in" a door, by wedging a soda case over the doorknob so that the knob is tightly held inside the case (Simmons 1967: 228).

Especially in men's dorms and fraternities, many pranks expand on scatological and sexual themes. Rumps are exposed, undergarments are snatched, and references to feces are common. At Rutgers, Michael Moffatt observed a kind of male bonding in a group called the "Wedgie Patrol." "New male students and unpopular older ones were snatched from their beds, usually sleeping only in their underwear, and 'hoisted' by the tops of their 'wares' until the garments shredded, leaving them naked and confused, sometimes with cloth burns on intimate parts of their anatomy, at the center of a circle of laughing attackers.... The correct manly response to a wedgie attack, according to its perpetrators, was to take it in good humor" (Moffatt 1989: 86). As in other boys' play such as "Smear the Queer," and some argue, football, the initiate shows his masculinity by metaphorically withstanding homosexual attack (Dundes 1987b: 178-96).

In a related custom at Berkeley, popular men are "pantsed." According to a student's observation, "First someone says, 'knock, knock' and others respond by saying, 'who is there.' Then the first person says, 'roll on' and the others say, 'roll on who' and the first person will give a name of a person. When this person's name is said, everyone runs to that person, gets him or her on the ground and takes off the socks and shoes and finally the pants and hides them. As the clothing is taken off this song is sung: Roll on you Golden Bear, For victory is in the air. For California's fame we'll be winning the game, And for Alma Mater fair" (Folklore Archives, 1978; see also Yohe 1950).

Some of the scatological pranks—such as covering toilets with plastic wrap, filling toilets with gelatin, coating black toilet seats with shoe polish, covering other toilets with petroleum jelly or shaving cream, and feeding a cat a laxative and placing it in a car or room—take the form of orchestrated attacks. In the student's folk categorization these examples of ritual pollution are reserved for rival hall or fraternity and sorority groups. In student lingo, these more malicious acts go by the name of "borassing," "ratfinking," "ratfucking," or simply "R.F." (Egan 1985: 179-80; Poston and Stillman: 1965: 193; Simmons 1967: 227). To complete the raid, students may fling toilet paper across the front of the house or expose their buttocks to the rival students in an act of "mooning." In this category, too, is the mock sexual attack of panty and jock raids known for many years on college campuses.

Besides polluting rivals, students baptize their own with water. On their birthdays, and in pledging ceremonies, students are regularly thrown into showers, fountains, and ponds. Special dunkings occur on a student's twenty-first birthday or engagement. Unlike the whacks one received as a child, dunkings do not count age as much as recognize status within the group. The immersed birthday person is simultaneously set apart and brought into the group, humiliated and honored; he or she is now given new life by the water. The birthday person or pledge must rise from the dunking and come anew as if by evolution onto dry land. At the University of Washington students are dumped into Drumheller Fountain, also known as Frosh Pond; at Indiana University it's Showalter Fountain; at Texas it's Littlefield Fountain. At the University of Alabama, the traditional tapping ceremony for Jasons, a men's senior honorary society, includes a good dousing with muddy water (Wolfe 1983: 226).

Some traditional pranks involve student theatrics. One well known prank is the chemistry experiment with food. In 1970, a student at Berkeley reported it this way: "A chemistry major introduced Paul to the 'salt and butter reaction.' He put salt on a pat of butter and told Paul it was an exothermic reaction, giving off heat. Paul thought heat really would be coming from it, so he put his hand over it to test the temperature. The chemistry student smashed his hand down on Paul's, so that Paul's smashed on the butter." And in 1989, I received the following from a Millersville University student: "I would gather various substances in cafeteria, such as mayo, catsup, and mustard, and add ice. I would tell other people at the table that I had done this fascinating chemistry experiment. Then I wave my hand over the gooey mixture and say 'Yeah, it seems to be getting warmer.' Keep doing this until curiosity overwhelms the unsuspecting onlooker. When someone waves his hand over the mixture, slam it down!" The prank is meant to reveal someone's gullibility, especially in a college setting where fellow students all seemed learned. Be alert when in the company of people with B.S. behind their names!

Another theatrical practical joke involves some collaborators. Former President Ronald Reagan related a version of this prank he and some fraternity brothers pulled on pledges at Eureka College. After they sneaked into a nearby farm's watermelon patch, a blinding light showered the pledges and they heard a shotgun blast. A fraternity brother clutched his stomach and burst a ketchup-filled balloon onto his clothes. He yelled, "I'm shot!" Actives excitedly told pledges to go get help. By the time the pledges scurried back to town, the fraternity brothers, including the shotgunned "victim," were there to greet them (Egan 1985: 61; see also Brubaker 1987: 126).

In a variation, the prank is also known as "Going to See the Widow," and commonly played on a braggart who extols his sexual abilities. The braggart is led by pranksters to believe that a widow (or O'Reilly sisters, trucker's wife, brakeman's wife, or prettiest girl in the county) who lives a few miles from town is interested in making his acquaintance. He is warned, however, that the widow has a suitor whose jealousy has been inflamed by rumors concerning her conduct. Once out at an isolated farmhouse, the group gets out of the car and walks up to the house. A series of blasts from a shotgun ring out in the darkness, followed by shouts and threats. One of the group pretends to fall wounded. The braggart runs until informed of the joke played on him (Cohen 1951: 223; Grotegut 1955: 51-52; Hand 1958: 275-76; Sobel 1951: 420-21; Randolph 1957: 17-19; Starr 1954: 184).

Leaving one's mark

Students also use their artistic abilities to make their presence felt on campus. Every campus, it seems, has a rock, bridge, fence, wall, cannon, or water tower repeatedly given a fresh paint job. The painters traditionally come do their work in the middle of the night, so as to surprise the campus community in the morning. Fraternities particularly like to leave their Greek letters or spirited messages on rocks, and classes often leave their special colors. Eastern Michigan's rock receives a paint job from fraternities and sororities every few days. It is estimated that the rock receives more than fifty-five hundred coats of paint during the school year. When college officials removed a frequently painted rock from the courtyard at Northwestern, students answered with a papier-mâché model where it once stood ("Tradition Crumbles" 1989: 35).

At MIT, students regularly paint messages and "Smoot" marks—slashes of paint spaced five and a half feet apart—along the half-mile long Harvard Bridge. The marks date back to 1958 when Lambda Chi Alpha pledge Oliver Smoot agreed to lie down and be the measuring unit for the bridge's 364.4 "Smoot" lengths plus an ear (Egan 1985: 127; Geeslin 1989: 93-95; cf. Dodge, et al, 1982: 19). What's the point? Well, ever been in Boston during the winter? "Smoot marks make it possible for students to know how far they are from the other side without looking up," the frat president explained, "and you can stay huddled down in your jacket and still know how far you have to go." "Besides," Smoot himself added for good measure, they're "no more illogical than feet or yards" (Geeslin 1989: 94).

College officials did not always look kindly on what they called "painting vandalism," however. When Vanderbilt engineering students early in this century painted the school colors on a much-venerated downtown cannon, officials dismissed three upperclassmen and suspended three freshmen for a year (Conkin 1985: 142-43).

Games to drink to

Students are more likely, though, to be out painting the town than cannons or bridges. When they do, they may gather for a drinking game or two, or three. During the 1940s and 1950s, students, particularly men, popularized the "chug-a-lug," in which each drinker in a group downed a glass of beer in one fell gulp. Whoever failed to do so had to buy the next round (Dorson 1959: 265). It was a show of manly achievement, and at the same time, of bonding with buddies (Spradley and Mann 1975: 138-39). "Chugging" now generically refers to finishing off the glass and is the main penalty in many folk games played by students, both male and female.

Among the games that can be played in large groups is "Thumper." Students clap and thump on a table rhythmically while one person asks, "What's the name of the game," to which the group responds, "Thumper!" The questioner says "How do you play?" and the group responds "Fast and Dirty!" "Why do we play?" the person asks, and the crowd answers "To get fucked up!" At this point the person provides a signal, such as pulling on an ear or snapping fingers. The next person repeats what this person has done and adds a signal, and so on down the line. If someone forgets a signal or botches the order, then that person must chug his or her beer.

The game can also be played by the demand to name something rather than give a signal (Duda 1987; Griscom, et al, 1984: 39; Egan 1985: 167-68). Examples are cigarettes and cars. In a variation called "Bizz-Buzz" that uses numbers, players count off numbers in sequence from one. For all multiples of five, a person must say "bizz" and for multiples of seven, a person must say "buzz." If a player misses, then he or she has to chug (Duda 1987; Griscom, et al, 1984: 79-80; Egan 1985: 168). These games play on the effect of drinking on memory and concentration.

The ability of drinkers to articulate is tested in a tongue twister game, Turtles, with antecedents in English pub contests. In the game, usually played in smaller groups, the object is to repeat what the first person says. If this can't be done, everyone must drink, and the person who made the mistake must try again. The game can be made more challenging by being played in round, so that the caller starts off with the first line and waits for all to repeat it. Then the participants drink to the completion of a round (Douglas 1987: 55; cf. Egan 1985: 170). The lines are:

One fat hen
A couple of ducks
Three brown bears
Four running hares
Five fat fickle females sitting sipping scotch
Six simple Simons sitting on a stone
Seven Sinbad sailors sailing the seven seas
Eight egotistical egotists echoing egotistical
    ecstasies while eating an eggroll
Nine nude nublings nibbling nuts, nats, and nicotine
Ten I never was a fig-plucker or a fig-plucker's son but I'll pluck figs till a fig-
    plucker comes.

Adding stimulation to the game is the slurring of the last line, which causes the repeated utterance of a taboo word.

Other games test physical dexterity. The most common of these is Quarters, a game with many variants. The object of the game is to bounce a quarter into a cup. If the player makes it, he or she can order another student to chug. Super Quarters uses two full cups and one empty one, and players square off against each other—if a player inadvertently lands a quarter in a full cup, he or she must drink its contents. In Chandeliers, each player has a full cup and one sits in the center of the table. Players try to bounce quarters into opponents cups. If one makes it, the opponent must chug. If a quarter lands in the center cup, everyone must drink together (Duda 1987; cf. Griscom, et al., 1984: 73-74; Griscom, et al., 1986: 53-55).

Several games seem designed to be played in a dorm or at a party. They often depend on signs and numbers, whether from cards, dice, or television. In an "advanced" drinking game, "Up and Down the River," a dealer hands players five cards face down and then the dealer turns a card from the deck face up. If the card in a player's hand matches, then he or she must drink that number of times. Sometimes, reversals are allowed; the player with a match can make someone else drink (Duda 1987; Griscom, et al, 1986: 94-99). Combining students' fondness for social television watching and drinking are "Hi Bob" and "Cheers." Students pick a name before the airing of "The Bob Newhart Show" or "Cheers." When the name is said on the show, then the player must drink (Egan 1985:173).

In "Mexicali" or "Liar's Dice," two dice are placed in a cup. One player rolls the dice inside the cup and slams the cup to the table. The player peeks under the cup and tells the next player the result of the roll, perhaps truthfully, perhaps not. The non-roller has the option of believing the roller, rolling to beat the call, or calling "bullshit." If bullshit is called, the cup must be lifted to reveal the dice. If the roller is caught bluffing, he must drink and it is the next player's turn. If the roller wasn't lying, the player calling bullshit has to drink and the roller goes again. If a 3-2 shows up, then everyone must drink, and 21, or "Mexicali," is the highest roll possible (Duda 1987; Dundes and Pagter 1975: 5-7; Griscom, et al, 1984: 71-72; Egan 1985: 171).

Paul Douglas documented sixty-five drinking games in 1986 from Towson State students, and comparable collections exist at Indiana, Western Oregon State, Penn State, and Wayne State. Douglas found that previous generations of students knew of drinking games but did not engage in the frequency and variety of games as do today's students (1987: 57). Drinking games are played normally by underage drinkers from high school to college, but usually trail off as one nears graduation. Drinking in these games is made social and playful to initiate young drinkers; alcohol, after all, is an acquired taste. Many of the new drinkers, Douglas found, were women who felt more at ease drinking beer and engaging in publicly assertive behaviors by participation in games. Fifteen percent of the students, Douglas found, played these games at least twice a month.

For some, the games are not about drinking but about socializing. In a college setting where one meets strangers, they allow for relating to others; they break the ice, as students are fond of saying. The attitude reveals a pattern in modern American culture of people needing mood-altering substances to mediate their social relations with strangers. "Fun," used so often to describe what students are after, first means engagement of others through conviviality, and second, the release from everyday reality, which suggests the loosening of inhibition.

In drinking games one finds mixed messages toward America's favorite mood-altering substance. While many of the games carry the warning that drinking adversely affects memory, concentration, activity, and speech, they also make it the source of play, a definition of friendly fun. The games aren't designed to select a winner as much as to isolate a loser. Typical of many pranks, players will in fact "gang up" in these games on someone they feel can't handle drinking. The sickness that one may suffer is the ultimate embarrassment, and at the same time a sign of initiation. Another special characteristic of drinking games is that they focus on *how* the game is played rather than on the achievement of the winner. Is the message then to avoid drinking, or to drink heavily if one is to fit in? For many the answer is ambiguous.

Killing and being killed

Other games in college, sobering in their content, are categorized as "serious fun." "Killer" and all its variations swept college campuses during the 1980s. Variously called "The Hunt," "Assassin," "KAOS" (Killer as an Organized Sport), "Gotcha," "Kisser," "Eradicator," and "Seventh Victim," the game appears to be an outgrowth of the 1965 movie "The Tenth Victim" although most players of the game are unaware of the source (Johnson 1980: 81-101; cf. Fine 1983). The movie was set in the twenty-first century when huge wars have been replaced by millions of small ones. Computers pair players who play alternately as assassins and victims in ten games. In some reports, a student at the University of Michigan is given credit for introducing the game there after the movie came out (Editors 1982: 84). Regardless of origin, the fact remains that the game is played with rules often passed by word of mouth by students from one coast to the other, in colleges big and small. Here are some versions taken from responses to my surveys:

Assassin: Each person in a dorm has a water gun and picks a person out of a hat that they are supposed to kill with the gun. When you kill your person they have to give you their person. Then you go after that person. That goes on until there is one person left, who is the winner (Hood College, 1988).

Gotcha: Everyone gets an index card. You wrote your name on it, and then they are collected and mixed up. They're distributed so that everyone would have someone else's name. Everyone is given a dart gun with suction cup darts, and they're supposed to "kill" the person on the card with the dart gun. You had three tries to get someone. When you "killed" someone, you got their card and had to "kill" the person listed on their card, too. There were prizes for the winner (York College, 1984).

KAOS: You fill out a form describing your class schedule and habits. You have to stake out your victim, take him by surprise, and shoot him before he catches you. You have to make a kill in seven days or else you're terminated, taken off the roster. There's an obituary list where scores are registered, and the obits are pretty funny with sexual references and creative prose. Awards are given for the best shots as well as the survivor (UCLA, 1980).

Students didn't describe the game setting futuristically, but rather as a spy or nihilistic fantasy. Many students described the game as a way to meet other students, especially of the opposite sex. The student at Hood added that it brought a dorm together, and was complemented later in the semester by another secret-identity custom: Secret Santa. Sociologists commenting on the game cite the growing tolerance for violence in America which allows such a game to thrive (Johnson 1980: 92-93).

Folklorist John William Johnson, however, is kinder to the game, and points out that the game provides an outlet for "surrogate sin," feeding on new freedoms young students are finding in college, "but in a very safe way." He interprets the game in its college context, suggesting a "cathartic function." He explains: "Such a game lends itself readily to the highly tense atmosphere of university life, which involves many forms of academic pressures: deadlines, exams, identity crises, term papers, and the questioning of traditional mores and values. The establishment of life-and-death scenarios totally within the realm of fantasy can help relieve the tension of college life through the medium of Killer, especially at the moment of killing or being killed" (Johnson 1980: 92-93).

I also suggest that the text of the game itself provides a model of success in a modern world. It stresses more than other games the role of individual alienated from any group. Faced with the prospect of diminishing expectations of success, each person looks out for him or herself, simultaneously acting as attacker and victim. It is a role protecting privacy yet remaining always vulnerable. It is simultaneously and tensely competitive and cooperative. To a large degree, the modern college with its intensity and divisiveness accentuates this individualistic character of the "me" generation, and, many would argue, its paranoid style (see Sennett 1977; Bellah, et al, 1985).

The Greek life

A traditional place in the college where "me" becomes "us" is in Greek letter societies. In fraternities and sororities, one sings the praises of fellowship, ritually honors "brothers" and "sisters," and parades the value of commitment. For a long time Greek organizations represented sociality and school spirit to students at small colleges. When students thought of a haven within the multiversity, they looked to the Greek houses. So why not now? Although membership in Greek organizations is up, fraternities and sororities are clearly on the defensive. They are being scrutinized, restricted, reformed, suspended, and at many campuses, banned. The secret world of fraternities and sororities, long the bastion of old-time college tradition, is out in the open; it is changing in a society watchful for instances of abuse in any form.

Social fraternities on campuses blossomed after the early nineteenth century. Evolving from literary and debating societies, and the model of Greek honor societies such as Phi Beta Kappa, the early fraternities first provided fellowship outside the control of the college. Students saw an advantage in forming fraternities, often ten or fewer in a chapter, where the support came from one another in an intimate setting. In the often repressive atmosphere of the old-time college, the fraternities sought out a social, fun side of college life. Sometimes they attracted members looking for escape from the depressing lot of dormitory life in the nineteenth century. Greek houses appeared much more attractive and independent.

Fraternities also promised something for the long term: the business contacts one needed after college. The fellowship of the Greek society would last a lifetime, members vowed, and serve to garner favors. This led to the second important characteristic of fraternities, and later sororities—their exclusiveness. The undergirding principles were about the privileges of a fraternity of like-minded, like-acting, and often like-looking members. Invoking Greek civilization in their name, fraternities held up lofty ideals of educated, privileged youth.

In their rivalries with one another, they perpetuated the competitiveness of the old-time college. But they often acted together in college politics, leading many student governments across America, and they stood up for student concerns against many college administrations. "Rushing" to attract fraternity and sorority members became a major campus event to rival the old scraps and rushes. Pledging and gaining a fraternity pin were signs of status indeed. To serve their social ends, the Greek letter organizations instituted initiations, rituals, and customs to select appropriate members. The Greek customs saw to it that close friends were made quickly, more quickly than students thought they ever could back in the dorms.

The dramatic social widening of colleges to include more traditionally excluded groups changed the role of the college fraternities and sororities. They were still about fellowship and exclusiveness, but with the number of "independent" students growing, they could not exert the control they once did, and they no longer represented the voice of the student body. (Horowitz 1987: 82-150). To maintain their social niche, fraternities, sometimes as large as two hundred members to a chapter, threw the big parties, gained status in athletic competitions, and drew out a lively college spirit, often at a considerable cost to intellectualism (Egan 1985: 223).

Civil rights legislation of the 1960s frowned upon discriminatory racial practices of policies in the fraternities. More and more colleges responded to complaints about the exclusiveness and rivalry in fraternities in the midst of calls for an open democratic society. In addition, the parties—particularly at fraternity houses, sometimes packing in hundreds of students—often caused problems with violence, alcohol, and sexual abuse. Meanwhile, coed dorms diminished some of the appeal of the frat as a place to mix with the opposite sex, especially in the iconoclastic 1960s.

Though some pundits expected that frats would face extinction in a new age of college life after the 1960s, a resurgence of the frat occurred during the 1980s (see Horowitz 1987: 273-79). Undergraduate fraternity membership went up from more than two hundred thousand nationwide in 1980 to four hundred thousand by the end of the decade, and more than a thousand new chapters formed. Sorority memberships increased similarly to a total of two hundred forty thousand (Betterton 1988: 179). Still, more than ninety percent of college students today are not Greek, though at many campuses Greeks dominate college life. Greek organizations claim more than forty percent of the student body at some forty-five colleges. DePauw is the most Greek at around eighty percent, and other campuses with strong frat representation are Washington and Lee and the College of William and Mary (Yale 1990).

Although many of the colleges with strong Greek systems tend to be of moderate size, at larger universities, the frats and sororities are also making inroads. The intimacy of the Greek house sometimes seems more attractive to students facing mass campuses of more than 30,000 students and dorms holding hundreds of students. Another factor influencing the resurgence of frats is that when drinking ages rapidly moved up from eighteen to twenty-one and colleges cracked down on alcohol in dorms, many Greek houses became underage drinking clubs. Fraternity and sorority membership opened up to more campus types.

Many fraternities during the 1980s reduced the length of their pledging periods, and softened or eliminated their hazing practices. Some sororities meanwhile benefited from women forsaking the coed dorm and its atmosphere of sexual competition. Students also reported to me the need to have a small group to rely on and support, a surrogate family, that would nurture them through what they perceive to be difficult social as well as academic years. The perception that future financial security is a primary goal of college had an influence on other students. The feeling that jobs are more competitive, especially in business, also restored the role of fraternities and sororities as a place to make future professional contacts.

But if the independence of the Greek organizations was going to be maintained under renewed administrative, faculty, and even community scrutiny, the image, and some of the roles, of the fraternities would have to be changed. Yes, maintain tradition, give students a peer support group, encourage community service and college spirit, administrators admonished, but don't harass, exclude, or abuse other students. At Bucknell, Gettysburg, Colgate, Colby, Amherst, Franklin and Marshall, and Middlebury, faculty voted to eliminate the Greeks altogether after reports of sexual and racial harassment, injuries caused by hazing, and drug and alcohol abuse. Two national fraternities—Zeta Beta Tau and Tau Kappa Epsilon—moved to improve the Greek image by eliminating pledging. Zeta Beta Tau also closed two chapters, including one at Ohio State accused of violations of rules for drinking, drug abuse, and hazing. While maintaining pledgeship, four other national fraternities—Alpha Gamma Rho, Kappa Delta Rho, Phi Sigma Kappa, and Alpha Epsilon Pi—announced programs to eliminate hazing (Quinto 1989: 27-28).

In the 1990s fraternities and sororities are shedding their "Animal House" image on the one hand, and clean-cut elitism on the other. Students seeking Greek status typically now need minimum grade point averages, and will not be turned away on account of race and religion. Fraternities and sororities are accenting the positive, and trying to point out that the abuses are rare and shouldn't reflect on all Greekdom. The Greek organizations play up the service roles they take on in the community, the brotherhood and sisterhood they offer in the anonymous, individualistic world of mass university life, and the cultural passage they provide through a turbulent period of a student's development.

Pledging

Today much of the feeling of initiation of old-time flag and cane rushes can still be found in the fraternity and sorority rushes. So as not to distract new students, many colleges prohibit rushes until at least the second semester of a student's freshmen year. Others insist on waiting until the sophomore year. Students choose from a number of fraternities and sororities, many with reputations for a certain ethnic or racial membership, social atmosphere, and outside interests such as athletics or business. The Greek organization offers the prospective student a "bid" to pledge with the fraternity or sorority which the student can accept or refuse.

Alpha Chi Omega for many years held a formal dessert in which a piece of "dream cake" was given to rushees. A story and song accompanied the cutting of the cake; they concern a lonely princess who dreamed of having many friendships. The rushees are told to take a piece of cake and wish upon it before they go to sleep; if they receive their bids, their wish will come true and they will have many friendships (Christner 1967: 11-12; Glavan 1968: 195). Some frat members have a custom called a "shakeup" or a "jolly up," celebrating the acceptance of a bid by lifting the student over their heads and tossing him around (Egan 1985: 28). Many sororities throw a pledge dinner honoring the students accepting bids (Washburn 1976: 2; Glavan 1968: 192-98).

Sororities usually more kindly call it Inspiration Week, Initiation Week, or the euphemistic Help Week, but it's still Hell Week—the climax of activities designed to initiate the "pledge" into the fraternity or sorority. For weeks before Hell Week, the pledge has learned songs, followed rules of address and etiquette, and fashioned special clothing or emblems. Pledges are assigned big brothers or sisters and as a "class" they take part in sports, drink-offs, barbecues, "walk-outs," and singathons (Egan 1985: 45-46). To hear a national frat executive explain it, "Pledging is the period of time when prospective members of fraternities participate in planned, non-esoteric activities to familiarize themselves with the organization and its members before they make the decision to be inducted as a full member for life. In the great majority of cases these activities are developmental and supportive of the pledge/associate member. Hazing is an aberration of this process" (Martin 1990: B3). Nonetheless, actives during Hell Week often resort to hazing to test the mettle of pledges, to instill values of the organization, and to build unity before crossing over to the status of "active" brother or sister. Many critics question how much hazing involves mental or physical abuse; most chapters, however, view initiations not as hazing but as invoking traditional tasks and ceremonies to bring out the special status of Greeks in close fellowship with one another.

Chapters usually require pledges to clean and repair the Greek houses. Chapters may also require pledges to wear special clothing, rarely humiliating anymore, but certainly conspicuous. Pledges might carry a pledge brick and wear ties and jackets, for example, or, for sororities, pledge ribbons with the house colors and symbols. Pledges also sleep—or spend sleepless nights together—in the house during the week, and may be mobilized for a "borassing" raid on a rival house. Anytime day or night pledges may be herded to a "line-up" or, as sororities know it, a "call-out" (Egan 1985: 42-45; Acri 1989: 5; Glavan 1968: 197). At the line-up the actives remind pledges of their lowly status, calling them scums, worms, slime, lowlifes, maggots, pledgettes, and rats. The actives bark esoteric questions to pledges arranged neatly in line. Some examples are "What is my middle name? Where do I come from? What am I majoring in?" (Dalkoff 1974: 5). If the pledge doesn't know the answer, the active punishes the pledge by some kind of physical task, such as push-ups or work detail. In addition, the pledge may have to withstand teasing about some personal characteristic, such as being short, skinny, or stout, and submit to accusations of sexual inadequacy (Raphael 1988: 83).

Other physical demands on the pledges may include forced cold showers taken while singing a fraternity song (Raphael 1988: 82). Some frats will require members to make runs through town or campus, sometimes dressed down to undergarments (Britton 1987: 6-7; Egan 1985: 230). Or there's the controversial use of the symbol-laden fraternity and sorority paddle. Although typically outlawed today, hitting pledges on the rear with a paddle in initiations surfaces in reports (T. 1976: 6-7; see also Egan 1985: 57). One old fraternity prank that plays on this fear involves taking a pledge into a closed room while the other pledges wait outside. The person in the room is told to yell and scream each time the paddle is hit on a table and chair, thus creating anxiety among the waiting pledges. One pledge after another is taken in to the room, until all are in on the joke (survey response, York College, 1989; see also Raphael 1988: 88).

There may be more going on in fraternity practices such as shots on the rear with a paddle than at first meets the eye. Because the bonds among the men are supposed to be intimate, a fear arises that this may suggest homosexuality. Thus many of the demands placed on pledges to appear sexually aggressive to women, or the taunts hurled at them for acting like "fags," compensate for the risk of physical intimacy among the men. The strike on the rear with the paddle is, in essence, a homosexual attack which the pledge withstands to show his masculinity.

One former pledge described a variation from Beta Theta Pi, whose symbol is a winged dragon: "A guy would say to me, 'I am the Brother of the East who brings you the blessings of light and knowledge.' And, 'I am the Brother of the North who brings you strength and fortitude. Now prepare yourself to meet the dragon!' So they took me over to what they called the dragon's balls, some kind of round, smooth spheres. They told me to take my pants down and lean over to grab hold of the dragon's balls. Then they took my blindfold off and showed me this huge guy with a polished hack-paddle, wood, about two feet long. They told me that my final test would be to take one hack with that paddle. They said that people had been injured in the past, so I'd have to pull my balls up and cup them with my hands. So I pulled my own balls up and leaned over." The paddler gives his most threatening advance and the actives give their best screams to scare the pledges waiting outside, but the pledge ends up getting a light tap on the butt. Then the actives announce, "You made it! Congratulations!" (Raphael 1988: 88).

A similar relief comes from an initial line-up reported by Robert Egan: "the pledges are requested to bring a carrot to the line-up—an innocent vegetable in itself, but an instrument of loathing to wide-eyed pledges who have heard those stories about frozen hot dogs during Hell Week. The pledges' worst fears seem to be justified when, as soon as the line-up begins, they are asked to take their pants down. Not to worry. The actives just want to see, in the words of one brother, 'if the pledges are wearing 'grown-up' boxer shorts or if Mommy still has them in Fruit of the Looms.' Nothing happens to the guys in boxers—but the guys in 'Fruits' get wedgies until they say they will change their evil ways. Then the pledges eat the carrots" (1985: 43-44).

Although related, the demand on pledges to undress probably suggests different social lessons. To be sure, pledges learn not to treat the state of undress as a sexual threat to one another. Line-ups, for instance, are frequently held in showers (Egan 1985: 43-44). Further, it lends a feeling of primitiveness to the young pledge, in contrast to the clothed "active." As a prospective fraternity member, the pledge is reminded that he is different from non-members. Successfully running through quadrangles in undergarments turns what could be an embarrassment into a socially shared triumph. The pledge has proudly defied the expectations of others. As with tasks asking for physical strength, the "undies runs" ask for mental strength. With the support of his brothers, the pledge has triumphed over his own inhibitions.

One young man who experienced rigorous frat hazing—and might have been expected to resent it—described it this way: "Hell Week brings the pledges together. It forever gives them a point of departure, a common center with which to identify. By the mere fact that a pledge class goes through Hell Week together, each pledge cannot help but feel a certain kinship with his fellow pledges. And the importance of this cannot be overestimated. In a fraternity that survives because its members consider themselves brothers, unity is vital.... The activities associated with Hell Week thus serve to divert the tension surrounding the pledge's introduction into the house. When the week has ended, pledges and actives are fully familiarized with one another" (Klein 1975: 19).

Similar responses were recorded by Ray Raphael in his study of men's initiations during the 1980s. As one informant told him, "I have good, strong memories of the comradeship that the fraternity developed. We had a real acceptance of each other. You did not have to prove yourself anymore—after you had proven yourself during Hell Week" (p. 89). A former pledge also told me of Hell Week, "I thought it was going to be stupid, and at first I probably did feel silly sometimes, but, you know, as I accomplished more things and went through it with my brothers, it gave me strength. I did something special and I had an identity others didn't have. I never felt lost again like I did when I was a freshman. I belonged to something, and others belonged to me" (interview, 1989).

While fraternities have generally toned down hazing, some of the cases pending show the risks when hazing goes overboard. At the University of Lowell, six fraternity members were charged under the state's anti-hazing law over a stunt that sent a pledge to the hospital with a body temperature of 109 (Members had bundled him in a sleeping bag and turned on heaters nearby); a fraternity chapter was disbanded after the alcohol-related death of a pledge (he and thirteen others were required to drink kamikazes, a potent vodka concoction); and a pledge at the University of Delaware claimed in a lawsuit that someone dumped caustic oven cleaner over his head during a fraternity "Hell Night."

Besides denouncing hazing for its potential mental and physical abuse to pledges, feminists at the University of Pennsylvania decried fraternity initiations for perpetuating a "phallo-centric sexual culture" that sanctions violence against women. One anthropologist cited a 1983 incident in which pledges were blindfolded with a sanitary napkin, stripped naked, and forced to put a heat ointment on their genitals while other fraternity brothers urged them not to act like "fags" or "wimps" (Collins 1988: 3B).

To Lionel Tiger, the reason for this aggressive testing of pledges is the special need men have to clarify their ambiguity about socio-sexual roles in adolescence—especially in American society, which does not provide society-wide rites of passage for a boy to become a man (Tiger 1969: 190-92). While many recognize the need for cultural passage during adolescence, reforms have been suggested to stress the positive aspects of initiation (Quinto 1989: 27-28). Eliminating hazing altogether is one; another is to bring back the kind of strong in-house supervision by faculty or professional housemothers that was common during the 1950s (Krattenmaker 1989: 9, 12). Still other reforms involve reducing or eliminating pledging, instituting coed fraternities, eliminating separate residences for Greeks, or providing stronger social alternatives in the dorms.

In the name of building brotherhood, fraternities are nonetheless hanging on to their ritual "dousings" and "reversals." Some houses use dousing in a nearby pond or in the showers to mark the passing from a pledge to an active; others use it during Hell Week. At Duke, one student recalled, "the threat of being hauled away encouraged you to move in packs," thus forcing pledges to rely on one another. Tempers did flare occasionally, however, and punches were landed (DeParle 1988: 45).

One way for pledges to release this frustration is reversal weekends. During this time, the pledges act like actives; they are relieved of work details and pledge tests, and they get the run of the house (T. 1976: 6-7). In other versions, the pledges borass the house or lock out the actives by constructing elaborate barricades. Another ploy is to kidnap an active and take him along on a walkout to another campus or site; they leave behind a message in the form of, say, taking all the silverware and dishes from the kitchen (Free 1982: 3). In a variation, the pledges take the kidnapped active to a hiding place and give the other actives clues to his whereabouts. If the actives discover the victim before receiving the last clue or before time runs out, the pledges have to throw a party for the actives; if they don't make the discovery, the actives serve the pledges dinner (Egan 1985: 50-52).

The discovery of a missing item, namely the active, by figuring out clues is a reversal of the longstanding fraternity tradition of scavenger hunts for pledges during Hell Week. Often held dusk to dawn, the scavenger hunt requires pledges to bring back, by a deadline, items on a list prepared by the actives. The hunt challenges pledges physically and mentally, and forces them to work together intensely. Sometimes the items on the list are open to interpretation; an example is the request to bring back a "bird," which was answered by pledges extending their middle finger at the actives. As the example suggests, many of the items are sexual in their nature. Frat pledges bring back large bras, contraceptive devices, and autographs on bodily parts (Egan 1985: 53). Another common requirement is to bring back instant photographs of deeds accomplished ranging from "mooning" a hotel to hugging a policeman.

Then there are "walks" or "dumps." In this custom, actives take pledges miles away from the house to a remote spot, often take away some of their clothing, or give them some outlandish clothing to wear, and tell them to make it back by their wits and small change. In a variation, the actives "walk" the pledges, requiring them to do tasks along the way, or to check out places associated with ghostly legends. At DePauw, pledges had to throw their shoes and socks into a pile, and the footgear was mixed together. The pledges were given only a few seconds to retrieve their goods before setting out. The mad dash meant that the pledge often ended up wearing another person's shoe (Berkeley Folklore Archives, 1975). Reversal is possible here, too. Tradition sometimes calls for pledges to dump or walk the rush chairman (Egan 1985: 62).

Distinguishing pledging in historically black fraternities is the use of "lines," "step shows," "signals," and occasionally "branding." Although pledges now rarely are shackled or tied together "on line," as they once were, they still walk across campus in formation with military-style synchronized steps. Pledges line up in size order, wear uniforms—often of their own making—and speak in unison. Many chapters require black pledges to refrain during the pledge period from drinking alcohol, eating sweets, having sex, and/or speaking with non-members (Egan 1985: 44-45). The distinctive features of black pledging provided the backdrop of Spike Lee's movie "School Daze" (1987), in which he brings out the severe regimen of being "on line." For many, being "on line" is designed to develop even more unity than found in many historically white fraternities. The idea is conveyed that the pledges, as minorities among the frats, as minorities in society, have to be tougher, more creative, more united than members of other organizations. Also at stake is a lifelong commitment, for while many white fraternities and sororities serve their main purposes in the college setting, black Greeks maintain their activities well after college in community chapters (Gadson 1989: 34-36, 136-37).

"Step shows," a member of Alpha Phi Alpha explained, "are the soul and spirit of black fraternity social life" (Nomani 1989: 1). Based on African-American musical forms, the stepping by six to nine pledges is a study in coordination and unity. Pledges in their lines break into a series of precisely synchronized steps which create a syncopated beat. The pledges accompany the steps with chanting and singing proclaiming loyalty to the fraternity or sorority. As a Hampton graduate explained, "Stepping is a form of precision and motion. It's competition, it's publicity, it's emotion. It relates back to Africa, to

Black pledges "stepping on line," Indiana University, 1977. (Simon Bronner)

African tribes and the movements they do. It's a tight bond we have of being brothers" (Gammage 1989: 2B).

When I first encountered a step show at Indiana University during the 1970s, it was a private affair for other black fraternities and sororities. The show started about 1 a.m., and for a few hours, distinctively costumed lines from different fraternities presented songs, dancing, and recitations to the sharply syncopated beat of their marching. Besides proclaiming their loyalty to a particular fraternity, the lines also hurled barbs at other frats, and the audience noisily encouraged them. Despite the distractions, negative or positive, of the vocal crowd, the pledges were expected to maintain their serious, concentrated looks and continue their routines. During the 1980s, competitive step shows have gone public, being presented to the whole campus community at Virginia, Michigan State, Northwestern, Penn State, and North Texas (Anderson 1987; Gammage 1989; Nomani 1989: 1, 4; "Fraternity" 1989; Moore 1989).

Different black fraternities and sororities have distinctive hand signals and yells they often sound at parties and picnics. Omega Psi Phi members bark "Woofa, Woofa!" and form an inverted Omega with their hands over their heads. Deltas make a triangle with their fingers and holler "Oo-ooo-oop!" (Egan 1985: 120-21). The different signals, signs, and yells are likely to be apparent at massive reunions that black fraternities and sororities run in many cities. In addition to social activities, the fraternities and sororities mobilize politically during these reunions. For instance, the eight black Greek organizations worked together to spearhead the letter-writing campaign to declare Martin Luther King's birthday a legal holiday (Gadson 1989: 36).

A controversial practice among some black fraternity members is branding as part of initiation rituals. Members voluntarily take twelve-inch heated irons and shape Omega or Sigma symbols on their arms or backs. At Michigan State, Omega Psi Phi received criticism from the local press for the practice, and responded by saying, "It's just an individual's way of showing how much he loves his fraternity," and "It represents a common bond of brotherhood" (Boettcher 1980; Egan 1985: 67).

Sorority pledging, black and white, is often a variation building on the themes of family and expressiveness (Young 1962:379-96). In comparison with the grim ceremonies of male fraternities, sorority initiations are more socially than individually oriented, and involve considerably softer physical demands on pledges.

"When I became a sister," one student explained, "it was like entering into a big family. Every pledge got a Big Sister and the pledge class had a Pledge

Mom. Pledging usually lasts about six weeks and begins with an induction ceremony. This ceremony begins with the sisters in an open circle, which means that they are united but welcome new members. They all recite the creed of the organization and they have candles. One person lights a candle and the flame is passed on. Then the pledges receive their pledge pins and ribbons to wear throughout the pledge period" (Acri 1989)

Sororities place great demands on pledges to show caregiving qualities and creative abilities to one another. Fraternities, often in manly military style, reward values of toughness and dominance; sororities reward creativity and cooperation. For the sororities, the risk of intimacy is not perceived to be as great, since women are socialized to express themselves more physically and emotionally toward one another, and they tend to avoid imitating the implicitly homophobic practices of the frats.

In some sorority chapters, pledges must earn "pearls," twenty-two in all, which symbolize the pearls placed in their sorority pin once they are initiated. Pledges earn pearls for passing pledge exams, attending campus events, and doing service work. A progressive search for clues is used to lead pledge to her "new mother." As a sister explained, "The clues lead the girls through the house and finally to the informal living room, where the sorority moms are seated under sheets to which their social security numbers are pinned" (Washburn 1976: 7). Sororities, though, have their share of pranks and escapades as well, especially "walkouts" and "borassing." At Shippensburg, actives took pledges to a remote cemetery and related a ghostly legend about the founding of the sorority. Pledges were blindfolded and ushered to the grave of a woman who supposedly founded the sorority. Actives tell the pledges that this woman wants to meet them. With her heart beating fast, a pledge steps forward and a skeleton hand with clay and a sponge around it is put in her hand, causing her to scream (Barrick Folklore Archives, 1989).

Another sorority tradition is the humorous skit produced by the pledges for the actives. The material pokes fun at the actives, especially at their vanity and their relations with men. If the skit goes off well, the pledges are given pledge points or smaller work loads (Egan 1985: 49). Song is another important artistic expression. Although fraternities also require singing, sororities tend to use it more extensively. Pledge classes serenade the actives at dinner, in front of the house's fireplace (occasions called "firesides"), on the lawn at night, and at other houses (Egan 1985: 49; Christner 1967; Taboada 1967; Maurer 1976). Some critics complain, however, that pledges are sometimes made to serenade in undergarments or bikinis.

Songs of the greeks

Beyond this occasional hazing, songs are used as forms of address as well as entertainment. Sororities have songs for welcomes, congratulations, farewells; songs explain the significance of pins and activities, and voice the values of the sorority. Spaced out through the week, serenading can take on a different character depending on what night it is. Monday night songs are typically formal and inspirational. One example refers to the "lyre," the sorority pin (Christner 1967:7; see also Glavan 1962: 194-95):

> *Our love is faithful to the lyre*
> *The symbol of our lives.*
> *Together let us seek the heights*
> *Together let us strive.*
> *Alpha Chi, Alpha Chi,*
> *To you we'll always be*
> *A steadfast loyal guardian of*
> *Our precious symphony.*
>
> *And so our pledge is made.*
> *Our harps are found.*
> *The harpstrings of our lyre*
> *Ring forth again to tell the world of our fulfilled desire.*
> *We dedicate this song to you,*
> *Our dear fraternity.*
> *To Alpha Chi, to Alpha Chi,*
> *Everlasting loyalty.*

Congratulations and other informal salutations are offered in song during the week. Here, for example, is a congratulation song from Alpha Chi at UCLA:

> *Here's to (name)*
> *We'll never let her down!*
> *Here's to (name)*
> *We'll never let her down!*
> *And when she hits that line,*
> *There'll be no light at all!*
> *There'll be a hot time in the old town tonight!*
> *Here's to (name)! Yeah!*

Many of the songs express the distinctions between the many sororities, such as this song from Kappa Kappa Gamma (Taboada 1967: 36):

Oh honey, would you love me any
Better if I lied like a Gamma Phi
If I partied like a Delta Delta Delta
Or cheated like a Pi Beta Phi, Beta Phi
If I danced like a Chi Omega, ugh
Or strutted like the Thetas do,
Or shot a hot line like the damn
Delta Gammas 'stead of kissin' like the Kappas do?
Incidentally I'm a Kappa, too
Let's go out and pitch a little woo!

Friday night is reserved for "rasty" songs often about sex and drinking (Christner 1967: 20):

Who says Alpha Chis never stay out late?
Who's that swinging on the fire escape?
Just another Alpha Chi with her lovin' date
She came home early for a class at eight. Oh-h

Alpha Chi girl… Gotta have her lovin'
Alpha Chi girl…Just another smooch.
Alpha Chi girl… Gotta have her lovin'
She came home early 'cause she ran out of hooch,
Ran out of hooch boys!

To this kind of selection must be added a host of risqué fraternity songs full of braggadocio on drinking and sex (Reuss 1965; Teplitz 1976; Craig 1974). A perennial favorite is a parody of Cornell's "High Above Cayuga's Waters":

High above a Pi Phi's garter well above her knee
Stands the symbol of her honor, her virginity
Roll her over, oh, so gently
Down in the grass
This is what men fight and die for
A piece of Pi Phi ass

(T. 1976: 18; see also Egan 1985: 195)

The same song can be used against a rival fraternity:

Far below Acacia's standards,
There's a motley crew
One hundred and twenty sons of bitches
Known as Sigma Nus
Half the world is white and pure
The other half is Sigma Nure

(Reuss 1965: 154)

Another song that's been around a long time with many variations is a convivial parody of "Put On Your Old Gray Bonnet":

Bring out that old silver goblet with the ZBT on it,
And we'll open up another keg of beer,
For it ain't for knowledge that we came to college,
But to raise hell while we're here.

In one common variation, the last line is sung as "prevent virginity" (Reuss 1965: 160-64).

Survey responses tell me that the group singing tradition among the brothers and sisters has declined to a few occasions, and to be sure, more than a few hall men and women know their share of bawdy songs as well, but Greeks especially use singing to showcase their many voices singing as one. Their shared knowledge of the songs points to their shared cultural bond; it is a form of ritual communication and release.

Parties in Greekdom

Besides singing, Greeks are often known for partying. They have the houses for it, and as a mark of distinction, each frat commonly devotes its organizational skills to giving the parties creative themes. Given their association with scant dress, vacation, and released inhibitions, tropical themes are favorites for campus parties. As might be expected, Phi Gamma Delta, called "Fijis," take special pride in throwing parties encouraging students to go native. Great effort goes into making the house over into a tropical isle complete with huts and war shields. Other tropical parties brag "Give Me Samoa," "Let's Get Lei-ed," and "Taiwan On" (Egan 1985: 143-44).

The movie "Animal House" (1978) saw to it that toga parties have become old hat by now, but other ancients—Vikings, Neanderthal Man, Egyptian kings, Medieval knights—are celebrated in fraternity parties (Egan 1985: 145-47). American popular culture gets its due in Wild West, Barn Dance, Las Vegas, and Hollywood parties. The Bowery Ball was a popular Phi Delt party at Penn State until animal-rights groups protested the custom of swallowing salamanders.

Sigma Alpha Epsilon is known for its annual Paddy Murphy parties, which uses a Prohibition-era theme. Murphy, according to legend and song, is an Irish drunkard hero given to womanizing and rowdiness (Reuss 1965: 302-6; Dorson 1949: 676-77; Egan 1985: 150-51). Murphy is given a mock funeral procession and Irish wake, surrounded by guests dressed in Prohibition-era outfits. The party that follows often includes the singing of Paddy Murphy songs, mock sermons, and theatricals on Murphy's life or ghost.

To the chagrin of critical observers of Greekdom, animated parties like Murphy's often build on ethnic stereotypes. At the University of California at Davis, a "Sombreros and Cervezas" party outraged the Chicano community, who protested the party's stereotypes about alcoholism and laziness in Mexican society, and a "Godfather Night" stirred outcries from Italian-Americans (Mechling 1989: 295). At Juniata, a "Bridal Party" raised eyebrows when the mock wedding caricatured Poles; the party had beer, Kielbasa, and polka music, and participants took on faked Polish names (survey response, 1989).

"Greek Slave Auctions," a longstanding fundraiser for fraternities similarly drew fire when a black member was auctioned at Davis (Mechling 1989: 292-93). The intent was to build on the Greek theme to offer the services of a member for a day to a high bidder, but to a public, the event was taken as an insensitive reference to the enslavement of Africans. A Davis faculty member's description of the controversy is revealing for its commentary on the different worlds of the fraternity and the campus community: "The fraternity members, including the black member, were puzzled by the outcry. The fraternity was integrated and, indeed, united in conducting the event. To have excluded the black member from participating in the auction would have been discriminatory in the eyes of the fraternity members. Where the fraternity had miscalculated was in its assumption that it could move a ritual from the relatively high-context, private world of the folk group into the public realm of strangers who did not share the group's intimacy or their frame for interpreting the ritual... What the fraternity took to be an expression of solidarity was interpreted as racist and divisive" (Mechling 1989: 293).

Greeks engage in many community service and charitable fundraising events, and point to them as the civic benefits of fraternity and sororities. It is estimated that fraternities and sororities raise nine million dollars a year for charitable causes (Egan 1985: 134). Greeks sponsor health fairs and blood drives, serve in Big Brother and Big Sister programs, and volunteer for community projects and hospital duty. Fraternities and sororities are also typically among the most active organizations helping the campus. They often serve as campus ambassadors, guiding visitors through campus, and ushering events.

Holiday telegrams are a favorite fraternity and sorority fundraiser for charity; for a price, Greeks will personally deliver a note to another student on campus. Around Valentine's Day, it's a Cupidgram; for Christmas, it's a Santagram; at Hallowe'en, it's a Pumpkingram. You can also buy "wake-ups" or "tuck-ins" for friends: the sorority sister will wake the person and present him or her with a card and a cup of coffee, or tuck him or her in with a stuffed bear and read a bedtime story (Egan 1985: 134). Greeks sponsor marathons, special olympics, and contests of dubious achievement (e.g., ugly bartender, kissing). On some campuses, fundraising and fun combine in versions of Greek Week or Derby Days. During Greek Week, you're likely to encounter chariot and bed races, eating contests, and keg tosses, all for a good cause (Egan 1985: 115-18). Derby Days, Sigma Chi's fundraiser, includes wacky field events and the Derby Chase, where sisters get points for plastic derbies grabbed off a Sig head (Egan 1985: 140).

Fraternities and sororities don't have a monopoly on fun and games on America's campuses, and they are not the only sources of community. The identity and solidarity they provide are appealing for many, but less so for others who find social and expressive outlets elsewhere, frequently well away from campus. The social side of college life is found in a number of places from the stadium to the dorm. In these different settings, students search for social connection on campus in the face of an increasingly individualistic culture. They seek cultural as well as academic passage through their absorbing, exhilirating, and frightening experience on campus. They seek emotional release and self-discovery at a formative age when they feel they have to define human relations, morals, and limits for themselves. From the tussle of class scraps to the intrigue of futuristic games to the wackiness of Greek field days, students realize social lessons.

"Remember the Homework that Never Got Done"

The college campus resounds with talk of the strange and wondrous. A walk through campus with students inspires the tell-tale spirits of college life. After all, passing through the gates of the college typically creates the impression of entering a mythical kingdom, a new arcadian domain. Past the bustle of streets and stores one finds a winding path through nature and around proud edifices often showing medieval faces. In this commercial-free zone, there seems to be a unity of purpose, a march of thought. The march stretches from the dormitories around the library and past the halls of academe. Giving focus to the domain are campus markers—the clock and bell towers, columns, obelisks, statues, and quadrangles.

Students coming to a campus feel a need to adjust to this environment by connecting themselves to those that have come before. The continuity provided by the "real story" of folklore allows them to understand the personality of a place, to learn the lessons of the ancients, and to know the portents ahead. Imposing buildings are humanized, and so made accessible. Fellow students and other strangers become familiar. When stories are told, students stop and listen.

Fears and joys of campus life come out in stories that can edge toward laughter or tears. Whether ghostly legends or bawdy jokes, they raise emotions, they entertain and teach, and they offer release in the grind of life around the sobering college landscape. They allow the expression of feelings, values, and hopes. In the special frame that folklore provides, fears and joys are translated into symbols and telling events, and given plenty of room to operate. The stories may be told as true, but more often as half-truth with the elaboration of a twice-told tale. That doesn't detract from their value. Indeed, it adds to it, for the "truth" of the stories lies in the belief and sentiment expressed—the cultural perception, if you will—in this "unofficial" version given from one student to another in folklore. Students favor legends and jokes because they invite participation or response. There's usually enough moral ambiguity built into legends that listeners often initiate discussion about the lessons in them.

Lore of the land

A number of campus legends make reference to the Native American presence that gave way to the college. Such legends often are given romanticized literary treatment. When students take in the landscape around them they often get a dose of Indian lore to explain the human relation to old trees, streams, and hills, so dear to the early inhabitants of the land. In their retellings, the stories evoke thoughts of love and romance, so dear to the hearts of students. At the University of Texas, the "Battle Oaks" still standing on the northwest corner of campus are said to have learned the Indian tongue. "Later the tree brought happiness to an Indian brave by whispering to him of the maiden who loved him, for beneath the branches of the tree she had cried out her love for the warrior.... The University grew and the oaks became a favorite spot of the students" (Berry 1983: 58-59).

At Tennessee Wesleyan College, an Indian story is told about hackberry and oak trees on the north end of campus which serve now as a meeting point for young lovers. According to this legend, a hunting party of Cherokees found a young English officer wounded not far from where the college stands. The Indians brought the officer back to their settlement, and there the officer was nursed back to health by No-ca-too-la, the beautiful daughter of the chief. The two fell in love, and the officer was given the name Con-ne-sto-ga, meaning "The Oak." The officer met a tragic end when a jealous warrior ambushed and killed him, and the Indian maiden killed herself rather than live without the officer. The grief-stricken old chief placed a seed in each of their hands—an acorn in one and a hackberry in the other. From these seeds grew the two trees, symbolizing undying love and devotion.

Miracles and follies

Historical legends about buildings on campus often provide reminders of the college's mission. Houghton College in upstate New York is an evangelical Christian institution, and some of the stories of its expansion suggest divine intervention. When the main auditorium was built, students hear, bad weather over a weekend prevented completion of the roof and snow threatened the interior. The building superintendent called for prayer and workers. When workmen braved a snowstorm to come to the rescue of the building, they strangely found no snow on campus and were able to seal the roof. The story is also told of the college's need for native river stones for its buildings. The stones were in a field owned by a farmer demanding a sum much higher than the college could afford. "For that price we'll just let the water wash over 'em," he told them. Through the winter the water did wash over them, and moved them

Old Library Tower at SUNY at Binghamton.

onto another farmer's land. The new farmer gave the college its much-needed stones.

Convinced that colleges construct their buildings on a shoestring, and have, despite their reputation for intelligence, a knack for fouling things up, students on almost every campus have architectural folly stories. I went to school hearing that the old library tower at SUNY at Binghamton was leaning or would topple over sometime soon because the site attracted the fiercest winds in the region. Maybe mistrust of the building arose because it was the tallest building on campus, and students suffered as they braved winds to enter its grim doors. The University of Massachusetts library is the tallest building in that part of the state, and it attracts similar stories. Students assure each other that the structure is sinking into the ground. After all, they offer, the architects failed to compute the weight of the books into their designs. That must be why many shelves are left unfilled to this day (Carey 1988: 9).

Sometimes building stories are about the modern rivalry between architects and engineers. At Penn State, right on College Avenue by the entrance of the school, is the Hammond Building. Built in 1958 as an engineering hall with severe straight lines and unfriendly glass and steel, it stretches along the street for what seems like an eternity (it's 609 feet long). To explain this monstrosity, voted the ugliest building on campus, students tell the tale that architects designed the structure to be nine stories tall. Realizing that engineers had misrepresented the ability of the ground to hold the structure, the architects had to divide the building into three side-by-side sections. In a variation that adds a student comeuppance theme, it is said that after the first three floors were built, graduate students went over the calculations and found the mistake. The original design is, in fact, the blueprint for the building that went up, but that doesn't stop students from pointing out its legendary folly.

At the University of Arkansas, freshmen are told that the North Tower of Old Main is taller than the South Tower because the architect was a northern sympathizer in the Civil War. The fact is that Old Main is a replica of University Hall at the University of Illinois, unbalanced towers and all (Parler 1984: 26). At Penn State Harrisburg, the one-level residences for upper-division students in an area called Meade Heights have large, drafty sliding doors. In blustery northeastern winters, students complain of the chill. They explain the situation by pointing out that there's a second Meade Heights in Georgia (or Florida). When the two housing areas were being constructed, the plans for the houses must have been mixed up, for the ones down there look like northern fortresses against the cold.

Hammond Building, Penn State University at University Park.
(University Archives, Penn State Room)

At the University of Pennsylvania, students swear that the Irvine Auditorium, referred to as "that bizarre pile," was designed by a student who flunked out of the University of Pennsylvania's school of architecture. According to many versions of the legend, the student's father gave it to the school as revenge (Hine 1980: 1). Well, the story doesn't check out, but it highlights folk narrative's power to point out deviations from the norm, especially in imposing structures such as public malls and museums as well as lofty college buildings (see Brunvand 1989: 253-58; McCulloch 1987: 109-16).

Legend asserts that the buildings—and by extension, engineering "progress" past human scale and control—have it backwards. At SUNY at Stony

Brook students look to the "bridge to nowhere" to make their case. Built in 1970, the bridge leads from the second floor of the union building to the north wall of the library where it stops in a dead end. According to legend, the bridge was supposed to go into the library but the library was built backwards. Why, "there are skylights in there that point the wrong way," students say (Birnbach 1984: 262). Jan Harold Brunvand meanwhile reports the case of an apartment building built for students on the Bloomington campus of Indiana University which students maintain is "backwards." It "was supposed to have been curved the other way to be more in harmony with the shape of the hill." It must have been the fault of the engineers, students observe, because "the architect was very disappointed when he came to Bloomington and saw what they had done" (1989: 257).

Sometimes in collegiate legendry, rifts between university trustees and a builder cause problems. The bid for rock work on Old Main at Howard Payne was given to someone whom the board suspected of tipping the bottle. They decided to fine him one hundred dollars every time he was caught drinking on the job. According to legend, he owed the college money by the time the work was finished. Legend has it that prudish trustees at Indiana University objected to the extra endowment given the breasts of a sculpted female figure in the central fountain. The sculptor spitefully responded by making things worse: he placed fish between the figure's legs (Waymire 1978: 2-3). It is true that at Hamline University, trustees worried about undignified art ordered the removal from a residence hall of a gargoyle that portrayed a freshman, beanie and all. The eventual fate of the whimsical statue is a matter of folkloric speculation. At Case Western Reserve University, freshmen avow that the gargoyle facing west from the Gothic chapel sticks out its tongue at Case's trustees (Cramer 1976: 355).

Suicidal ghosts

By far, most legends about buildings on campus get students where they live, including the dormitories and fraternity houses. As if to both personalize the place and underscore its strangeness, new students are introduced to a resident ghost. There's often a warning embedded in the stories—the spirit may belong to a student who met a tragic end by studying too hard or not enough, or by loving too much. The ghosts are rarely malicious, but they do act up enough to let their presence be known.

At the University of North Alabama, students tell of Priscilla, who committed suicide in a women's dormitory. Some say she was distraught over failing exam grades; others whisper she was involved in an unhappy love affair with a professor. Some say she jumped down the stairwell; others are sure she hanged herself in the second floor elevator shaft. Her ghost haunts the halls of the old dorm, especially around exam time.

From Oberlin comes a related story about the spirit of a student who committed suicide during the 1950s. "She was having trouble dealing with the high pressure situation in Oberlin; it was near the end of the semester and the work was piling up. The weekend before finals her roommate was gone and she had a huge fight with her boyfriend. Feeling lonely, frustrated, and depressed, she took an overdose of sleeping pills. She was found the next afternoon by her boyfriend when he had come back to apologize. She is said to return to the room periodically looking for her boyfriend. Her sobs drift through the room and her shadow can be seen in the window, beckoning for someone to help her" (Penn State Folklore Archives, 1980).

Suicides in legends far outnumber those in real life. In narrative, they serve to warn students about letting the pressure do them in, especially in this modern day when students seem more self-absorbed and competitive. An abundance of cautions can be heard in a legend told by a student from Bethany College: "It was said that some years ago, a Bethany College student had leaped to his death from the tower that overlooks the campus. It was rumored that the student had recently broken up with his girl, was on academic probation, and was under pressure from his family to excel in school. It was spring and finals were only a week or so away and he wasn't prepared for them. He left a note in his dorm room apologizing for not being able to live up to everybody's expectations. Ever since that night, people have said they have seen his ghost near the bell tower during final exam times. Some people even say that the ghost has made the clock strike the wrong time or not ring at all, causing many a student to miss his final exam" (Penn State Folklore Archives, 1978).

Student storytelling doesn't always use a ghost to bring the point home. An example is the suicide legend recorded about Schulze Hall at Penn State. "She had been dating a guy quite seriously," a student explained there. "It was expected that at any time an engagement would be announced. One night these two lovers had a real bad argument. Everybody thought it was just a lovers' spat. Evidently it was more than that, at least to the girl involved. Nobody heard or saw the girl that night or the next day. Finally a maid opened the door and had quite a surprise waiting for her. The girl had hung herself" (Penn State Folklore Archives, 1977). Although there's no ghost, students sometimes add that grass didn't grow on the poor girl's grave (cf. Carey 1988: 9).

At Bethany College students tell of a lone grave up on a hill overlooking campus. According to legend, a coed pined so over a broken love affair that she died and was buried at the spot where she went to cry. A trip to the grave is a favorite social excursion for new students who come to check out the legend.

Lovers' ghosts

With courtship such a prevalent distraction for students, it isn't surprising that lovers' ghosts frequently haunt campuses. At Stephens College in Columbia, Missouri, students still recount the story of a young woman who found a wounded Confederate soldier in the tower of Senior Hall. The student nursed the soldier back to health, and the two fell in love. The couple decided to elope, but when they crossed the Missouri River the woman fell in and the soldier died trying to save her. It is said that the ghosts return to Senior Hall where they found their happiness. In a more cautionary variation, a student offered that the soldier left the student, vowing, however, to return to marry. "I've heard one thing," the raconteur emphasized, "that she had his baby and he never came back and she went crazy. It was just her ghost that comes back each year" (Shutan 1972: 5).

A similar story is told about Norland Hall at Wilson College—like Stephens, a women's college. The college's location in Chambersburg, Pennsylvania, site of a Civil War battle, is the backdrop for several stories of Colonel Alexander McClure, builder of the elaborate Victorian-styled Norland Hall, and his beautiful daughter (who, by the way, never existed). A Union soldier with whom the daughter was in love came back to warn the family to flee because the Confederates were coming to destroy the town. The daughter hid the injured soldier in the attic and fled. When she returned, she found him dead. He is said to be buried in the garden, and red flowers tended by the daughter mark the spot. It is also said one can hear his ghost knocking in the tower attic room. In a variation, students say the Colonel hid the daughter from a Confederate soldier. The Colonel chased the soldier into a tunnel, and when the tunnel collapsed, both were killed. The daughter committed suicide in the tower room after hearing that her father and lover were killed. The ghost of the daughter haunts the tower, while the ghosts of Colonel McClure and the soldier roam the tunnel which is now Prentis Hall (Ohlidal 1981).

Resident ghosts

Strange noises and occurrences on campus are typically blamed on ghosts. If there's a pattern to the finger-pointing stories, it's that the revenants were vulnerable young women meeting a tragic end, often by their own hands. At Kutztown University, unusual sounds emanating from the top of Old Main are explained by the story of a coed who took her dog to the top floor. She hanged herself and the dog was found dead later. The sounds must be the young woman's dog who is howling for her. That's why you can't go up to the top story today, students say to support their case (Penn State Folklore Archives, 1979). At Indiana State University, a whole cycle of stories is told about Burford Hall. Students report hearing moans, laughs, cries, and even vomiting sounds made by a resident ghost (Baker 1982: 219-21).

At Wayne State University, the ghost of yet another suicide case is blamed for unusual happenings: "She was supposed to have the other side of the room and keeps coming back, pulling things from the cupboard and making a pest of herself. I guess her spirit never rested, she was so unhappy" (Kreston 1973: 4-5). At Olivet College, students refer to "Ellen" or "Eileen" of 307 Dole. Stories range from security guards hearing orchestra music to someone whispering names when no one else is in the room (Sigler 1988:1).

At Georgia College a woman who hanged herself in Sanford Hall is blamed for spooky lights appearing on the vacant third floor, sounds of footsteps, and warm spots in the east wing. At Coe College, a freshwoman dying of pneumonia—"Helen," as she's called—is the guilty ghost. She hangs around a grandfather clock donated to the college in her memory and kept in the drawing room of her dormitory. According to legend, Helen would appear once a year at midnight in the old clock. After the clock was moved in 1980, it began to break down at exactly seven minutes to three—the time of Helen's death, or so it is rumored. Meanwhile, students living in her former room reported mysterious rearrangement of their things. Today, Helen inhabits the old dumbwaiter in the dorm. The women report hearing strange noises coming from behind a sealed door located on the first floor.

One may wonder about students being on a first-name basis with their ghosts. Women often treat the ghost as a resident guest, albeit a sometimes difficult one. She's often a lost, plaintive soul struck with heartbreak, and thus her antics are understandable, students say. Women at Brenau College, for example, have "Agnes"; at Smith, there's "Lucy" at Sessions House. These figures, like those from Wilson and Olivet, have similar legends told about them. In the Smith variant, there's the extra mysterious feature of a secret staircase to add intrigue to the tale. As George Carey collected the legend, "In revolutionary times British General Bourgogne stayed in Sessions House and while there fell in love with the owner's daughter, Lucy. To keep their affair hidden, they met as frequently as possible on the stairway. Another account has Lucy falling in love with a soldier in Bourgogne's army, again using the secret stairway for their trysting place. In this version, her lover eventually leaves with the unfulfilled promise to return, and Lucy pines away. To this day her ghost returns to startle students near the stairway and in the house. Residents returning to Sessions at night have seen a light in their room and a figure standing there looking out. They reach the room only to find it dark, and their roommate gone from the building" (1988: 8).

Sometimes the ghost reminds students of the need to reach out to one another. At Huntingdon College in Alabama, students talk about "Martha," also known as the "Red Lady," who wanders around Pratt Hall. Forced by her father to leave her New York home for the school in the Deep South, Martha, whose trademark was wearing red garments, had trouble adjusting to her new environs. One roommate after another left her, calling her behavior "strange" and "aloof." Even the dorm president made a gallant try, and when she prepared to leave, Martha cried, "I was beginning to think you really wanted me to be your friend—but you hate me just like the rest." After her departure, Martha slashed her wrists and bled to death. Students today report seeing flashes of red shooting out into the corridor (Windham and Figh 1969: 97-103). Students make various interpretations of this story, from a daughter's sad lot when she can't express her wishes to her father, to the need all residents have, no matter how different, for a friendly presence in the dorm, and finally to the intersectional differences that sadly divide students.

Men aren't immune to the ghostly bug. At Michigan State's Holmes Hall, students reported seeing a ghostly male figure standing by the door at the end of the hallway and they called out, "Hey, you." They followed the figure out the door and down the stairs, but he was nowhere to be found. They then figured that the spirit was none other than that of fabled computer whiz James Egbert, a seventeen-year-old student who committed suicide in 1980. Also at Michigan State, the story circulates about the ghost of a male student who died on the fifth floor of Wilson. "Now the elevator always stops there," a student explained. "Whenever you press the button it has to come down from the fifth floor first. They hired elevator workers to come in and find the problem, but the workers could find no mechanical reason for the elevator continually stopping on the fifth floor" (MSU Folklore Archives, 1985).

Greek ghosts

Fraternity and sorority house ghosts tend not to be suicide victims. Selfishly taking one's life would go against the spirit of brother- and sisterhood prevailing in Greekdom. But like so many "real-world" ghosts, fraternity spirits are restless because of an unnatural death, often in a car accident, and they come home to the Greek house where they seek comfort. Lurking in the fraternity or sorority house, in the best tradition of Greek high jinks, the ghost commonly causes disorder. He or she opens windows after they've been closed, turns on lights in the middle of the night, and mischievously knocks over books or dishes.

According to a student from Bucknell, "One of the first things you learn at Bucknell is the story of the ghost on the Beta Gamma suite in Hunt, situated on the third floor." The ghost was a sorority sister who was called back home. Her house had burned, and when she arrived she discovered that her parents were dead. She decided to return to school, but the way was treacherous. Heavy rains soaked the road on her nocturnal trip. She lost control of the car and was killed in the accident. "Now, on stormy nights," the student told me, "people sometimes see a young woman wearing a drenched raincoat standing in the stairwell of the Beta Gamma suite" (survey response, 1989).

Many accounts of ghost legends are told as personal experiences. It's not enough to say how the ghost came to be; you need to describe an encounter with the ghost to affirm its reality, even if it happened to a friend of a friend. That student from Bucknell, for example, made sure to add: "A fellow Beta Gamma was in her room studying one stormy night, with only her desk light on. It was late and she was just about to fall asleep when she heard a knock on her door. Wondering who it could be at such a late hour, she opened the door and saw someone standing there in a raincoat, dripping wet. I don't recall if the stranger talked or not, but Cathy somehow understood that she wanted to use the phone. Leaving the door open, she turned around to get the receiver (she was going to dial for her), but when she looked at where the girl had been standing, she wasn't there. She knew she wasn't crazy because there was a wet spot on the floor from the rain off her coat. Cathy stepped out into the hall to see if she could see her, but no one was there."

Shades of the Vanishing Hitchhiker! You've probably heard of that internationally known story of the young woman hitchhiking along the side of the road, often in the rain. When she's picked up, she asks to be taken home, but when the driver stops where she's supposed to go, he discovers that she's gone. Confirming her presence, however, is a wet spot or sometimes even the raincoat. The hitchhiker, it turns out, had died on that very night, often as a result of a car accident (see Brunvand 1981; Goss 1984; Bronner 1989: 146, 307-8; Baughman motif E332.3.3.1). As the hitchhiker legend often points to the security of home during teenage years when the rebellious youth seeks to drift away, so the vanishing sorority sister avows the significance of her Greek home.

It's not uncommon for student raconteurs to confirm the fraternity spirit by identifying the pitiful student out of a yearbook or fraternity composite photograph. At Penn State, students at Alpha Sigma Phi talk about Lou (or John) Amici (or Ameche). "He was there during the 1960s," a student told me in 1981, although more recent residents bring the date up to the 1970s. "He was a good athlete and involved in all house activities. All of the brothers were very fond of him. After graduation, Lou moved from State College and settled down somewhere else, where he was killed in a car accident. One night when a brother was asleep in his bedroom, he was awakened for no apparent reason. He opened his eyes to see Lou's ghost kneeling at the side of his bed. He lashed out with his arm but felt nothing. A cold wind began to blow through the room. A week later he was looking through Alpha Sig's yearbook. All of a sudden he noticed a picture that looked very familiar. It was the same person who was kneeling down beside his bed."

From another fraternity brother comes a variation: "One time, a brother was asleep in his room with the door locked, as he locked it every night when he slept. When he awoke the next morning, all of the furniture in his room had been rearranged. He happened later to look through some pictures of old brothers and found a picture that matched the image he had seen. It turned out that the ghost had lived in that room" (Penn State Folklore Archives, 1981). Again there's a connection to the Vanishing Hitchhiker tale. In many versions the driver accompanying the ghostly passenger recognizes the ghost after seeing her picture inside the home to which she had asked to be driven (see Brunvand 1981: 28-29).

At Indiana University, members of Sigma Phi Epsilon relate similar encounters with the ghost of Michael A. Frang. He's the fraternity house's version of the headless horseman (Baughman motif E422.1.1) As the story goes, Michael died during a homecoming parade during the late 1960s. He was atop the Sig Ep float when the cannon aboard misfired and decapitated him. After that tragic end, Michael came as a revenant to the fraternity house, lurking mostly in the dark basement where he once lived. As one might imagine, strange occurrences down there in what was called "the swamp" were blamed on Michael's restless—and headless—spirit. As one student lamented, "Most of the problems would never have happened, most people believe, if that cannon wouldn't have blown off Michael's head." Several accounts mention books flying off a shelf of a bookcase in the "swamp"; others swear that drinking glasses mysteriously fell off another shelf. One student called attention to a venetian blind that fell. "The window wasn't open so it couldn't have been caused by the wind," he explained. Several students talked about lights going on after they had been turned off and doors mysteriously unlocking after being locked. And then there's the time the trophies from the locked case mysteriously were strewn about the room (Battreall 1987).

The University of the South at Sewanee also has a headless ghost, who belonged to a fraternal organization called the Order of the Gownsmen, although students treat this figure from the more distant past less reverently than the Sig Ep brothers do Michael. The gownsman lost his head when fisticuffs with fellow students ensued after some late-night studying (overstudying, and the pressures that go with it, students speculate). Notwithstanding that the college public relations office assured me the headless gownsman hadn't made an appearance lately, it was reported as late as the 1970s when this account was taken: "Each year someone claims to have some sort of scuffle with the ghost or sees the ghost in his room. It is said to come down the stairs and then count the stairs as it comes down, always the right number of bumps per the number of steps it comes down. Normally, it only shows up during the exam period" (McNeil 1985: 74).

The spirits of sad characters who are not fraternity brothers or sorority sisters are known to roam Greek houses. Once again the scene of the crime is the basement. At the Sigma Chi house at Penn State, various stories are told about an unsolved murder that occurred there. According to legend, the house cook and her daughter were viciously murdered by an unknown assailant when it was a sorority house. In some tellings, the cook belongs to the fraternity and the daughter to the sorority. Supposedly the restless ghosts appear around four in the morning when a brother is alone in the house. In a variation, the ghosts are carryovers from the days before the house belonged to the fraternity. A devil-worship cult inhabited the place, and one night a member was found on the back steps with his throat cut. The murder was never solved, but the cult was cleared out of the house. "Through the years," students report, "various brothers have heard strange sounds and happenings. The house is haunted by the murder victim. Brothers are afraid to stay in the house alone or over vacations because of the ghost" (Penn State Folklore Archives, 1978). As one may surmise, being in a fraternity, or a fraternity house, is not about being alone.

Fraternity houses that mysteriously lock and unlock, windows that open and shut without someone there to do the task, and lights that come on and strangely disappear are also found at Indiana University. Indiana has its share of strange noises, but one, the sound of babies crying at a house occupied at different times by several fraternities, receives special attention in legend from students. Again, the story refers back to the days before the house was inhabited by a fraternity. "The story I have most often heard concerning the ghost," a student reported, "is the one involving the baby. From what I have heard, a doctor and his wife were some of the first inhabitants of the house. The good doctor supplemented his income by performing abortions. Because abortions were illegal, the operations were performed in the basement, at night, with instruments which were crude by design" (Rosemeyer 1976: 11). There are many variations. Sometimes the doctor is thought to be linked to the builder of the house. After all, "signs" exist in the basement, such as a newly bricked-in area in the shape of a roughly made cross, or the thick steel doors. Sometimes, as the story goes, the doctor performed the abortions on sorority members. He was variously arrested after slipping up, or he went insane, or he killed himself. Crying sounds are attributed to fetuses he threw in a coal bin or buried behind a wall (Lecocq 1980: 265-78; Rosemeyer 1976; cf. Baker 1982: 84-85, Murdered wife buried in wall of the Preston House; Baughman motif E334.2.1g, Ghost of sailor haunts house where his skeleton was buried in wall).

Again, one hears the personal experience stories to chronicle the hauntings: "I was in my room studying late at night for an exam and I believe everyone had gone to bed. I was becoming drowsy. Suddenly I heard someone begin walking from south to north along the long second floor hallway. The walk was not normal. One step was muffled as if one foot or leg was crippled. It ended its march down the second floor hallway and stopped by the stairway door. Everything was silent. I waited to hear the door slowly being opened onto the stairway. I waited perhaps to hear a brother step out of heavy shoes and scamper barefoot back to his room, laughing to himself hysterically. I heard nothing" (Rosemeyer 1976: 13-14). Beyond the personal experience, there's the appeal to the experience of others: "From what I've heard, while the house was empty for one and a half years before we moved in, many persons claim that, as they walked down the sidewalk next to the house at night, they would hear crying coming from the house" (Rosemeyer 1976: 12). The coincidence of the legend with debates over legalized abortion in the United States is noteworthy, for in the telling the legend frequently sought comment: Was the detail that the doctor performed abortions the horror, or was it that he was forced to do it illegally? (cf. Dundes 1987: 3-14)

In another legend with a modern ring to it, some resourceful fraternity spirits call in their orders. Here's the way the story was told at Penn State: "Each morning at precisely 6:40 a.m., the house phones at the Phi Kappa Psi fraternity on Locust Lane begin to ring. And each morning they ring just three times. If answered at any time before the three rings are up, there is heard from the other end of the line nothing more than a common dial tone. It's been happening for about two years now...ever since the death of the house's founder John Henry Frizzell. John Henry, as the boys all used to call him, had practically devoted his entire life to his fraternity. Next to his family, Phi Psi was his true love. It is said that John Henry himself is responsible for ringing the phones each morning, each ring representing the mystic Greek words that are represented by the letters Phi, Kappa, and Psi" (Penn State Folklore Archives, 1979).

The phone call from the deceased is apparently a circulating motif. Ronald Baker collected several stories from Indiana State University students about a phone installed in a nearby mausoleum. In one version, the deceased, before he died, had promised his wife that he would call her. Several years later his wife suddenly died of a heart attack, and when the police found her, she was still holding the phone in her hands. When they checked the mausoleum, they found the receiver off the hook (Baker 1978: 72).

Murder most foul

Students out on their own, away from the protection of home and family, listen particularly attentively to mysterious legends, sometimes ghostly, of unsolved murders on campus. Franklin College in Indiana has its murder legend which has persisted among students for more than fifty years. Many variations exist, but the plot usually centers on a student, sometimes a sorority pledge, who is found dismembered in a dresser drawer, trunk, or wall. When the story uses the character of the sorority pledge, it typically follows in the telling that after an argument a crazed active fatally knifed, chopped, and put away a pledge. Otherwise, the identity of the assailant and details of the motive remain a mystery, students say.

But there must be reports in newspapers or college records of this bizarre case, you say? Well, students add that there was a cover-up of the grisly crime. "You can find the yearbooks over in Hamilton and the picture will be gone. You can go down to the administration office and check back records and nothing's in there either. Everything's just been removed. It's really strange...you know that room is still here, except it's been changed. It's no longer lived in" (Till

1976: 189). In students' minds, it's either the college or the daughter's rich father worried about his reputation who's responsible for keeping it all hush-hush. Some students ask "Could it be because the daughter was pregnant?" The location of the crime, Bryan Hall (a women's dormitory), is thus susceptible to strange noises produced, naturally, by the ghost of this victim (Till 1976: 187-95). The story has the earmarks of a migratory legend, for the dismembered victim with similar circumstances supposedly resided at Kentucky and Indiana universities.

In a variation stressing the need for harmony among roomies, an Indiana University student told this story: "There was a strange noise coming from one end of the hall. I never thought much about it 'till the next night when I heard it again. I asked some guys on my floor about it the next day, and there was this one guy, an upperclassman, that told me that one night a long time ago when there were some girls living in Bryan, there were two girls who were room-mates. Well, they got into a fight and it ended up one girl killing the other, stabbing her with a knife. After she did this she put her behind some panels, or something behind the wall, and no one even noticed. Well, a couple days later some girls started complaining of a smell. They thought it was rats or something, so they had an exterminator come, and when he came he found the girl, and I guess the other girl was convicted or something. But the funny thing about the whole thing is that you can't find anything about her even being here at I.U. It's a real mystery" (Waymire 1978: 4).

Far back in collegiate history, students resided with the spirits. Statesman and scholar Edward Everett recalled his freshman year at Harvard in 1807 with this story: "Just at the corner of Church Street (which was not then opened), stood what was dignified in the annual College Catalogue—which was printed on one side of a sheet of paper, and was a novelty—as 'the College House.' The cellar is still visible. By the students, this edifice was disrespectfully called 'Wiswal's Den,' or, for brevity, 'the Den.' I lived in it my Freshman year. Whence the name of 'Wiswal's Den' I hardly dare say: there was something worse than 'old fogy' about it. There was a dismal tradition that, at some former period, it had been the scene of a murder. A brutal husband had dragged his wife by the hair up and down the stairs, and then killed her. On the anniversary of the murder—and what day that was no one knew—there were sights and sounds—flitting garments daggled in blood, plaintive screams—*stridor ferri tractaeque catenae*—enough to appall the stoutest Sophomore."

The "Den" is also the setting for a nineteenth-century Harvard legend about Mr. Wiswal's second wife, who raised suspicions because she happened to be the nurse for the recently deceased first wife. Students speculated that the first wife got her revenge in the "Den." As the story goes, when the second wife opened a dresser drawer filled with the first wife's clothing, a ghost or even the Devil himself appeared and drove the second wife to insanity and eventually death (Hall 1968: 156-57).

The cadaver arm

Although the victim in the old legend from Harvard is guilty until proven innocent, the motif of an innocent victim ending up insane or dead, often as a result of a practical joke, is common in student lore. Folklorists even give it a motif number (N384.0.1.1) and call it "The Cadaver Arm." Here's a version from Indiana University: "One year in McNutt Quad, some girls played a joke on another girl that lived on the same floor. They put a severed hand in her room one night, and when the girl came back to her room they didn't hear her scream or anything, so they went to her door to see what happened. When they got there they found her chewing on the hand" (Waymire 1978: 3). Often the detail is added that the victim's hair turns white, he or she makes gurgling noises, and sometimes even that the victim dies of fright (see Parochetti 1965: 53; Barnes 1966: 305-6; Baughman 1945: 30-32; Carey 1971: 80-81). The story tells partly about the risks of pulling pranks, and it also offers a lesson about the vulnerability of students, especially new female ones, who seem to live closer to the edge in the strange college environment than most realize.

The most common variation of "The Cadaver Arm" concerns medical students. It often involves a novice medical student or student nurse who doesn't quite cut it. In most versions the student is also given antisocial characteristics; he or she is an arrogant snob, a loner, a grind, a braggart, or a snoop. From Berkeley, for example, comes this account: "This is a new med student. He went out on a date and got back late and his roommate and a bunch of the fellas decided to play a trick on him. This guy was really struggling and he was a new student, and the pressure of all of it. And they didn't like him very well—he was kind of a study type—he worked late in the lab and he was really trying and he was kind of a teacher's pet kind of creature, not a very strong character. And they put the hand of one of the cadavers that they had worked on that day in his bed. And they're all waiting for some huge noise or something and nothing really happens. So they go in, and they find him and he's sitting in the closet chewing on the hand and his hair's all white" (Berkeley Folklore Archives, 1974).

In many versions, the pranksters tie the arm to the "light switch in the lab," "turns the lights out, and wait in the next room." As a former pre-medical student from Butler University elaborated from there, "The unsuspecting student enters the lab as expected, reaches for the light switch, and inadvertently grabs the arm. The pranksters next door hear a blood-curdling scream and rush into the lab, laughing hysterically, but their fellow student is nowhere to be found. Neither is the arm. They search all over to no avail. Finally, someone hears a faint gnawing sound. They open a cabinet door to find their 'victim,' his hair turned white, crouched down in the cabinet, stark raving mad, chewing on the cadaver's arm" (survey response, 1990).

The backfiring prank also comes up in a variation where students work a cadaver's arm into a sleeve and attach money to its palm. Then they drive to a toll booth (or subway token stand) and extend the arm to the tolltaker. When they zoom off, the tolltaker is left with the arm and, according to legend, dies of a heart attack (see Brunvand 1989: 299-301). In a version that adds elements from crusty professor anecdotes, police come in after the event and trace the arm to a school lab. "The anatomy professor and the police matched the hand to the body, then confronted the students with the incriminating evidence. The pranksters supposedly weren't expelled—but the professor flunked them in anatomy, since they had put a right hand into a left coat sleeve" (Brunvand 1989: 300).

Students of medicine and anatomy, so used to dealing with the dead, typically appear, well, cold as a cadaver in such legends. Consider the story of the students who plugged electrodes into a cadaver and left the switch near the entrance of the room. That evening while the janitor was cleaning he touched the switch and the cadaver sat up. The janitor, so the teller says, "nearly had a heart attack" (Berkeley Folklore Archives, 1979; cf. Baker 1982: 50). In other stories, the recently deceased cadaver sits up by itself and occasionally even utters a word (cf. Dorson 1967: 328-31). There's the one about medical students who replaced the cadaver with one of their very alive colleagues under a sheet. When the professor stepped to the body, the student sat up, frightening the professor to death (cf. Hafferty 1988: 347).

Medical students also tell of bringing a cadaver to a homecoming football game where it shocks a vendor or someone in the stands (Hafferty 1988: 347). In a related story, medical students arrange two cadavers in a sexual embrace and cover the two with a sheet. When an unsuspecting victim removes the sheet to begin work, a scream reverberates through the hall; sometimes it is simply a male member that is inserted into a female cadaver. Carrying this sexual theme further, a story circulates about a condom on a cadaver's penis which provokes shock in a wet-behind-the-ears student. (Hafferty 1988: 347). Another variant questions student insensitivity when confronted by a familiar face. Usually identified as a new medical student, the protagonist is about to work on a cadaver when he or she realizes, in horror, that the body is none other than a relative, usually an aunt.

As with most legends, the built-in moral ambiguity of the narrative allows for several interpretations depending on how the story is told and to whom. The cadaver stories may remind medical students that death and dismemberment, while second nature to the world of medicine, are horrifying to most people. Indeed, the medical student who works with dead bodies to take care of the living, according to the gruesome ending of the legend, appears to be a short step from cannibalism. The stories may suggest a cold attitude necessary for success in medical school or anatomy class, while maybe mildly reminding students to be sensitive to the other world marked by an emotional response to medical sights. To medical students, the cadaver is depersonalized; it is neither capable of having a personal identity nor of having sex. When located in a lab, the stories draw attention to the inappropriate behavior of screams or emotional expression.

Commenting on the stories in a scholarly journal for health professionals, Frederic Hafferty emphasized that "cadaver stories stress that within the culture of medicine, the cadaver should exist as a learning tool and an object for manipulation rather than as a formerly living human being. In these stories, students who fail to behave accordingly, and thus threaten the emotional equilibrium of lab, are held up to ridicule and to the possibility of further torment at the hands of their peers" (1988: 350). Hafferty points out that the stories additionally deal with an issue of gender of significance to health professionals. Most stories show males as the "emotionally transcendent and detached perpetrators," and cast women as the "emotionally vulnerable victim," a further reflection, he claims, of traditional attitudes in the culture of medicine (1988: 352).

Further, when the victim is not a fellow student or professor, it is often a blue-collar worker such as a janitor, vendor, or tolltaker. The stories reinforce the superiority of the medical professional over the common worker. Although the worker is often depicted as physically tough, the medical professional's mental and emotional toughness gets the, well, upper hand.

Medical students are not the only characters that use cadavers and other grisly sights in college legendry. In fact, "The Cadaver Arm" story commonly involves sorority members, and less often fraternity pledges. In line with the interpretation of the story's medical school form, the fraternity and sorority connection again points to the exclusiveness and toughness associated with Greek membership. Here's one of the early versions collected by Louis C. Jones at the State Teacher's College at Albany (now SUNY at Albany) in 1946: "Shortly after having entered college as a freshman this girl was asked into a sorority. She went on pledge and she always did what the other girls told her to do. What's more, she always did her pledge duties willingly and promptly— never lacking nerve nor showing any signs of being afraid. Finally the girls decided that something must be done to frighten this poor pledge to make her worthy of joining. One night the girls broke into a nearby hospital and carried off a pickled arm. This arm was placed in the girl's bed one night. The following morning they waited hour after hour for her to get up so that they could laugh and joke about it. But the girl didn't come out of her room and so later in the day they took it upon themselves to go in and get her. When they entered the room, they found the girl still in bed—now, grey-headed and gnawing at the arm" (see Dorson 1949: 674-75). In a common variation, the arm is hung from a light switch in a closet. The result is predictable: "To their shock they found her eating the arm, and her hair had turned white and was on end" (Baker 1982: 216).

Fatal initiations

As fraternity and sorority lore, "The Cadaver Arm" is part of a general cycle of stories about fatal initiations. The most common one in my collection takes the listener to the site of a haunted house. Here's the way a student told it at Penn State:

> There were three fraternity pledges who had to spend the night in a haunted house as part of pledging. So a few of the fraternity brothers took them over. They unlocked the door, and the three guys went in. They told them all they had to do was spend the night, and the brothers would come and get them in the morning. So the brothers locked the front door so the pledges couldn't get out, and started to leave. They were walking down the front steps, which were really rotting, and the steps collapsed underneath them. The guy that was holding the key dropped it though a crack in the stairs, and they couldn't get it back. Well, while they were trying to get it, they heard these screams coming from the house—they really sounded like desperate screams, not just scared screams. So they ran back to the car to get a crowbar, and they jimmied open the door. All they heard was a weird,

steady creaking noise and a constant banging coming from somewhere. They ran through the ground level, and there wasn't anybody there. Then they ran down to the basement, and there wasn't anybody there. They ran upstairs and started checking the bedrooms. When they got to the second one, the creaking noise got real loud, so they went in. One of the pledges was hanging by his neck in the center of the room, above a pool of blood; his arms and legs were cut off. The creaking came from the rope swinging back and forth from the ceiling. They still heard the banging noise, so they ran into another bedroom that had a big closet. They opened up the closet, and it was empty, but there was no ceiling to it; it was just open to the sky. So they pushed one guy up, and he got up on the roof. He found the second pledge up there on his back—his hair was stark white, and he didn't have any eyes left; they were gouged out. He had a hammer in one of his hands, and he was just banging it on the roof. They never found the other guy.

In its formulaic structure, this fatal initiation story is reminiscent of playful horror tales often told at summer camps (Bronner 1989: 154-59). In these tales, a ghost comes closer and closer to the final victim until the teller startles the listener by grabbing him or her or feigning death. Adapted to the college scene, what might be called the "initiation curse" story is sometimes told as a personal experience by actives to pledges: "Three pledges and I had to go into this haunted house. Each one had to enter the house by himself, armed with only flashlight. The first guy went in and we watched him shine his flashlight through the entire first floor. We watched his light on the second floor, but when it should have appeared at the middle window, we didn't see anything. We waited some time, thinking it was a joke, but he still didn't shine his light. Finally we decided that, pledge project or not, we were going to go in together. We followed his footsteps through the downstairs to the second floor. It was very dusty in the place, so we had little difficulty. His steps led to a door. Frightened, we opened the door, only to find an empty closet. No one's ever seen this guy since. That was ten years ago. Since then, something has happened to everyone else. Two years after this guy disappeared another was killed in an automobile accident. Five years after that, the third was killed in a boating crash. Now I'm the only one left and AAAARRRRRRGGGGHHH! (teller screams and feigns death)" (Penn State Folklore Archives, 1980; see Baughman 1945: 50, motif N384.0.1a; Carey 1971: 78).

In most of the fatal initiation stories, the pledge's imagination produces the final frightening blow. In a story known internationally to folklorists as Aarne-

Thompson Type 1676B (and Baughman motif N384.2a), a pledge goes to a graveyard to stick a knife into a grave. As a Colgate student tells it, "Some of his fraternity brothers drove a pledge to the cemetery, watched him lean down to plunge the knife in, and then drove off. It was a cold, foggy night with snow on the ground. The initiate was wearing a muffler and heavy overcoat. He leaned down, stuck the knife in, and started to walk away. He took one step, felt someone grab at his coat tail, and fell dead of fright. Alarmed at his absence, his fraternity brothers checked for him at the graveyard the next morning. They found him dead, with the knife stuck through the tail of his coat (Berkeley Folklore Archives, 1964; see Baughman 1966: 373; Bronner 1989: 146, 307; Baker 1982: 76-77).

A series of fatal initiation stories concerns the fate of blindfolded pledges. One of these with a long lineage is sometimes called the "pseudo-decapitation" (Baughman motif N384.4c). According to the legend, actives decide to give a pledge, often characterized as particularly disobedient, a scare. They tie him to a chair and show him an axe. They blindfold him and strike him on the neck with a wet towel. When the actives lift him up they discover that he died from the shock (see Hartikka 1946: 80; Baughman 1945: 52-53; Bronner 1989: 169). The tale has been traced back to British university tradition in the eighteenth century (Hobbs 1973: 183-91).

In a variation, "the brothers told this guy they were going to slash his arm and let him bleed. What they did was to run something cold and sharp across his arm but they did not cut him. They had water dripping off of his arm into a bucket so that he would think they had really cut him. Everyone then left the room for a few hours, and when they came back they found him dead" (Penn State Folklore Archives, 1978; see Baughman motif N384.4a; Baughman 1945: 51-52). Another variation has the pledge threatened with branding. After the pledge is blindfolded and tied to a chair, a hot poker is pressed against raw meat at the same time that a piece of ice is held on the pledge's skin. The pledge smells the burning meat, and thinking it's his own, crumples up dead (Baughman motif N384.4b; Dorson 1949: 674; Hartikka 1946: 79).

The fear of being trapped, especially by the legendary motif of being tied up in a scary situation, is the subject of several fatal initiation stories, typically told by non-fraternity members. An example is the frequently collected legend about the pledge who is tied to a railroad track. The actives drive away, certain that the train wouldn't be coming or would come on the opposite set of tracks, and they return to find the pledge dead from fright after hearing the train (Indiana University Folklore Archives, 1970; Mac Barrick Folklore Archives,

Shippensburg University, 1979).

Some versions of the "tied-up pledge" story have a grisly ending. Here's how a Penn State student related an example: "A young pledge was given his initiation one night. He was tied to a chair in an old abandoned house and left there. To become a member, he must free himself within one hour. This was impossible because of the ropes and the knots used by the frat brothers. Determined, however, the young pledge decided he would cut them off on the broken glass in the window. As he started to try to cut the ropes off, he slipped and fell on the window and beheaded himself" (Penn State Harrisburg Folklore Archives, 1983; Baughman motif Z511; Baughman 1945: 52-53).

Some of the horror stories use the familiar scary feature of the cadaver arm to get revenge on the actives. From Indiana University, for example, comes the story of a pledge at an isolated cabin in the woods who is tied up in a chair. The actives produce blood-curdling noises from the outside of the cabin throughout the night. When they check on him in the morning, they discover that he's no longer in his chair. His ropes are broken and his chair is overturned. The actives then hear a creeping noise coming from the attic, so an active goes up to check it out, but he doesn't come back for a good while. Another active then hears something dripping from the attic and goes up to investigate. He finds the active lying dead, his arm removed, and blood dripping down to the floor. The now-crazed pledge is beating the active with the arm (Indiana University Folklore Archives, 1968; cf. Bronner 1989: 148).

Told in college, the horror variety of initiation stories is frequently offered to explain why a campus does not have fraternities or sororities. Reporting "scary stories" from Purdue, for example, JoAnn Parochetti recounted the belief legend that fraternities were forbidden after a boy was killed when a tombstone to which he had been tied toppled over, crushing him (1965: 52-53; cf. Baughman 1945: 50-51; Baughman motif Z512; see also Baker 1982: 221-22). As place legends, however, such stories, with variations usually stressing the grisly details of the crime in an isolated, treacherous, or dreary location, are often heard well before students enter college. They often relate to specific mysterious places in a teen's life, which include devil's elbows, haunted hollows, cemetery ridges, spook light hills, not to mention lovers' lanes. Heard at slumber parties, camps, and summer outings, the stories may inspire heartbeat-raising trips, complete with retellings, to the scene of the crime (see Dégh 1969: 54-89; Thigpen 1971: 204-5; Hall 1973; Ellis 1983: 61-73; Meley 1990).

Legend trips

The trips are sometimes re-enacted in college settings by upperclassmen taking green freshmen or pledges in tow along with a generous supply of beer. I vividly remember my legend-trip experience at Indiana University. It was a foggy summer night with a full moon just barely visible above. Inspired by a round of talk about haunts in the area, a group of students jammed into a car to search for an out-of-the-way graveyard where, according to legend, the outline of chains appeared on a tombstone after a man killed his wife with a chain, although some argued it was an overseer who killed a slave (see Baker 1982: 72-74; Clements 1969b; de Caro and Lunt 1968). We discovered that indeed it was out of the way, but it was hardly a lonely site, since it attracted several other carloads of teens who arrived at the cemetery from different points about the time we did.

Back East, George Carey tells about a favorite student rendezvous outside Baltimore called by the haunting name Druid Ridge (1971: 83-96). There students seek out the resting place of "Black Aggie," a spot once inhabited by a grieving statue with the word "Agnus" embossed on the bottom. A variety of stories, many with gruesome details of a horrifying murder, circulate to explain the notoriety of the grave smack in the center of the cemetery. Here's one: "A long time ago the caretaker of that cemetery lived right there on the grounds with his wife. Her name was Agnus. Before she died she asked her husband to bury her in the middle of the cemetery. Well, he buried her where she wanted to be and he had this big statue put over her grave. That statue is cursed because Agnus had a sister who moved in with her husband after she was dead. She was his housekeeper at first, but later on she became his mistress. Since she was buried in the center of the cemetery where she could see everything, she noticed this affair was taking place and wished to take revenge on her sister. So one night at midnight, Aggie's body rose out of the grave and killed her sister. I've heard that the two of them are buried head to head under that statue of Black Aggie" (Carey 1971: 83). Hmmm, the story has a striking resemblance to early nineteenth-century stories, which I discussed earlier, of Wiswal's Den at Harvard (see Hall 1968: 156-57). The theme of infidelity, along with the message of crimes discovered and exposed, especially when teens are increasingly asked to make independent moral decisions and face issues of commitment, apparently holds attention through the years.

Carey also reports that when the statue was up, fraternities and sororities called for pledges to pass the night in the statue's lap or to look into the statue's eyes at midnight. "The rigors of the exercise increase," Carey points out, "as the helpless victim hears accounts of what has happened to others who faced the same catharsis. He is told, perhaps, of the two Towson boys who went and sat in the statue's lap. When nothing untoward occurred, they jeered loudly, jumped back in the their car and left the cemetery. As they pulled back out onto Reisterstown Road, a truck plowed into their car and they were both killed instantly. Other accounts held that if you sit in Aggie's lap at midnight, her arms will unfold and squeeze you to death. Steve Bledsoe of Baltimore tried it on a fraternity hell night. Just at midnight his friends, who were waiting nearby, heard his screams: 'It's moving, it's moving,' but fortunately he slipped Aggie's grasp before she had a good grip. Another pledge was not quite so lucky. His fraternity brothers left him in Aggie's lap all night and when they returned in the morning, his corpse lay at her feet, the hair snow white" (Carey 1971: 85).

The legend-trip with its air of excitement and discovery, and its frequent recounting of morality plays in story, brings students face to face with the challenges of reaching out beyond their safe campus havens to the haunting situations out in the real world. On these trips students talk to one another about situations under the cloud of legend, and they experience for themselves the reality of the legendary sites, even as they confront their own cloudy fears and doubts.

The white witch

Parking in a lover's lane is a situation found frequently in student legendry. The lovers' lane stories have the earmarks of the horror tale recounted early in adolescence and later elaborated in a legend trip or group setting. Typically the backdrop for the legend is a couple out parking, that is, necking in a car in a secluded spot. As the lovebirds pursue the pleasures of embrace, all sorts of dangers lurk outside. The dangers outside, of course, point to the danger inside the car of going too far sexually. The car has metaphorically gone too far by being parked by the fertile woods, high on a mountain, or out beyond town by a cemetery.

One frequently mentioned danger is the "white witch." At Berkeley, she appears in Tilden Park; at the University of Arizona, it's a lonely road from Patagonia; at Indiana, it's a limestone quarry off a country road. The "white witch" or "white lady"—sometimes a ghostly jilted lover or rape victim, sometimes a real-life maniac—has her ways of driving couples from the parking spots. At Berkeley, "she would try to scare them away by tapping on the roof or windows with her long diamond fingernails. It seemed that her daughter had been raped while while parked up there and the White Witch's goal in life was to prevent the same thing from happening to other girls" (Samuelson 1979: 18). At

Indiana, "if you are out on a date with a girl and you park your car alongside this quarry and at midnight on a moonlit night, this girl who was abducted and raped will come running over this hill and she'll be throwing rocks at your car. She'll go to the girl's side of the car and start beating on the window." Near Altoona, Pennsylvania, the ghostly white lady is so called because she appears in a wedding dress. She is part of a couple who eloped, but traveling down the Buckhorn Mountain, the car went out of control and crashed. The girl's body was never found, and she haunts on the mountain on dark and rainy nights scaring away young lovers (Bronner 1989: 147).

In these various stories, the woman bears the responsibility for keeping limits on the romantic enterprise. It is her window that is scratched, and it is the young female victim (and sometimes the victim's mother) who returns to clear the spot of lovers. In many versions, the woman is more violent and seeks revenge on the men. At the University of Arizona, students tell of men picking up what appears to be a beautiful woman by the side of the road. But she turns into a devilish figure and kills the men (survey response, 1989; see also Leddy 1948: 272-77; Chambers 1983: 31-39).

The wrath of the white witch is often aroused because of the brutality of rape. With the concern of college women out at night alone, it is common for them to tell cautionary tales, sometimes ghostly, of the dangers of rape on campus. Many of the tales concern places on or near campus where ghostly screams can be heard at scenes of the crime. At Indiana, women tell of strange ghostly cries at midnight coming from a small stream that runs through campus (Waymire 1978: 3). In New Orleans, students say that a cloud or mist that comes down in City Park late at night and makes crying noises is the spirit of a rape victim (Chambers 1983: 34-35).

At Colorado State University, the motif of the crying as a warning is built into a white witch legend concerning an outdoor theater. In one version, the victim's mother swore that she would get revenge for her daughter's fate. As a student told the tale in a dorm one night, "Supposedly she waits on the stage of the ampitheatre at night with a hatchet to kill anyone who comes there. Her bloodcurdling screams can be heard as a warning to stay away. It's been said that people have died up there—not from falling off the rocks" (Samuelson 1979: 36).

The hook man

The most loathsome male figure to haunt lover's lanes in student legendry is the "hook man." In these legends the locales change but the plots follow similarly. A couple parks in a secluded spot outside of town or campus. The guy puts on the radio to set a seductive mood. The couple is getting deeper in embrace when a flash comes over the radio. It warns that a maniac or killer has escaped from a nearby institution (sometimes an insane asylum, sometimes a prison). The dangerous character can be identified by a hook replacing one hand. The woman typically becomes scared, but her date assures her that there's nothing to worry about. She persists, so he agrees to take her home. He zooms off, perhaps showing his disappointment. After he pulls up to the house, he comes around the car to open her door, and to his horror, sees that a bloodied hook—presumably from the escaped maniac—is in the door handle (see Bronner 1989: 148-49, 310-12; Dégh 1968: 92-100; Barnes 1966: 310-11; Carey 1971: 78-80; Thigpen 1971: 183-86; Baker 1982: 78-79; Brunvand 1981: 48-52).

In her observations of the telling of the legend, Linda Dégh mentioned that the legend is frequently told by men to scare girlfriends while they are parked in lonesome spots, while others elaborate on the natural dread of the handicapped (1968: 98). Alan Dundes has made a case that from the point of view of the women, the story is a warning about the aggressive sexual advances of men. "The 'hook' could be a hand as in the expression 'getting one's hooks into somebody,' but a hook could also be a phallic symbol. The typical fear of the girl might then be that a boy's hand, signifying relatively elementary necking, might suddenly become a hook (an erect, aggressive phallus)" (1971: 30). Dundes supports his claim by pointing out that "if the hook were a phallic substitute, then it would make perfect sense for the hook to be severed as a result of the girl's instigating the sudden move to return home. The attempt to enter the 'body' of the car is seemingly a symbolic expression of the boy's attempt to enter the body of the girl" (pp. 30-31).

Then why, Dégh asks, would the telling of the "scary" story by the man, as she observed, result in the woman drawing closer to the man, "seeking protection from the 'fearless male'"? (Dégh 1971: 65-66). One answer might be that the story has in it a social map of teenage transition between childhood and adulthood. The car, a sign of teenage mobility and maturity, is parked on the fringes of the community, far from authority or constraining forces. Indeed, the car is often located near an "insane asylum" or "mental institution," indicating that rationality is absent in this outlying zone. The radio bulletin, emanating from town, warns the couple to head back to the fold; the female, usually stereotyped as more cautious and homebound, typically insists that the couple return. When the couple return home, the boy acts more like a gentleman. They have traveled the road of transition from the home to the edge of the community, from childhood to the freedom of adulthood. In some versions, the narrator comments that the girl "was laughing at herself for being so silly" as to have childish fears, but discovers in her driveway that the dangers are real and she need not feel embarrassed about wanting to go home (Bronner 1989: 311-12).

Knock, knock, who's dead?

The "fearless male" might also wish he had stayed home in a legend called the "boyfriend's death" that often complements stories of the "hook man" and the "white witch." In the most frequently collected version of the story, a guy drives a car with his date out to a country road surrounded typically by woods. The car with the necking couple runs out of gas or is somehow otherwise incapacitated. The man volunteers to go in search of gas, but the woman is scared for him as well as scared of being left alone. He assures her he will be fine out in the dark, and devises a knocking signal that he will use for her to let him back in. If she doesn't hear it, she is to lie down out of sight in the back seat. The guy doesn't return for some time, and in many versions she falls asleep. She hears a scratching or dripping sound coming from the roof and she shrinks in her seat in fear. At daybreak, the police rescue her (sometimes it is still dark and she is aroused by the headlights of the police car). They lead her out of the car but warn her not to turn around. She of course then turns around and sees her boyfriend hanging dead from a tree above the car. The noise coming from the roof is explained by toenails (fingernails if he's hanging upside down) or blood dripping (see Dégh 1968b: 101-6; Thigpen 1971: 174-77; Barnes 1966: 309-10; Baker 1982: 201-3; Carey 1971: 79; Roemer 1971: 12-13; Amick 1980: 1-17; Bronner 1989: 148, 310; Glazer 1987: 93-108).

Most commentators have cited the story as a cautionary tale about the dangers of parking, especially during a period of increased sexual freedom during the 1960s and 1970s. After all, the boy "gets it in the neck" for his wish for necking. But another theme is the disregard of the boyfriend's attempt to re-enter the car. So the story has the message to the boy of being less foolishly macho and to the girl of being more aware of what is happening outside the car.

This last theme is especially evident in a spin-off of the boyfriend's death story to one about dormitory life. In the "roommate's death," a woman's roommate leaves late at night to study. Fearful of a maniac attacking the roommate, but really fearful of mistaking the returning roommate for the maniac and opening the door, the woman requests a knocking signal. Late at night, the woman hears a scratching at the door which she does not answer. But when she opens the door in the morning she discovers her roommate dead on the floor (frequently with an axe lodged in her head), and her fingers on the door as if she had been desperately trying to get in the room (see Dégh 1969: 55-74; Brunvand 1981: 57-62; Barnes 1966: 307-8; Carey 1971: 75-77).

In a variation, two women stay in different rooms in a dorm over Christmas or Easter break, while everyone else has gone home. Because of their fears of being alone, they decide to call each other on the phone if help is needed. Sometimes a report comes over the radio that a hatchet murderer, a man who kills girls, is on the loose. The phone goes dead, and one woman locks herself in her room, sometimes going so far as to move furniture in front of the door. She hears a body dragging upstairs or a scratching at her door. When all is quiet in the morning, she opens the door (sometimes there is a male, blue-collar rescuer) to discover the other woman dead with an axe in her head and her fingers bloodied from trying to scratch at the door for help (see Grider 1980: 147-78; Waymire 1978: 3-5; Baker 1982: 217-18; Parochetti 1965: 53-54).

The lingering question for the listener, then, might be whether responsibility for the tragedy belongs with the victim who took the risk of going out late at night or with the person in the room who did not answer the door because of her fear of the murderer. The issue of responsibility commonly underlies the climax of both the boyfriend's and roommate's death stories, and in each type, extreme fear and courage could each be shown to create problems in this age of adolescent independence.

The roommate's death story's attachment to women suggests other nuances. The story creates a feeling of horror because of the presumption of women's vulnerability and the expectation of violence against them when they are out alone or late at night. But there's also a question about the responsibility that women must take for one another in the potentially intimidating setting of college, and the values they must hold there. Many of the victims in these stories get it in the "head," die with masculine tools like axes embedded in their brains. In many stories, the woman is threatened because she has chosen to stay in the dormitory over vacation while everyone else has joined their families. When she is attacked, she is typically out studying late (or smugly going out partying after the semester is over), therefore defying obstacles to her use of intellect. Stumbling back to her room, she loses her feminine fingernails scratching for help. For Beverly Crane, "The points of value implicit in this narrative are then twofold. If women wish to depend on traditional attitudes and responses they had best stay in a place where these attitudes and responses are best able to protect them. If, however, women do choose to venture into the realm of equality with men, they must become less dependent, more self-sufficient, more confident in their own abilities, and above all, more willing to assume responsibility for themselves and others" (Crane 1977: 147).

Yet another variation of the "roommate's death," especially prevalent in my collection from the 1980s, tests the various interpretations of the legend. From Shippensburg comes this version: "These two girls did everything together. They studied together, ate together, and partied together. They were always together, up until one night. The one girl decided to stay in and catch up on school work. The other went out. When she returned to the room, she was very careful not to wake her roommate. In the morning, she found her roommate dead and on the mirror, written in blood was 'Aren't you glad you didn't turn on the light last night?'" (Barrick Folklore Archives, 1986).

Sometimes a blind date is blamed for the murder, as in this version from Berkeley: "A girl who was a student at the University of Chicago had gone out on a date one night and gotten home fairly late. As she was standing in front of her dorm room looking for her keys she debated whether or not to turn on the lights to her room, but she decided not to because she didn't want to disturb her roommate. So she got ready for bed in the dark and then went to sleep. The next morning she woke up and looked over to her roommate's bed, and saw her roommate hacked apart into bloody pieces. There was a note pinned to the sheets of the bed which read, 'If you had turned on the lights last night you would have looked like this too.' It turned out that her roommate had gone out on a blind date that night and had invited him back to her room, and the guy had turned out to be a psycho, and had still been in the room when the girl had gotten back that night" (Berkeley Folklore Archives, 1984; see also Baker 1982: 218-19; Britton 1987: 2). Women reported hearing the story in conversation about the hazards of dating in a world of strangers, and fears emanating from the sensational news of handsome men such as Ted Bundy who dated college women before insanely killing them.

The story also came up in conversations about dorm security. In fact, a detail is sometimes added to the legend that the two agreed, foolishly, to leave the door unlocked because one didn't have the key. In these instances, the story strongly conveys warnings to undergraduates. But in other ways, the story bears out the "points of value" given by Beverly Crane. The woman who is killed by the male attacker is often studying, but to say that we have an anti-"grind" motif here is probably off the mark. The woman is variously dating and studying, and either way she is hacked up like "meat"—an offensive slur often hurled at women. So, is the woman who doesn't turn on the light feeling guilty for her decision to "stay in the dark," or is she relieved? The answer is left for the listener to provide. When I turned the question back on tellers of the story at Penn State, I heard that the roommate who had been out should feel responsible for the one who stayed in. Indeed, the detail of one roommate being spared, and the fear that it inspires in the telling, seems like a punishment for going out, usually on a date, with its implicit dependence on men.

Murderous rumors

Axe murderers also figure prominently in a story about a psychic who predicts a mass murder around Hallowe'en at a college campus. According to the story, the psychic gives clues that lead students to believe their campus is the one that will be victimized.

From Shippensburg, for example, came the rumor in 1986 that "the psychic predicted that there would be a mass-murder in a Pennsylvania state school. It would take place on Halloween night in a single-sex dorm which is near railroad tracks" (Barrick Memorial Folklore Archives, 1988). Sometimes the psychic was identified as Jeane Dixon: didn't she predict, students asked, the massacre by a crazed gunman at the McDonald's restaurant in San Diego?

Similar rumors were heard at the same time at East Stroudsburg University, Lehigh University, Dickinson College, Slippery Rock University, Bloomsburg University, Penn State University, Susquehanna University, Mansfield University, and Kutztown University, all in central Pennsylvania (Donovan 1989). According to some students, the attacked dormitory was a freshman dormitory, or the largest dorm on a campus, or a women's dorm where the attacker was predicted to rape as well as kill. The psychic was said to have appeared on Phil Donahue, David Letterman, Johnny Carson, Oprah Winfrey, or Joan Rivers. The killer was variously a crazed student, professor, maintenance worker, escaped convict, or maniac from an insane asylum. The psychic (usually identified as Jeane Dixon) appeared on none of these television shows, and the weekend passed with no incidents. Nonetheless, some students took no chances and rushed home for the weekend. Others laughed it off and went to Hallowe'en costume parties dressed as murderous hatchet men. After the weekend was over, one enterprising student sold shirts showing a bloodied undergrad with a hatchet through his skull and the message "I Survived the Kutztown Massacre."

It wasn't the first time for this hatchet-man scare. Linda Dégh reported a massacre rumor circulating among American college students in 1968. She connected the rumor to media attention to the brutal murder of nine student nurses in their Chicago rooming house. The features of the psychic's prediction and a hatchet murder are consistent with the latest scare. "Didn't Jeanne Dixon predict Kennedy's death before she told of this massacre?" students asked. The Indiana University student newspaper ran a story on the rumor less than three weeks before Halloween 1968: "A rumor reportedly rampant on campus that seer Jeanne Dixon has predicted the axe murder of 10 coeds on a midwestern university campus has been quashed by her New York publishing syndicate office. Robert Gillespie, who handles Miss Dixon's material for Newsday syndicate, said she has never made a prediction of that nature. Gillespie said the rumor started about six months ago in Oklahoma and had spread throughout the Midwest. In various forms, the rumor depicts an axe slaying on either a Midwestern or Big Ten campus" (Dégh 1969: 71; see also Baker 1982: 219). The rumor made it out to New York State where reports said the prediction held that the attack would be on, variously, a women's dorm, starting with an A (or B,C, or D), at a state school, at a private school, near a mental institution, and between nine p.m. and midnight (Degh 1969: 70-74).

As the 1968 rumor seemed to be about fear of real-life horrors repeating themselves in the vulnerable world of institutional dorm life, so other rumor cycles made indirect references to the news. In 1983, a rumor circulated around campuses from California to Massachusetts about a hatchet murder predicted by a psychic, but with the strange twist that the attacker was going to dress up as Little Bo Peep at Hallowe'en (Ernstberger 1983). At the University of Massachusetts, the rumor additionally called for an attack at a Hallowe'en Party at a sorority house. The rumor was taken seriously enough there to cause several parties to be cancelled (Berberoglu and Hilliard 1986). It is true that in June of 1983, news magazines gave splashy coverage to the hatchet murder by an escaped prisoner and former mental hospital patient Kevin Cooper. He attacked an innocent family at a California horse ranch, leaving only an eight-year-old, his neck slashed, barely clinging to life. According to *Newsweek*, "Local police called it the most gruesome murder scene in memory" (Alter 1983). Previously he had attacked and raped a seventeen-year-old in Pennsylvania, although the crime did not occur at a college.

In January 1978, two women were murdered and three others beaten in a Florida State University sorority house, but the reports did not spark a new wave of massacre rumor that spring. Rather, an outbreak occurred in the Midwest before Hallowe'en 1979 (Mitchell 1982: 89). And the "Bo-Peep" connection? In 1983, tabloids had a field day with a sensational transvestite murder case in New York City, although the cross-dresser was the victim rather than assailant (Wadler 1983).

One also has to wonder about the influence of popular "slasher" movies, typically appealing to adolescents, and the incorporation of traditional legendary motifs into their plots (Danielson 1979; Schechter 1988: 25-48). *Halloween* (1978) and its many sequels are perennial teen favorites; they regularly feature a knife-wielding attacker escaped from a loony bin, who with Hallowe'en mask in place, slashes a young woman. Many slasher films, such as *Black Christmas* (1974) and *Final Exam* (1981), use college settings as backdrops (see Egan 1985: 122-24; Danielson 1979: 212). The Draculas and Frankensteins of popular horror films past have been traded in for ordinary-sounding Freddies, Michaels, and Jasons. Today's monsters in legend and life roam around reality (Russo 1990: 10).

As students were arriving at school in 1986, they probably heard the news report of a massacre by a gunman in Oklahoma. A letter carrier unexpectedly opened fire on fourteen fellow workers in the Edmond post office (Pedersen 1986). There was no college connection in the news of massacre, but one still detects in the resurfacing rumors how students sublimate horrifying incidents into the celebration of Hallowe'en: they make the murderer one of the campus's own. The coincidence of the rumors with the darkening fall season, the mistrust of the security of institutional life—especially for students away from the haven of home—and the setting of many campuses in isolated arcadias undoubtedly feeds the rumors.

It is probably not a coincidence that the heyday of the rumors paralleled the era of eased restrictions on dormitory visitation. With colleges giving up their role *in loco parentis*, the campus seemed a more open but less protected place. It was potentially open to dangerous strangers. When the massacre rumors were related by students, they become folk tests of fear, invitations for commentary (both serious and humorous), and reminders to keep alert generally, particularly in an individualistic culture where students feel out on their own (see Rosnow and Fine 1976: 54-62).

One can detect some change in the pattern of the rumors over the years. Whereas the victims in the early rumors were typically women, suggesting the questioning of the adaptability of women to college life during a period when numbers of women were increasing, later rumors added victims of either sex in "large dorms" and "state universities." This additional detail raised the insecurity students felt as smaller and smaller cogs in steadily bigger collegiate wheels. And the ubiquitous psychic in all this? Jeane Dixon, the legend's most popular seer, as a woman herself, projects the concerns of women's vulnerability onto the prediction. She adds a touch of the supernatural appropriate to the season, to be sure, but she also speaks to the future, at a time when students are looking ahead with uncertainty and seeking predictability in their fates.

Murder in the stacks

Rumors of a murder about to happen or having just happened are often attached to campus libraries. At many campuses, the library is the largest structure and comes to represent the mad mix of students coming and going. Women are often victims and the stories include the frightening detail of screams not heard because the building was so large or students so indifferent. From Indiana University, for example, comes the account that "the library is so big that this guy came up to her and grabbed her and threw her on the floor. She screamed once but then he pulled a knife and she stopped screaming. No one who was studying around her came to see what the scream was about and so the guy just raped her" (Indiana University Folklore Archives, 1974).

In 1969, the fatal stabbing of a female graduate student actually occurred in Penn State's library, and it provided the basis for cautionary legends going by the name of "the murder in the stacks" ever since, especially because the culprit was never found. "Stay away from level two," freshmen are warned each fall; "maybe the murderer will come back some day." Often the date of the murder is moved up to "just last year or so," and it is sometimes predicted that it might have been the first in a serial killing (Anthony 1989: 1, 4).

In narrative versions, the dead woman (sometimes a senior, a graduate student, a narcotics agent, or policewoman) is usually not discovered for days. The student reportedly was "minding her own business," "doing research," or "doing undercover work." In a variation, a student said: "This girl got locked in the library and she went to sleep or something and she woke up and heard noises and there was this guy in there. She saw him and she ran away into the stacks. And he finally caught her and he had a huge knife and he dismembered her body" (T. 1979: 5).

Students sometimes explain the failure to land an arrest in the case with an administrative cover-up—probably, they surmise, because drugs were involved, and maybe the university was even hiring students to spy on others. (This last motif surfaces elsewhere: at Brigham Young University, a Mormon-affiliated school with prohibitions on alcohol and tobacco, rumors fly about paid informers in the dorms on the lookout for the contraband; see Bart 1983).

Despite the deviation from the known facts, the legends reveal the truth of student attitudes toward the dangers of large public places, especially for women, and by extension, the danger of the university's growth in general. Echoing motifs of the dormitory hatchet-man stories, in "murder in the stacks" legends, students have, as a result of the university's growth, become indifferent to one another's welfare and even distrustful of their comrades. Additionally, recently told legends voice a concern for the threatening intrigue of drugs on campus.

Phantoms in the theatre

Besides resounding through dorms and libraries, word of strange incidents often comes from the campus theater. The drama, mystery, and pathos enacted there lend to speculation about phantoms lurking in the darkness. Besides, theaters, usually intimidatingly cavernous, often have trap doors, mysterious basements, and multiple dank passageways. At the University of Delaware, students point to Mitchell Hall, which houses the theater, as such a place. Students in the theater department tell of "Elmo," a revenant who hangs around the theater. According to legend, Elmo was a stage technician who met a tragic death after he slipped and fell from the crow's nest into the concrete sub-basement that now bears the label "Elmo land."

Elmo's spirit now watches over the place, often looking out for accidents and their victims, usually thespians. In an often-told story, an actress is running through her steps ("running some blocking," in theater lingo) on stage. She heard a mysterious voice from stage left. She ignored it, but the call continued. She headed over, just as an immense light crashed into the stage where she had been standing. Had Elmo saved her from a nasty end? Could be, but he is also blamed for mischief such as resetting control panels behind closed doors. Stories of Elmo bring out the dangers and responsibilities of technical theater work and bind technicians through lore. Technicians often feel upstaged by thespians, and get a chance to show the reliance of actors upon technicians in narrative (Roskin 1988).

Actors have their spirits, too. Usually they are so devoted to the theater that they stay in costume around the stage late at night. Hamline University has its "Pink Lady," for example, fabled to be an actress from the old theater which was later replaced. She wore a flowing pink gown that has become her ghostly trademark. Upper Iowa University's best known ghost belongs to Zinita B. Graf, who died in 1950. A devoted alumna of the school, she went on to become a professional actress. During her lifetime, she returned to the school during the summers to reside. Her spirit mischievously likes to move things around in Colgrove-Walker Auditorium, especially before opening night, but she is gener-

Michigan State's statue of the Spartan, 1989. (Simon Bronner)

ally benevolent. Her costumes still reside in the theater closet, and play programs thank her spirit for aiding the production. Theaters also seem to attract suicide legends. At West Virginia Wesleyan, students talk about the strange sounds coming from Atkinson Auditorium. There a young student supposedly hanged himself during the tumultuous 1960s and now his disturbed soul haunts the balcony and sometimes moves to the Long Dock under the stage. Often students feel his spirit during rehearsals. Maybe the talk of his presence displaces their anxieties about the performance they need to perfect. Consider the report of the student who said: "We were on stage for 'A Man for All Seasons.' While Mr. Presar was giving us directions, we both saw something walk into the light booth, yet we knew there was no one else in the auditorium. Somehow our eyes were both drawn to the same point in the balcony above" (Barlow 1989).

And if a virgin passes...

Outside the theater and dorm, students are likely to rehearse explanations attached to the many towers, statues, and columns that typically dot campuses. They are not likely to reiterate the stately official meanings of these proud structures, however. They have their lighthearted accounting for these intrusions on the landscape. The structures stand so rigidly because they are monuments to the sexy student body. In the unlikely event that a virgin graduates, or walks by the structure, students hyperbolize, bizarre things start happening. At the universities of Missouri, Michigan, and Cincinnati stone lions roar. The statue of the seated Pioneer Mother at the University of Oregon and of the seated Lincoln at the University of Illinois stand, while at Michigan State the statue of the standing Spartan sits. At Upper Iowa, the statue of the Green Goddess bows; at Duke, the statue of James Duke tips his hat. At Cornell, the statues of Andrew D. White and Ezra Cornell leave their pedestals and shake hands. At the University of North Carolina, a statue of a Minuteman fires his musket; the statue of Italian patriot Garibaldi at New York University draws his sword. At the University of Nebraska, classical columns crumble and at Penn State a proud obelisk falls. At the University of Arkansas, Old Main collapses. At Bucknell and Southern Illinois University at Carbondale, a venerated cannon fires. At Indiana University and Bucknell University tower bells ring for all to hear.

Students put one another to the test. They jokingly dare friends to walk by the all-knowing structure to see if it stays still—and of course it does, confirming the teen's badge of honor: awakened sexuality. It is significant that the very

The Green Goddess at Upper Iowa University.

Indiana University Clock Tower. (Simon Bronner)

symbols used on college campuses to mark their proud intellectual heritage are converted in student lore into sexual monuments. In a kind of parody play, students thus imply that the school really belongs to them, or that beneath the stiff intellectual exterior sex is the primary preoccupation.

Yet despite this general interpretation, the fact remains that the virgin test is most often directed at women. Most of the venerated statuary are phallic—cannons, obelisks, towers, and columns. Especially during the 1960s, the accounting of the statuary was accompanied by legends of the "one remaining virgin," usually a woman. At Knox College, for example, when the last virgin walked by the statue of a wounded soldier, it "would rise up and chase her out to the outlying cornfield to personally alleviate this condition" (Berkeley Folklore Archives, 1969). At Southern Illinois University, "it is said on campus that each time the cannon has been mysteriously painted during the night another unwise girl has succumbed to masculine persuasion and has lost her virginity" (Indiana University Folklore Archives, 1966). The outline of green hands above a former women's dorm at Berkeley is sometimes explained with the tall tale that the Campanile (the "campus phallic symbol," according to student accounts) wandered over to the dorm looking for sex (Berkeley Folklore Archives, 1979, 1986).

Barre Toelken points out that these accounts are "a revealing expression of male concerns over the rapidly developing status of women at universities for

Indiana University Well House. (Simon Bronner)

Coeds walking by the Penn State Polylith, 1950s.
(University Archives, Penn State Room)

Campanile at the University of California at Berkeley. (Simon Bronner)

the 1940s onward. The movement of women into domains previously thought of as male and rapid changes in women's habits (smoking, drinking, voting) have often brought out charges that sexual promiscuity was also somehow involved" (Toelken 1986: 522).

Charmed spots for romance

To emphasize the importance of courtship on campus, students also point to spots inspiring romance. Indiana University and Franklin College have well houses that have long been used for the purpose. "I heard that if you're sitting in the Well House," one student said, "and you're not doing anything romantic, the fountain will gurgle." Most often reported, however, is that "a girl isn't a coed until she's been kissed by an upperclassman in the Well House for the full twelve strokes of midnight" (Waymire 1978: 1-2).

Spoofer's Stone at the University of Arkansas. (Special Collections, University of Arkansas Libraries, Fayetteville)

At Michigan State back in the 1940s, Richard Dorson reported that "a girl becomes a coed when kissed in the shadow of Beaumont Tower at the stroke of midnight" (1949: 674). At the University of Michigan as late as the 1960s, coeds became "official" when they had been kissed under the arch in the engineering building (Cannon 1984: 42). At Eastern Michigan, the ritual kiss occurred under the lamp posts on the college mall. Cedar Crest women had "Wishing Steps" behind what was once the president's home. Some students claimed that wishes came true if the man and woman each counted the steps silently and arrived at the same number before sealing the wish with a kiss.

The University of Arkansas has a "Spoofer's Stone" where couples met. This piece of limestone was left next to Old Main after its construction in 1872. When campus rules early in the century prohibited "all intercourse between boys and girls," the stone proved useful for the leaving of love notes on the sly. Later it evolved into a favorite resting spot reserved for upperclass couples (Wylie 1933: 192-96). Oregon State also had a rock, of marble, a gift from the class of 1901 placed under what was known as the "Trysting Tree." Grove City College had several "sweetheart trees" on campus where couples left their mark by initialing the tree with a pocketknife (Gray 1969-70). Bethany has "Centenna Stones" in the center of campus marking the spot where the first college building stood. According to tradition, relationships are ready to commence when they have kissed while standing atop the stones.

Other spots invite communing with nature. Western Oregon State had its "Cupid's Knoll" and Northern Colorado its "Inspiration Point." Loving students at Juniata College went to the "Cliffs," a high rocky area overlooking the Juniata River. At William and Mary couples kiss on the bridge over Crim Dell Lake. (Some say this is a sign of future marriage—unless the woman throws the man into the lake.) Rutgers in New Brunswick still has a pond romantically minded students fondly call the "Passion Puddle." These spots inspire the kind of sentimentality typical before the days of "coed" dorms.

With segregation of sexes and visitation rules in dorms largely dropped during the 1960s, the romantic rendezvous was more likely to occur indoors. The coed dorm has relaxed sexual prohibitions, but arguably has also improved attitudes between the sexes. As Michael Moffatt points out, men in coeducational situations tend to treat women less as sexual objects, and to build intellectual and social friendships (1989: 45-49, 181-86). Indeed, Moffatt reports that "the sexual ambience of the coed dorm floors—the conventions of the mixed-sex groups in the lounges—was in curious ways more like older American erotic sensibilities than one had any reason to expect" (p. 182).

Through traditional signals, students show that sex is still a private affair. One might still encounter a white towel used by women or a tie used by men on the doorknob as a signal for a roommate to stay out. For the less formal, a sock around the doorknob gets the message across. On a Saturday night especially, it is customary to knock three times before walking in on your roommate.

Courtship codes

The long list of slang words for courtship in college argot shows the cultural coding of the romantic enterprise today on many college campuses. According to today's custom, women as well as men are liable to "scope," or check out potential mates in public places. Some women even establish "hunk alerts," when desirable men come by. What was once called "girlwatching" or "piping the flight" now sounds like a scientific exercise (see Dundes 1968: 27; Acheson 1987). At Worcester Polytechnic Institute, "scope" is considered the first part of a mating process marked with the letter "s." A "scam" is a find, a "scoop" is the meeting, and the "scromp" or "score" is the sexual engagement (Hancock 1988: 16).

Students hardly refer to "dating," although they do very much the same thing, just more informally, when they "go out with" or "see" someone. And while students don't talk much about "going steady," they do wonder who's "serious" or "tight" with whom. If not getting pinned, women will still wear a sweatshirt or ring of their beloved. There's also speculation about whether beads in the popular "add-a-bead" or "collect-a-bead" necklaces (gold chains to which are added gold, onyx, lapis, or tiger's eye beads) worn by many college women signify their exceptional "scores."

With a return to many traditional values during the 1980s, including to the institution of marriage, colleges witnessed a rejuvenation of some engagement customs that were once special events. Most common are women's "candle-lighting" or "ringing" ceremonies. From Bryn Mawr comes this account: "the women sit in a circle and pass a lighted candle from hand to hand. The candle is usually decorated with flowers and ribbons, with the engagement ring attached in some way. After a number of complete circles around the group, the engaged woman blows the candle out and then receives congratulations from the other women" (Briscoe 1981: 11).

At many colleges, candlelighting belongs to the tradition of sorority life. Typically the identity of the engaged woman is a secret until she blows out the candle. Usually only the best friend, housemother, or chapter president of the engaged sister knows, and she summons the others to the candlelight. In many sorority ceremonies, each pass of the candle represented the progression of a relationship often to the accompaniment of a sweetheart song; one time was for laveliering, twice for pinning, and three times for engagement (see Glavan 1968: 193-94; Hale 1968: 274; Toelken 1986: 515-16; Preston 1973: 271-74; Egan 1985: 131; Cochran 1981). Some houses today add a pass of the candle for friendship.

On some campuses, bells announce an engagement. Wheaton College in Illinois has an elaborate bell-ringing custom. Atop Old Main sits a tower bell once used to summon students to chapel. Today, when a couple get engaged, they gather their friends around and the group climbs five floors of rickety stairs, through the attic, into a small area with a ladder up to the bell. Tradition calls for the couple to ring the bell three rounds of seven times for good luck. While the couple rings the bell, their friends paint their names wherever they can find a spot on the ancient wood. Some couples hang their pictures or other mementoes from the rafters.

Both engaged men and women have a forced shower or ponding to look forward to. Often the shower occurs for women after the candlelighting ceremony. In a sign of community, women might also dump an engaged sister in a bathtub full of perfume donated by everyone in the house (Hunter 1977: 25-26). Men when they're dumped are likely to emerge with a less flowery odor. Typically a lake is chosen for the ritual event. At Union College, an engaged man's cronies kidnap him during the night and dump him in Holmes Lake near campus. It is also customary to remove his pants and if the engaged man goes in the lake alone he will get them back before returning to campus. If he manages to pull in someone with him, that person has to walk back to the college with the engaged man.

At campuses with a strong Greek life, the exchange of fraternity pins is an event just a notch below engagement. It may be celebrated as engagements are with a good dumping or a "swirlie." In the swirlie, the poor fellow's head is held down into a flushed toilet. Afterward, according to one witness, "you run like hell, because he's going to come and get you" (T. 1976: 5). Pinned brothers could also face a "poling": "Six or eight guys will grab him at dinner, usually the plegdes, and haul him outside, tie his feet together, hang him up in the tree upside down and throw garbage on him and leave him hang there for about an hour" (T. 1976: 18). At West Virginia Wesleyan, the pinned brother or sister might be tied to a statue of John Wesley and have food and mud hurled at him or her (survey response, 1989). In a variation, a fraternity brother pinned to a Delta Gamma will be stripped and tied to the sorority's large anchor on the front yard. His brothers pelt him with food or dump water on him, until the pinned sister comes out and kisses him. In the meantime some of the sisters may also get into the act by photographing him and rating his attractiveness (Birnbach 1984: 112; Egan 1985: 133).

Food and sex

Wondering about the college's efforts to control students' courtship activities, rumors circulate every once in awhile that the administration slyly had the dining hall food saltpetered, particularly on Fridays. Students speculate that the reason the practice hasn't been uncovered is that administrators intercepted a sample sent to a lab by enterprising undergraduates (Hunter 1977: 131). The rumors may have sources in military lore, which veterans spread about doctored food in repressive training camps (Rice and Jacobs 1973; Wyman 1979: 88; cf. Hand et al, 1981: 552).

As soldiers had their jocular names for institutional food, so students also refer to the wonders of dining-hall cooking as "griddle pucks" (hamburgers), "garbage barges" (tuna boat sandwiches), and "mystery meat" (U.F.O.— unidentifiable food object). Many names carry castration references: "Pigmy dicks" (miniature carrots), "monkey dicks" (link sausages), and "horse cock" (ring bologna) (Egan 1985: 129; Aman 1984-85: 284). Further adding to the image of victimized students' plight, rumors regularly fly about fingers, worms, and insects in the food, and mice and cigarette butts in soda cans (Domowitz 1979; Wyman 1979: 88; Fine 1979).

If students complain that the food served them acts as a sexual depressant, they may counteract the effect with items believed to act as aphrodisiacs. One still hears about oysters, radishes, hard-boiled eggs, bananas, yeast, chocolates, and peppers stimulating sexual passion (Cannon 1984: 157; Hand, et al, 1981: 551). A whole series of aphrodisiacs known for some time are green: olives, celery, asparagus, and avocado (Hand, et al, 1981: 550). That might explain the rage during the 1980s for the latest and hottest aphrodisiac: green M&Ms. True, you don't get too many green ones in a pack filled with brown, yellow, and orange bits, and the few green gems (usually ten or fewer out of 57), and sometimes the red ones, are treasured by college students to induce sexual desire (Clarke 1987). Sometimes they are even collected in a dish for "special occasions" (Brunvand 1986: 111-13).

One detects a modern imaging of pills for mood alteration in this association of M&Ms as aphrodisiacs. Most college women are aware of medical birth control pills and devices, but have reportedly added to their contraception or anaphrodisiac measures by eating grated nutmeg and parsley, and douching after intercourse with cola, lemon juice and water, and vinegar (Fish 1972).

Although conception is to be avoided, appearing "sexy" is usually an admired trait. Convinced that looking pencil-thin makes one sexually attractive, women tell one another about "wonder" diets, using magical formulas of three or seven in structuring diets or relying on the fabled "calorie-burning" effects of grapefruit (Tucker 1978: 142-43). Perhaps making a feminist comment on the sexual implications of this dieting craze, the riddle-joke "What would women be without men?" is answered by "fat and happy." The obsession with magical diets is also ridiculed in photocopied lore about the "30-day reducing diet" (1 part Metracal, 1 part Ex-Lax, 1 part Spanish fly, 1 part Bourbon/Scotch). The result according to the sheet is that "you will be the skinniest, sexiest, shittiest, alcoholic in the world" (D'Pnymph 1988: 301; Dundes 1987: 236).

Sexual passion is not always desirable in college lore. College women may hear a cautionary tale about a drugging that results in unwanted seduction. In these stories, an underclasswoman, usually a frosh, goes on a blind date with a fraternity brother to a party at his house. During the course of the evening, the boy slips a drug into the woman's drink, which causes her to lose consciousness. In some versions, she wakes up just as he is molesting her.

In others, she wakes up the next morning and finds her clothes are gone. The teller speculates that she was raped or frighteningly didn't know what happened to her. Andrea Greenberg observed that the legend is a response to the tension of the coed arriving on campus on her own. She has a new-found freedom to experiment sexually but she often feels, even more strongly than men do, parental disapproval. "The opposition," she points out, "is resolved by a forced sexual experience which places all responsibility for the sexual act on the male, who then becomes a surrogate for past parental responsibility. In this way, the girl achieves both goals: sexual experience plus irresponsibility" (Greenberg 1973: 134). It is a warning for women to maintain control, particularly as women are believed to be more susceptible to the effects of alcohol than men. In addition, the legend reminds women that although they may be flattered by many social invitations in college, they may indeed be treated as sexual objects (or "hit on," in student lingo), especially, the story suggests, in male domains such as fraternities.

A passion for excess

Men meanwhile may hear a legend about sexual assertiveness by women. From Minnesota college men, Gary Alan Fine and Bruce Noel Johnson collected many versions of "The Promiscuous Cheerleader." The legend tells of a young female cheerleader who has sexual relations (often fellatio) with members of an athletic team. She becomes ill, sometimes while cheering at a game, and must be rushed to the hospital. There doctors pump her stomach, removing a miraculous amount of semen (1980: 120-29; see also Beezley 1985: 223). During the 1970s, a period of female assertiveness, Fine and Johnson argue, the legend is both a "warning to sexually aggressive women and the implication that it was perfectly acceptable for members of the team to take advantage of the cheerleader's sexual proposition" (Fine and Johnson 1980: 128).

As the "drugged and seduced" legend speaks to the fears women have of their sexuality being abused, the "promiscuous cheerleader" story tells of the fears men have of their sexuality being rejected. In the men's fantasy, the promiscuous cheerleader effectively saves the man from embarrassment about sexual maneuvering by offering herself to him. The cheerleader usually has a clean and wholesome image and here she seems to long for giving pleasure to men, particularly those that adhere to the masculine model of strength and dominance. The story thus reinforces the male bonding of the athletic team, which often comes to represent the school itself. Some ambiguity exists, however, in the appropriateness of the activity to the locale. Sometimes the story is offered as a derisive tale about the debauchery of a rival school.

The "promiscuous cheerleader" legend, like other collegiate stories, tells of excess. The main characters in the legend are suspect, because they represent an excess of brawn and spirit. With these excessive attributes, when compared to norms of the run-of-the-mill student, athletes and cheerleaders receive a tense mixture of disapproval and envy through the legend that begs for commentary. Students have doubts about overachievement in social pursuits, much as they do about it in academic performance. College life is supposed to be intense and excessive, students fondly offer, but they also voice worries about the limits of its hedonistic tendencies.

George Hornbein and Kenneth Thigpen, for example, captured a fraternity brother telling a variation of the "promiscuous cheerleader" legend in their documentary film *Salamanders* (1982). Commenting on his fraternity's ritual of swallowing salamanders at an annual party, a ritual replete with sexual symbolism, the brother told of a former member who had an extraordinary capacity for consumption of the amphibian. The heralded member complained of an upset stomach one day, so he went to the hospital. There an x-ray revealed slews of the creatures crawling around in his stomach. They live!

The theme of excess appears particularly in lore about drug and alcohol consumption. During the 1970s, many students heard rumors about the excesses of LSD. As Barre Toelken tells the tale, "six students were found totally blind on the side of a hill, where, under the influence of LSD, they had spent the afternoon staring at the sun. Each legend contained the name of the university the students had attended, and after the story got into the newspapers several times, there was a rash of denials by the universities concerned. Various journalists did local research on the story, but no one was able to come up with the 'real' occurrence. It may or it may not have happened, but for thousands of student-legend narrators, it allowed for the expression of fears and concerns that would have been considered 'uncool' among those who felt they needed to demonstrate their familiarity with the drug scene" (1986: 514).

For most students, alcohol is the drug of choice. The long list of terms for drunkenness offers an admixture of invitation and warning. Students smilingly refer to being "trashed," "wasted," "blottoed," "wiped out," "blinded," "pickled," "fried," "damaged," "smashed," and "shitfaced." They also freely give advice on ways to allow you to "drink others under the table": drink milk, milkshakes, and water before drinking; eat steak, ice cream, chalk, baked potato, and bread coated with olive oil. For that inevitable discomfort after "pounding" beer, "When you go to bed, put one foot on the floor and your arm on the bed. Swallow a raw egg and drink salt water to make you vomit" (Indiana University Folklore Archives, 1978). And there's the proverbial hair of the dog that bit you, or taking a stiff drink the next day.

As if to dubiously welcome the student into adulthood, his or her twenty-first birthday may well involve "taking shots" in front of friends to induce a ritual display of drunkenness. Legends of remarkable drinking feats meanwhile highlight dubious achievement. Berkeley, for example, has the drinking legend of John P. Ergman, reputed to have partied his way through school, always in the "recent past." "He was a notorious beer drinker, and he taught all the freshmen how to drink," one account begins. "J.P. was a true party man," another offers. At one of the parties, the beer supply ran out and J.P. was sent to get another 12 gallon keg, and did not return. Some days later his dead body was found leaning against a tree, and the keg was empty!" (Berkeley Folklore Archives, 1971, 1978).

Jocks, dumb and privileged

Often the legendary mass, indeed massive, consumers—of alcohol, food, cash, and cars—are the men's football and basketball stars. With their reputations for privilege and excess, these athletes present a dilemma in student lore. While praised for the esteem they bring to the student body, they are scorned for taking advantage of the system and distancing themselves from the "regular" student. Although much student lore taunts the studious grind, it can equally torment the non-studious athlete. The nature of the taunting has changed somewhat over the last two decades. The "privileged jock" has entered into student humor where the "dumb jock" left off (Beezley 1985). Wherever the jock is in these stories, the coach isn't too far behind.

Combining the stereotype of dumbness with excess is the joke about the new recruit who complained that the food at the training table was awful. "Every mouthful was terrible, just terrible," he went on, "and, to make it worse, the portions were too small."

Recruits are brought to the university, lore professes, for their brawn rather than for their brain. To make the point, a legend of a coach travelling the backroads of farm country to find players attaches to several Hall-of-Fame coaches, including Notre Dame's Knute Rockne and Minnesota's Clarence "Doc" Spears. As it is usually told, the coach asks plowboys he sees for directions to the next town. If they point the way with their finger, he continues on his way. But once in a while, there's the exceptional specimen who picks up his plow to point the way (Dorson 1949: 674; Baker 1983: 110; Beezley 1985:218).

Once brought to campus, recruits enter into lore when they find ways to get around the application process. A parody of the application form to the University of Pittsburgh begins by asking for the applicant's height (that means "how tall," the form explains) and weight ("to the nearest hundred," it requests) followed by the question "Do you play football?" If the applicant checks the box for "yes," he is instructed to proceed to the last two lines of the form. Those are the lines for the signature, you know, "that's a messy version of your printed name."

Lore has it that some recruits are given special oral entrance exams to bypass the normal academic route into college. Unfortunately, one star recruit gave the wrong answer of "eight" when asked to compute the sum of three and three. "Aw, come on," the coach pleads with the examiners, "he only missed the right answer by one!" (Beezley 1985: 216; Baker 1983: 110; Wyman 1979: 86). Using a similar scenario, the story is told about the Kentucky basketball player who had to spell "dog" on his oral exam. "D...d...d...," he stammered. Then the coach hit him on the back. "Oh, Gee!" he exclaimed. The player passed. From Wisconsin meanwhile comes the story of the tough oral exam where the football recruits were asked not one, but two questions: "What color is blue vitriol?" and "When was the war of 1812?" (Wyman 1979).

Today's privileged jock of folklore may be dumb but he isn't stupid, as the saying goes, for he's the one raking in bucks and having an easy time in college. And "How many jocks does it take to change a light bulb at Arizona State?" The answer? "Only one, but eleven get one course credit for it!" (Beezley 1985:

224). Many students at big-time colleges quip that they have the best teams money can buy. Rumors fly about the numbers of cars and other amenities athletes receive (Beezley 1985: 219). In many versions, the appetite of the athletes for tremendous quantities of food, alcohol, and women is equal to the generosity of patrons (Beezley 1985: 22-23). Many swear that once graduated into the professional leagues, a star student-athlete was introduced as "the only college player in history who had to take a cut in pay to turn pro" (Beezley 1985: 220).

There's a disturbing racial reference in some of these quips, especially as it is sometimes expressed that stereotyped black athletes get into big-time, predominantly white colleges to play for pay. After University of Maryland basketball star Len Bias died of cocaine intoxication in 1986, many "sick" jokes circulated, including "Why are so many blacks and other minorities enrolling at the University of Maryland?" Because they heard there is no bias there (Aman 1988-89: 271). Also during the late 1980s, a crude parody of a recruiting list made the rounds from photocopier to photocopier. In versions variously attached to the universities of Oklahoma, Wisconsin, Minnesota, and Miami, the list included the fictitious recruit Woodrow Lee Washington, 6 foot 8 inches tall, 198 pounds, from the Bronx, New York. "Third-generation welfare family. At 19 he is the oldest of 14 children. Mother thinks that possibly child No. 3 and No. 9 may have the same father. Expensive tastes; wants two floor-length mink coats and pink Mercedes to sign letter of intent" ("University of Wisconsin" 1986-87). The one from the University of Oklahoma was circulated in response to scandals involving football players arrested on criminal charges. It lists Cletis Quentis Jenkins, "running back. Set state scoring record out of Melrose High School, Charlotte, NC. Also led the state in burglaries. But has only six convictions. He's been clocked in the 40 at 4.2 seconds with a 25" TV under his arm."

Lore such as the parodied recruiting list draws attention to the business of sport at big-time colleges. Another piece of recent photocopied lore that offers this subtext parodies the schedules of colleges who play soft opponents to inflate their winning record and earn profitable tournament invitations. Although the names of the schools change the schedule of opponents is fairly consistent: Chicken Little Nursery School, Boy Scout Troop 99, Crippled Children's Hospital, School for the Blind, World War I Veterans Association, Brownie Scout Troop No. 13, High School Cheerleaders, St. Joseph's Boys' Choir, Korean War Amputees, and Veterans' Hospital Polio Patients. All the games are, of course, at home. The parody also lists important rule changes for the current year. Some of the notable ones are: The home team will be allowed to play with three footballs at the same time and 27 players can be on the field instead of the usual 11. The home team also has special rules tailored for the schedule. Implying that the home team would do anything to win, the rules stipulate that when playing polio patients, the home team must not disconnect iron lungs; when playing the Brownies, the home team cannot steal their cookies; and when playing the school for the blind, home team players cannot hide the football under their jerseys.

And the men who coach them

The pressure to win usually falls on the coach. In older collegiate lore, the coach often appeared confused or eccentric, but befitting the heightened role of collegiate sports, in today's lore the coach is mostly portrayed as aloof and egotistical. Among the older texts are those attached to Ed Diddle, long-time coach of Western Kentucky's basketball team. Complaining that his players were eating too well and gaining too much weight, his trainer suggested that the boys could cut down on their milk consumption. Coach Diddle "stood up and beat on the table with his fists and said, 'Boys, I got an announcement to make.' He said, 'From now on you don't get a quart of milk each meal. You just get two pints.'"

Another time, one of coach's stars asked the coach, "Hey, do you hear that noise?" "What noise?" Coach replied. "Illinois" was the joking answer. Coach liked that so much that he later tried it on one of his assistants. "Do you hear that racket?" he smilingly blurted. "What racket?" "Pennsylvania," the Coach offered (Dawson 1971:39).

Put in the context of contemporary collegiate sports scandals about the lack of education athletes receive, the humorous motif of the confused coach surfaces in stories such as the one told sometimes about Tom Osborne of Nebraska. Osborne was getting on Penn State's Joe Paterno about his disappointing season, and Paterno quickly responded by pointing out the high percentage of his seniors graduating. Osborne defensively referred to his student athletes at Nebraska. "You see that big red 'N' over there by Cornhusker stadium?" he said. "That stands for 'knowledge'" (survey response, 1988).

Students believe that coaches today have agreements with the trustees that they will always receive one dollar more, or astronomically more, than the president of the universities. After North Carolina's losing football season in 1978, North Carolina State students said that the NC coach received a $5,000 bonus because the school had a five-year plan to de-emphasize football and he did it in one year (Beezley 1981: 115).

Superstar coaches such as Bob Knight of Indiana, Dean Smith of North Carolina, and the late Bear Bryant of Alabama receive more than money; they get holy adoration. Witness a story and variations told with any of the three in the leading role. "There was a basketball player from Indy who died and went to heaven," one story begins. "When he got to heaven he told St. Peter that it was all right that he died as long as they played basketball in heaven. St. Peter said they did, but instead of numbers on the jerseys they used letters. The man from Indy didn't understand, so St. Peter said he would just show him. When they got to the court he explained that the man with the 'C' on his jersey was a center, the players with 'G' were guards, and since the man from Indy was a forward he would have an 'F' on his shirt. The player from Indy said he understood everything except who the man was with 'BK' on his shirt. St. Peter just laughed and replied, 'That's just God; he thinks he's Bobby Knight'" (Baker 1986: 173-74).

Sometimes the story isn't complimentary, as with this variation told by, not surprisingly, rival North Carolina State fans: "Basketball coaches Norm Sloan of State, Bill Foster of Duke, and Carl Tacy of Wake Forest died and went to heaven. As they were being introduced around, St. Peter told them: 'This is a nice place. Very few aggravations. About the only thing that might be considered unpleasant is the waiting. We have to wait in line for everything.' Sure enough, at dinner that night, there was a long line of angels. Suddenly there was a commotion as a line-breaker charged to the front, pushing other angels out of the way. He grabbed the food and began eating; soon he demanded to be brought seconds, and the angels meekly complied. 'Wow, who's that?' the coaches whispered to St. Peter. 'Oh, that's God,' said the saint. 'Sometimes he thinks he's Dean Smith'" (Beezley 1981: 115-16).

Pointing to, or knocking, the egos of coaches, there's the story of the group of northern sportswriters who came to Arkansas to see Bear Bryant's birthplace. Bryant took them to a small barn. "Is this where you were born, Bear?" asked one sportswriter. "Yep," answered Bryant. Another sportswriter said, "I thought you were born in a log cabin." "That was Abraham Lincoln," the Bear answered. "I was born in a manger." In another story about the coach's holy status, the Bear was taking a quiet, casual walk on the water, when he suddenly fell under. He gasped for breath and yelled for help, until along in a speedboat came the head football coach at Auburn, who assisted Bryant into the boat. "Now you won't tell anyone that I fell in, will you?" asked the Bear. "Not if you won't tell anyone that I rescued you," answered the Auburn coach (Boswell

1976: 77).

Sports, as the most visible part of the university to the public, figures prominently in stories showing the superiority of a school in collegiate rivalries. For many rivalries, the sports field becomes a way to settle the tension between "snobs" at the state university and the "hicks" at the land-grant college. The nation has many of these fierce rivalries, including those between North Carolina and North Carolina State, Michigan and Michigan State, Washington and Washington State. There's an old story at Indiana about how athletes at different big-time colleges introduce themselves to pretty coeds. "A Harvard player shakes the girl's hand. A Notre Dame player shuffles his feet. An Indiana player asks her for a date, and a Purdue player phones the coach for instructions." The story is told, too, about the Texas A&M coach who resorted to prayer to reverse his team's fortune on the playing field. His Aggies beat Baylor and SMU by big margins on successive weekends. Appealing to God once again before the big game against the Texas Longhorns, the Aggies' bitter rival, the coach came out on the field full of confidence. But the Aggies lost 99 to 0. After the game, the coach beseeched his Maker, "Why, oh Lord, did you let us down this time?" Black storm clouds gathered in the sky, a streak of lightning flashed, and a deep, solemn voice boomed, "Hook 'em, Horns" (*Best* 1976: 12-13; cf. Baker 1982: 173).

In this era of mass spectator sports, many rivalry jokes today concern the behavior of fans. There's the story told about the easy-going Michigan Stater who went to the lavatory at Michigan's stadium. He passed by some snooty Michigan fans on his way to the urinal. When he was done, he turned to leave the facility. The Michigan fans stopped him, and one scolded, "I don't know the way they do things at Old State, but here we wash our hands after we urinate." The Michigan Stater quickly replied, "Well, where I come from they teach us not to piss in our hands!" (cf. Beezley 1981: 112; *Best* 1976:150).

At Indiana, students say that Purdue fans wanted to tell everyone they were number one, but they couldn't figure out how many fingers to hold up. Purdue students meanwhile pass around photocopied sheets blaring "Not All Indiana Fans Are Assholes," under which is a drawing of a fan with a face strangely resembling a man's genitals.

Jokes about athletes, coaches, and fans address the importance of sports in big-time colleges. In many jokes, sports figures evade or triumph over the academic mission of the university. For many tellers, the stories thus carry a mixed message. The stories illustrate the public notoriety of sports for the campus as a source of pride for students, yet also demonstrate the abuses that reflect badly on the college's attention to the needs of students. At bottom, the stories about sports, usually told at large universities, are about the incorporation of the big-time colleges. Apparently driven by the profit motive, administrations have, according to students, exploited sports as much as athletes have exploited the colleges.

Further, the sports stories demonstrate the corporate structure of the contemporary multiversity. Coaches and athletes have specialized, professionalized roles in a hierarchical social system. Athletes and coaches are distanced from students in today's stories, whereas in older lore, they are part of a communal campus. Sports stories about greed, race, and class thus shed light on the professionalization of athletes in college, and use sports figures to refer generally to human problems caused by the corporate growth of larger universities.

Punchlines among rivals

At many universities, riddle-jokes abound to demean regional rivals, and students occasionally turn them on their own schools.

What's the difference between yogurt and Davis? Yogurt has culture.

What's an Indiana University martini? A beer with an olive.

Why doesn't State put Astroturf in the stadium? Because they wouldn't have a place for the homecoming queen to graze.

The last is one of many ridiculing a school because of its unattractive women. University of North Carolina students ask about the difference between a State coed and a trash can. The answer? Trash gets taken out once a week (Costner 1975: 111). State students meanwhile ask "What do you call a good-looking girl at Carolina?" A visitor (Beezley 1981: 114). Coeds at rival schools presumably compensate for their ugliness with sexual aggressiveness. University of Washington students ask, "What's the first thing Washington State girls do in the morning?" Pack up their things and go home. They also ask, "Why do Washington State coeds wear bibs?" So they don't get tobacco juice on their overalls when they spit. But State students might reply, "Why couldn't they hold a Christmas pageant at the University of Washington?" They couldn't find three wise men or a virgin (survey response, 1989; cf. Boswell 1976: 78; Beezley 1981: 115; Costner 1975: 111).

Similar barbs are hurled by students from women's colleges. Wellesley women ask, "What's the difference between a Smithie and a Ferrari?" Most men haven't been in a Ferrari (Birnbach 1984: 182). At Hood, one might hear "Goucher to bed, Hood to wed," while Goucher women say the reverse (survey response, 1989; cf. Carey 1988: 8).

If one of the rivals is an agricultural college, its supposedly hardy men may be accused of bestiality and its field-toughened women may be taunted for having masculine traits. The university men known for their intellectual snobbery, rather than manual labor, may be accused of homosexuality. North Carolina students, for example, are fond of taunting North Carolina State as a place where the men are men and the sheep are all nervous. North Carolina is meanwhile described as a place where the women are women and so are the men (cf. Mechling and Wilson 1988: 310-11; Birnbach 1984: 82; Wyman 1979: 82; Egan 1985: 128). And "how do they separate the men from the boys at North Carolina?" With a crowbar (Beezley 1981: 114). "Why did the guy from State marry the cow?" a UNC student may ask, and supply the answer, "Because he had to" (Costner 1975: 108). The reply to that from the NC State student might be "better ag than fag" (Beezley 1981: 114).

A whole sheaf of jokes, often built on numskull motifs, concerns Texas Aggies. As a book from Texas A&M professed, "The Texas institution that is talked about and bragged about—in addition to being joked about—perhaps more than any other is the Texas Aggie. Because Texas Aggies are not like the rest of the world (thank goodness), the 'Aggie joke' has become a part of the folklore of Texas A&M. People talk about Aggies because they are different, and Aggies are proud of it. Aggies tend to be 'a little bit square'" (Adams 1979: 4). The story is told, for example, about two Aggies who climbed a tree at the border of a nudist colony so they could see in. "Why you can't even tell the men from the women," one exclaimed. The other replied, "That's because they don't have any clothes on" (Mitchell 1976:518).

Usually told by students at the University of Texas, many Aggie jokes parallel the style of ethnic slurs, such as, "What do you call 144 Aggies in a room? Gross stupidity" (Mitchell 1976: 711; cf. Clements type E1.3; Dundes 1987: 134-35; Baker 1986: 109-24). A photocopied sheet circulates around many offices that asks "Did you hear about the Aggie who...?" Among the listed lines that complete the question are: "studied five days to take a urine test," "took a roll of toilet paper to the crap game," and "thought 'no kidding' meant birth control" (cf. Bronner 1989: 119-20; Sims 1944: 155-61; Davidson 1943: 101-4).

Aggies themselves may say "What do you call an Aggie five years after he has taken his first job?" Boss! (Adams 1979: 3). Or they may tell about the Aggie who got into a boasting match with some natives on a visit to Alaska. "We may not be the biggest state in the Union anymore, but we're still the toughest," declared the Aggie. The Alaskan laughed and said, "We Alaskans can't be beat. Every man here can drink a fifth of whiskey in one gulp, wrestle a grizzly bear bare, and make love to an Eskimo woman all in one night." "Shucks, any Aggie can do that," huffed the Aggie. So he downed a fifth of whiskey, and went looking for a bear. A few hours later, the Aggie staggered back with his clothes in tatters and bruises all over his body. "Okay men," bellowed the Aggie, "now where's that woman you want me to wrestle?" (*Best* 1976: 11).

Still, Aggies, again following an ethnic model, recognize the low regard often given those who follow an agricultural life (see Mechling and Wilson 1988: 303-17). Appropriately, Aggies have jokes to express their unfair treatment. In one, a University of Texas student approached St. Peter at the gate to heaven. St. Peter greeted him warmly, and said, "Welcome to heaven. We have a simple entrance exam here. Spell God." He spelled it with no problem. A student from Southern Methodist approached, and he took the same exam, which he passed. Then the Aggie came. "We have a simple entrance exam here in heaven," said St. Peter. "Spell Nacogdoches" (*Best* 1976: 151).

In a variation, an Aggie, a T-Sipper (derisive term for snobs from the University of Texas), and an Oklahoma Sooner were survivors on a wrecked ship in the middle of the ocean. When a helicopter came to rescue them, the pilot said, "There's only room for two. The two who answer my questions correctly can come aboard." The Sooner received the first question, "What was the famous ship that went down when it hit an iceberg?" The Sooner replied, "The Titanic." Next the pilot asked the T-Sipper, "How many people died on it?" "1,517," The T-Sipper smugly answered. The third question was for the Aggie: "Name them!" (*Best* 1976: 164).

Texas students have one with a numskull twist. It seems that an Aggie went to heaven, but was stopped by St. Peter when he started to enter the section occupied by Texas alumni. St. Peter cautioned, "You can't go in there; that's the section reserved for former Texas students." "Gosh, I'm surprised you practice segregation up here," the Aggie replied. "I thought college feuding ended a long time ago and everybody gets along with each other now. Why, I visited the University of Texas campus myself and lit the pre-Thanksgiving Day bonfire." "Really? When was that?" St. Peter asked. "About ten minutes ago," the Aggie replied (*Best* 1976: 10).

Texas A&M isn't the only state university to show a bit of inferiority complex when compared with other colleges. One example is a parody of a "Dear Abby" letter. "I have two brothers," the photocopied sheet begins, and then there are many variations, but it might follow like this one from my archives. "One attends Penn State University and the other was sent to the electric chair. Mother died in an insane asylum. Since I was three years old, my father has had a narcotics problem. One of my sisters is a successful and highly paid prostitute, the other is the common law wife of a local executive of the Mafia. Recently I met a wonderful girl (shortly after she was released from prison for smothering her illegitimate child). We are very much in love and expect to be married just as soon as her venereal disease clears up. My problem is, should I tell her about my brother who attends Penn State?" (cf. Clements type L5.10; Dundes and Pagter 1978: 15-16; *Best* 1976: 144; Beezley 1981: 113; Boswell 1976: 79).

Many jokes compare the various responses of students from different colleges in a region. In northern California, students like to say that in response to a professor's greeting of "Good morning," a University of California at Davis class writes the greeting down. At Stanford, the reply is "Good morning professor." At Berkeley the class retorts, "Hey, don't lay your trips on me!" (survey response, 1989). A variation is told in New England where Smith students typically write down the greeting. Mount Holyoke students stand up and salute, the ones at Amherst bark back "Prove it," and those at the University of Massachusetts respond, "Will that be on the final exam?" Finally, the students at Hampshire look at one another and say, "Hey man, far out!" (Carey 1988: 6-7).

In a similar vein, there is a story often told of a test of Ivy League chivalry in reaction to a pretty lady entering a room. A "Yale man" asks if someone else shouldn't bring a chair for her. The "Princeton man" dramatically brings one, and the "Harvard man" sits in it (Copeland 1940: 407).

Revealing graffiti

From where they sit in restrooms across the country, students also offer their humorous commentaries on school and the world in the form of graffiti. There where nature calls, students express their baser desires and concerns about sex, drugs, violence, and society. To be sure, campus maintenance regularly paints stalls and substitutes materials to challenge the bathroom writer. But somehow, traditional latrine rhymes and phrases appear anew. Triumphantly, the writer notes, "They paint these walls to stop my pen but the shithouse poet has struck again" (Mays 1980: 3)

Befitting the anal retention of academic work, the tension of student life in the institution may bottle up the writer. It shouldn't be surprising then that good places to look for graffiti are in the library and classroom buildings. One reads, for example, "Here I sit, broken hearted; came to shit but only farted" and "Here I sit, smelling the vapor, Because some bastard stole the paper; How much longer must I linger, Before I am forced to use my finger?" (Mays 1980: 3; Dundes 1966: 99).

Soiling the glorious image of the college degree, many writers simply write above the roll of bathroom tissue, "Diplomas, Take One" (Mays 1980: 5-6; Birnbach 1984: 265). Or the writer may advise, "If you can't go to college, go to State" (Egan 1985: 128). Men use bathroom walls to elaborate on life in the university: "State is like a dick, When it's soft you can't beat it, and when it's hard you get screwed" and "State is like a whore. Pay money and get screwed" (Mays 1980: 7-8; Nilsen 1981: 81). They may also wax poetically, "I wish I was a ring, Upon my true love's hand, Then every time she'd wipe her ass, I'd see the Promised Land" (Mays 1980: 4). If that's not bad enough, writers offer this meaning to the routine end of a thoughtful bathroom session: "Flush hard; it's a long way to the dining halls" (Mays 1980: 11).

Women have their own expressions to inscribe on bathroom walls. Often pointing to male dominance, women writers leave, "Balls said the queen; If I had them I'd be King." But they receive pleasure from lines such as "Here I sit, I have to pee, Just pissed out a member of R.O.T.C." and "Adam was only the rough draft" (Jachimiak 1978: 1). Writers often receive answers from those who take their place in the stall. At Indiana, a woman offered, "All females get rid of boys and war, hate, poverty, greed, and rape will die out. Matriarchal revolution is here. Women Unite!" "Unfortunately so will the human race," was the commentary inscribed underneath (Jachimiak 1978: 1). Another favorite political statement is "Eunuchs of the World Unite! You have nothing to lose." Women can match the men in expressing sexual play, "Long and thin goes further in, but short and thick does the trick," but they may also advise, "Look homeward pregnant angel" (Golden 1974: 5; Nilsen 1981: 84).

Some latrines express the distinctive wordplay of subgroups within the college. Again, the anonymity of the inscription allows for release and commentary. "I think I'm in love with my French horn," one might offer, to which the replies might be left, "It's the only thing worth being in love with" and "Horns are as fickle as any woman or man" (Gates 1976: 37). Or frustration might be expressed in rhyme: "Here I am to sit and ponder, While over these keys I do wonder, But right notes I just can't hit, I think this piano is full of shit" (Jachimiak 1978: 4). From a women's bathroom comes, "Voice students should practice topless, lets the chest breathe deep," while from the men's one finds "A concert violist named Leo, Was seducing a flautist named Cleo; As she took off

her panties, She exclaimed—No andantes, I want this allegro con brio!"
(Jachimiak 1978: 4; Mays 1980: 5).

Frat rats have been known to leave this motto: "When better women are
made, fraternity men will make them" (Egan 1985: 128). Independents may
respond, "Fraternities: The mind is a terrible thing to waste" (Egan 1985: 128).
Wondering about the society they will soon inherit, students may add
"The future of America is in your hands" (Mays 1980: 7). Contributing to
student cynicism since the 1950s has been the Cold War threat of foreign
nuclear bombs hanging over American heads. During the 1950s and 1960s,
writers offered, "In case of nuclear attack, hide under this urinal. Nobody ever
hits it" (Dundes 1966: 97). During the 1980s, however, students more aggressively used "nuke" to deal a decisive blow to various targets: "Nuke Iran,"
"Nuke Russia," "Nuke the Whale Hunters," "Nuke the Whales," and "Nuke
Steeler Fans" (Mays 1980: 9). Drugs receive comment in the commonly seen
line, "Reality is for people who can't handle drugs" (Mays 1980: 10; Lockwood
1978: 11). Showing cynicism about spiritual help, students may write, "God is
dead, but don't worry, Mary is pregnant again" (La Barre 1979: 275; Wyman
1979: 90; Gach 1973: 287). A reply to this last observation often is attached,
"God isn't dead. He just doesn't want to get involved" (Gach 1973: 287; La
Barre 1979: 275).

Graffiti writers also ply their trade on desk tops. "Oh, Oh! Somebody wrote
on this desk," one might find, or referring back to the latrine gallery, "These
desk top poets, so full of wit, should have their names engraved in shit"
(Lockwood 1978: 8; Gach 1973: 285). Some of the most common inscriptions
express boredom or frustration: "40, 35, 30, 25, 20, 15, 10 minutes to go of this
class," "I can't take it anymore," and "Let me out of here!" (Lockwood 1978: 4-
5; cf. Brunvand 1966: 21-22). Influenced by the television show "Star Trek," a
favorite of students writing on desk tops is "Beam me up Scotty!" (Lockwood
1978: 5).

Perhaps discouraged by the formica replacing old wooden desks and the
increased protection of bathroom stalls from the mighty pen, some creative folk
poets, identities still typically veiled, place more personally directed messages
in campus newspapers (and, I've noticed lately, on computer bulletin boards).
Student writers especially mark important rites of passage in the student
culture such as the twenty-first birthday and graduation. "Arteries are red,
Veins are blue, A year from today, You'll be 22!" one reads (Fagan 1981: 338).
Writers also honor holidays significant to students such as Hallowe'en, Christmas, Valentine's Day, St. Patrick's Day, and April Fool's Day. Many of the

messages, as one might expect, carry sexual references. From the University of Oregon, for instance, comes this sample: "The next time you want me to share your salami, take off the wrapper," "You are the tootsie roll in my candy bag of life," and "If you haven't had a ball until now you've got one comin'" (Fagan 1981: 340). Students might read the columns simply for its witty, off-color content, check the columns regularly to see if they received a message, and then figure out who it's from, or read messages to see if they recognize other recipients.

No wonder homework doesn't get done. Students have lots of distractions to deal with. Some have to do with the distinctive, often mysterious college environment, while others connect to the growing pains of the student's age. Legend, lore, and custom remind students of issues and decisions they need to face by themselves. As home, the campus presents students with more options, but fewer protections, than in years past. Students learn to be alert for hazards in the treacherous landscape they must cross from dorm to library, and the mindscape they must cross from adolescence to adulthood. Independent of parents and community, indeed often feeling unguided even prior to coming to campus, students share folklore with their peers to reflect on matters of sex, courtship, fidelity, drugs, and security. These matters are typically discussed outside of the curriculum, and they fill up much of the time students spend on talk—and on symbolic, dramatic narrative.

Through folklore, students confront their cultural status and that of others according to gender, race, region, occupation, age, and class. Through folklore, they are already learning about the specialized, professionalized roles of corporate life, and their social response to an individualistic mass society, which today seems increasingly open and tolerant. While that allows students many desired freedoms, it also challenges them to define moral limits. Appropriately, folklore helps students characterize the dangers and joys, and allows them to hypothetically explore the choices available. Rumors, legends, and jokes about the pressing questions students have are not just idle talk. By the time they receive their degrees at the big moment of graduation, students have received an emotional, cultural education from their peers.

Graduation

Graduation, after four long years, is the moment students have been working, waiting, and suffering for. To freshmen, graduation seems impossibly far away. That's the way it's supposed to be, because graduation comes after four years, rather than three.

While "three" in American society is a symbol of completion, "four" translates into a specific quantity representing thoroughness (Dundes 1980: 134-59; Brandes 1985). To travel "the four corners of the earth" is to see it all; to "cover all your bases" (four in baseball) is to go all the way from home and back; to win a series in four straight is to make a clean sweep.

"Three" suggests magical power, as in the phrase "third time's a charm," while "four" stresses rational human control, as in the basic building block of a four-sided square or the adage that wisdom comes with figuring out that "two and two make four." Maybe that's why there are normally four passing grades: A, B, C, D. Four is the number of seasons, after which another cycle begins. Especially appropriate to the idea of college as a transition from innocence to worldliness and from child to adult, is the idea of forty as a transitional journey away from home, often in seclusion with suffering often attached, to mark the passage from one stage to another. Moses travelled forty years in the desert; Noah withstood rain for forty days and nights (Brandes 1985: 74-77).

Arnold Van Gennep, who described the structure of "rites of passage" responding to life-stage changes, pointed out that such rites typically have three stages of separation, transition, and incorporation, but with the critical transition stage often divided into two parts, one can usually observe four components to cultural passage. Especially during initiation rites between puberty and adulthood, the transition stage comprises two sections of post-separation and pre-incorporation, both stressing the initiate's state of being at a threshold (Van Gennep 1960: 65-115). The initiate-child symbolically dies during this transition stage and is reborn with a new status as an empowered member of a special community. If "forty seems like a lifetime" and "life begins at forty" in American society, one can also observe the symbolic death and rebirth that occurs at "commencement," the ritual observing graduation after the four stages of freshmen, sophomore, junior, and senior life.

Moving up

Graduation ceremonies resound with the themes of rationality, transition, and rebirth. Ceremonies don't wait for the end of the fourth year, however. Befitting the symbolism of three as a natural cycle of completion, the recognition of graduating senior status begins at the end of the junior year. Students consider the junior, or third, year the roughest academically in their collegiate experience; they expect that senior year passes much more easily and is primarily devoted to preparation for moving up and out. Appropriately, a special occasion on many campuses, particularly smaller communal ones, is "Moving-Up Day." At Chatham College, Moving-Up Day coincides with closing convocation, in which classes receive the color of the class to which they are moving up. The dramatic climax is when the senior class bestows its color in the form of flowers to the juniors, who then become seniors. At Wells's Moving-Up Day, each of the three underclasses compose songs to sing to the departing class. In a sign of farewell, the seniors sing about their dorms and faculty. At Bryn Mawr, the four classes gather on the administration building steps. Seniors claim the central seats with the other classes in a hollow square around them. After a hearty round of songs about college life, the seniors sing the college's traditional "goodnight" song, and then they leave. The juniors move into the revered places held by the seniors (Briscoe 1981: 239-41). At larger campuses, where moving-up is less an honored tradition, students may joke about being on individualized "plans" ranging from five to seven years.

At Huntingdon College, a school in Alabama with fewer than a thousand students, an elaborate "Oracle Hunt" marks the traditional passing of the senior class title. Near the end of the school year, the seniors direct the juniors in a quest for the oracle. The seniors offer questions and progressively as the juniors figure out the answers, they come closer to the treasured item. When found, the oracle can only be touched by the newly elected senior class president. The officer presents the oracle to the outgoing president, who reads the scroll contained in the oracle and confers the senior class title. Intermittently since 1914, Shorter College seniors similarly hid a decorated wooden crook from the juniors, but they didn't encourage the juniors to find the stick. They pronounced their superiority by their ability to foil the juniors before they officially handed it over for them to guard as seniors (Gardner 1972: 196-98, 255-57, 322-24, 451-52).

At Vassar's spring convocation, "juniors officially become seniors and the new officers of the student government take office. The day is filled with much festivity as tradition requires juniors to ring the bell on the roof of the Main Building or they will die virgins" (letter, 26 April 1989). The "moving-up" of officers is a feature of older Moving-Up Days that has persisted through the change to larger and less unified classes in the old-time college. Sometimes called "Class Day," "Insignia Day," or "Senior Class Day," the event no longer marks peace among the scrapping classes at the behest of the departing seniors (Miller 1966: 396-97; Hall 1968: 68-76; Wyman 1979: 87).

On Class Day at Williams College seniors plant ivy to leave a permanent mark on campus and test their future fortune in a watch-dropping ritual. The ritual has students looking up as the watch is dropped from the chapel tower onto the concrete below. According to tradition, if the watch breaks, the class will be insured good luck in the future. On Class Day at most old-time colleges, classes united to honor the departing seniors, but now they might gather in an awards convocation often recognizing achievements in various departments and organizations.

A formal convocation frequently occurs during the fall to mark prepara-

Vassar seniors at spring convocation with their ribboned sticks, 1985.
(Ben Rayfield)

tions for the graduation year. At convocations such as Sweet Briar's and Cedar Crest's, seniors wear their caps and gowns for the first time, and join faculty and administration in the academic procession. Seniors at Vassar also join the faculty and administration by wearing their academic robes at fall convocation. Additionally carrying ribboned sticks, the seniors thus announce their separated status to the rest of the college community. The president of the college, the head of the Vassar Student Association, and a special speaker usually chosen from the faculty deliver addresses during the convocation. At Lawrence University the fall convocation is called Matriculation Day and the spring one is designated as Honors Day. At Hood, the fall convocation is followed by a "balloon launch" to signify the students' upward aspiration.

The "official" countdown to graduation often begins a hundred days before commencement. At Wells, seniors celebrate the first of "One Hundred Days" by wearing caps and gowns and sharing a champagne breakfast together in the dining hall. The freshwomen create a special calendar for the seniors counting down each day until graduation. Each day the calendar requires the seniors to do or wear something unusual, such as wearing their clothing inside out or wearing brightly colored lipstick. At Keuka, juniors ring the tower bell 100 times in honor of the seniors. At the College of Notre Dame in Maryland, "100 Nights" is the occasion for a special dinner followed by awards given by students to one another and a slide show meant to evoke laughter and some tears.

Some campuses have additional events a month or less before graduation. At Cedar Crest for many years seniors gathered on the steps of the administration building to be "vested." Dressed in white, they stood in a semicircle surrounded by their little sisters. The underclasswomen helped the seniors on with their robes. Then, one by one, the seniors were called forward to kneel on a white satin pillow embroidered with three Cs. The dean of students placed their caps upon their heads. A step-sing involving all the classes usually happened afterward. After vesting, seniors wore their caps and gowns to classes for the remainder of the semester.

At Texas and Eastern Michigan, a similar ceremony coinciding with "Class Day" was called "Senior Swing Out." At Texas, "retiring Cap and Gown officials removed their caps and placed them on the heads of the new leaders" (Berry 1983: 74). At Eastern Michigan, seniors wear their caps and gowns after a Class Day assembly until the end of the term. Most of these ceremonies fell victim to the iconoclastic spirit of the 1960s, but a gala step-singing affair at women's colleges still commonly occurs a few weeks before commencement, often in conjunction with May Day.

The end of classes or finals occasionally marks the beginning of some graduating senior activities. The morning of the last day of classes at Wells, seniors don their robes and dance around the old sycamore tree in front of the main building. The sophomore sisters present the seniors with roses, and then for luck they kiss the feet of Minerva in the front entrance to the main building. At Chatham, seniors burn early drafts of their senior theses in a bonfire in front of the chapel. Seniors at Wooster march in an annual Independent Study procession, which celebrates the completion of theses required of every graduate. Having submitted their theses to the registrar, students receive a Tootsie Roll and a gold button proclaiming, "I did it." In 1989, about four hundred students and faculty members joined the parade, complete with trumpeters, drummers, and a mock throne held up by brooms. One professor pulled a cart of old theses. Around his neck hung a placard with a final reminder for seniors about their as yet ungraded theses. It was a quotation from Mozart's opera *Cosi fan tutte:* "The beginning is amusing, but tomorrow comes the sorrow" ("Agony": 31). A similar procession celebrating the submission of the senior thesis at Reed College uses a costume theme, a fire-breathing thesis dragon, and a makeshift band (Betterton 1988: 172).

Particularly during the nineteenth century (when most students took the same classes) funeral processions as well as ritual burnings and burials for books and courses were much more common. At Berkeley, robed students carrying Chinese lanterns paraded caskets filled with Bourdon's *Elements of Algebra* and Minto's *Manual of English Prose*. The books were burned and buried, and a huge party followed (Stadtman 1970: 164; Dundes 1968: 21-22).

At Yale, the book so mourned was Euclid: "The huge poker is heated in the old stove, and driven through the smoking volume, and the division, marshalled in line, for *once* at least see *through* the whole affair. They then march over it in solemn procession, and are enabled, as they step firmly on its covers, to assert with truth that they have gone over it—poor jokes indeed, but sufficient to afford abundant laughter. And then follow speeches, comical and pathetic, and shouting and merriment" (Hall 1968: 41).

At Syracuse and Bucknell, particular courses were cremated and buried; at Syracuse it was calculus and at Bucknell geometry (Huguenin 1961; Oliphant 1965: 186). Well into the twentieth century, students at the University of Texas joined together in a huge book-burning at Class Day when each senior tossed in a book (Berry 1983: 73). Book burning by seniors ceased at Agnes Scott College during the 1960s. Commenting on the tradition's demise, the archivist told me that students had more control of their time then and became less inclined to remain on campus after spring exams. At Franklin and Marshall, the practice of cremating zoology and analytical geometry in elaborate ceremonies faded as the curriculum expanded and the whole class no longer shared a required course (Brubaker 1987: 36-37).

Being of sound mind...

In the spirit of "moving to the great beyond," another longstanding collegiate tradition was to leave wills and gifts to the college. "I, Charley Chatter, sound of mind, To making fun am much inclined," began one early will from Harvard. "So, having cause to apprehend, My college life is near its end, All future quarrels to prevent, I seal this will and testament." To "friends of science and of men" the writer left "naught but thanks bestow[ed]." The next lines explain: "For, like my cash, my credit's low; So I can give nor clothes nor wines, But bid them welcome to my fines" (Hall 1968: 476-79).

At Stephens, seniors leave the wills to their particular dorms. At Oregon State, seniors buried wills behind Education Hall. Returning to the college at the class reunion years later, the will would be read. The leaving of wills is still a part of "Senior Prank" at Hood. The wills mock professors and students; at Cedar Crest the tone became so harsh by the 1960s that administrators cracked down and ended the tradition.

Senior classes may still leave gifts to the college, often in the form of a class bench, tree, or statue. Of late, class gifts often appear less symbolic and more pragmatic in the form of equipment or a contribution to the scholarship fund.

In times of yore, gifts in the form of "transmittenda" were handed down from some lucky class member to the next. At Harvard, for example, a jack-knife was given to the ugliest member of the senior class who passed it on to a member of the next class. Apparently inspired by a tradition at Cambridge, Yale seniors offered the chair of the prom committee a wooden spoon usually implying that the recipient was the weakest student in the class; at Lawrence the wooden spoon belonged to the homeliest man (Hall 1968: 492-97).

Through the twentieth century, seniors puffed and ceremoniously handed down "pipes of peace" (Wyman 1979: 87; Miller 1966: 396-97; Pattee 1928: 5; Briscoe 1981: 11). Another symbolic gesture was to "bury the hatchet" by handing over a hatchet from the seniors to the juniors (Earley 1987: 27, 37, 52; Gardner 1972: 115).

While these war symbols ceased to be handed down with the fading of class scraps, other items representing school memories remain. Trinity seniors bequeath a wooden lemon squeezer that has traded hands since 1857. The squeezer had been used in the making of a renowned Trinity "punch," and inscribed with class mottoes and ribbons attached, the school pressed the relic into service as a symbol of class pride (Morris 1969). At Houghton College, the "Senior Chapel" concludes with the "passing of the mantle," a long strip of cloth to which each graduating class attaches its own embroidered insignia and graduation year done in the class colors. The graduating class also has a class banner which hangs in the auditorium at commencement, and is then given to a class which uses it as a homecoming decoration.

At Upper Iowa University's "Passing of the Gown" ceremony, the president of the senior class wears a special gown embroidered with the numerals of that year's class. The senior president delivers a brief speech about the state of the college and challenges the junior class. The gown is then passed to the junior class president, who makes a response. At that time the senior class gift is presented to the university president.

A common pre-graduation ceremony of transferral is a lantern procession. Every year on the Saturday night before commencement at Tusculum, seniors turn over robes and lanterns to the juniors to mark the passing of responsibilities for the college. While this is going on, the seniors offer the lantern song: "From thee, our Alma Mater, we depart, These our lanterns symbolize the glow that's in our hearts."

At Mount Mary College, seniors give juniors lanterns symbolizing the passing of the light of learning. Gathering around a reflecting pool in front of Notre Dame Hall, the seniors proceed around Madonna's circle with their lanterns. An induction of seniors into the alumnae association takes place, followed by the seniors moving to the front steps. There they sing farewell parodies to parents, faculty, and underclassmen.

Graduation week may also bring freshmen into the fold. At the Naval Academy, the freshmen, taunted as "plebes" and "the lowest of the low" rise to the top through a recognition ceremony to the delight of cheering seniors. Each spring, upperclassmen grease a 21-foot obelisk called Herndon Monument and place a plebe's white cap on top. Then hundreds of the fresh midshipmen try to climb the slippery stone and replace the white cap with an upperclassman's gold-trimmed hat. Resorting to teamwork, some plebes form a human webbing around the monument with legs resting on shoulders of midshipmen below. In 1989, a 6-foot-8 plebe finally made the climb after two hours and great pandemonium (Robinson 1989: 1,8). The midshipmen carried their hero to the steps of the Naval Academy chapel where the superintendent presented him with an admiral's shoulder boards mounted on a plaque. Tradition holds that the plebe to reach the top will be the first admiral of the class. "There are two main points in a midshipman's career—Herndon and graduation," explained one plebe, now declared a "fourth classman." Originally reserved for men, the ceremony is replete with male phallic symbolism, but beginning in 1977 midshipwomen joined the climbing ritual (Cohen and Coffin 1987: 191).

Senior chains and garlands

The "Daisy Chain" is the best known women's pre-graduation tradition. An emblem of fidelity, the daisy has many associations with women's divinations. Girls pluck its petals for fortune-telling charms to predict the identity of a future husband and the number of children the union will bring (Bronner 1989: 165, 329). At Shorter, sophomores gather daisies and make a chain leaving about six inches to a foot for every graduate (Gardner 1972: 454). Sophomores tradition- ally get the task because the seniors are their "big sisters." "How their backs ached from picking daisies," one reminiscence offers, "and how their hearts ached to see their seniors leave them." Another confessed: "We hunted daisies—we found daisies—we picked daisies—we made daisies—we hated daisies. But we made the largest and prettiest daisy chain we've ever seen" (Gardner 1972: 263-64). Of course, every class thought it made the prettiest and largest. For many years, the procession with the daisy chain united the class and marked their future orientation, as seniors used the occasion to tell their class history, dedicate their annual, and read their prophecy and last will and testament (Gardner 1972: 387).

Until the 1960s, the daisy chain was also a regular part of sophomore duties at Agnes Scott. By tradition, the sophomores began collecting late Friday or early Saturday morning and completed the 150-foot chain by 4 p.m. in time for a special ceremony at the May Day Dell. The seniors offered a class poem and the sophomores give the chain to the seniors who then formed it into an "S" on the dell (Agnes Scott College Archives, 1946, 1947, 1960).

At Hollins for many years, sophomores prepared the daisy chain to pass on to the seniors at the close of Class Day ceremonies. Then the seniors draped the garland over the lawn in the outline of the class numerals. At Vassar, a group of sophomore women chosen by the commencement committee of the senior class still carries a chain of daisies and laurel into graduation. At Howard Payne seniors choose a junior as a "chime-out partner" and in a ceremony the night before commencement under the college's bell towers, the garland passes from the seniors to the juniors.

At Hollins, women used willow, honeysuckle, and roses in their garlands.

The association of flora with spring femininity and fertility remained intact. Inspired by Vassar's daisy chain, Christian College (the oldest women's college west of the Mississippi) instituted the ivy chain after 1900 (Hale 1968: 131). In 1964, students changed the name of their yearbook from the *College Widow* to the *Ivy Chain*. The ivy combines Christian lore of the immortality of the soul and a more general association with femininity and fertility. The rose also carries special meaning for Christian College students because seniors carry loving roses on Class Day and write "rose notes" to favorite juniors.

Ivy chains were also used at Nebraska and Eastern Michigan (Manley 1969: 283; Eastern Michigan University Archives, 1927). Still relying on the symbolism of ivy is a graduation tradition today of ivy planting at Williams College and ivy cutting at Spring Arbor College. The Vassar daisy chain also inspired Texas's bluebonnet chain used on Class Day until 1963 (Berry 1983: 73-76; Berry 1980: 293). Reserved for women, a bluebonnet chain ceremony was part of "Senior Swing-Out," during which seniors passed a sophomore-arranged chain of bluebonnets, the state flower of Texas, to new junior leaders. Then the seniors marched out through the protecting bluebonnet chain into the "outside world." The juniors honored the seniors with a bluebonnet chain song: "We gather, dear seniors, to bid you goodbye/And wish you good luck in each task you shall try/Remember dear Varsity and we who remain/Are bound to you now by the Bluebonnet Chain" (Berry 1983: 74-76).

The big day

One difficulty with holding these multi-class events around commencement and after finals is that today underclassmen, and often faculty, want to leave campus as soon as they can. To keep the student body around for a show of community, some schools hold commencement before finals, from which the seniors are excused. At Oregon State University, the benefit of the free week for seniors since the 1930s was that the registrar's office had time to tally final grades and prepare personalized diplomas for the graduates. The benefit for students, as one explained, was having, "time to talk to professors, say goodbye to friends, find out where they were going to work" (Krause 1989: 12). But in 1989, a Faculty Senate edict threatened the tradition by requiring seniors to take spring finals. "The ceremony this year will take place on a campus that's not very vibrant," warned the senior class president. Students collected more than a thousand signatures calling for the retention of traditional commencement, but so far the university president has stood behind the edict.

Before commencement, many colleges recognize the special presence of seniors' families with strawberry (or sometimes champagne) breakfasts in the dining halls. Representing the auspiciousness of the day's graduation, the rich fruit is topped with sweets such as chocolate, cream, and sugar. The event can carry sentimental meaning, because, as a student from Hood explained to me, "It is the last time you eat at Hood as a student" (survey response, 1989). As part of the day's events, seniors may say their sentimental farewells to the college by making pilgrimages to favored college spots, occasionally requesting the presence of popular professors (Dundes 1968: 32). Professors are also part of a pre-graduation "garden party," a family affair on the campus lawn at Bryn Mawr. With the help of a "garden party girl," an undergraduate who ropes off a circle of chairs for the family and fetches professors the seniors would like her parents to meet, the graduating senior, often decked out in flowers along with her mother, invites faculty to join her family. To mark the end of her academic career, the senior may also enlist the garden party girl to help her to ring the college bell, a task that takes ingenuity since the building is often locked (Briscoe 1981: 69-72).

At large colleges, seniors typically divide by school, residence complex, or even department for an intimate morning ceremony honoring class leaders and offering brief orations before the massive commencement during the afternoon. At many colleges, the commencement procession often takes a symbolic route. At William and Mary students dramatically move from the "old" campus across a bridge to the "new" campus. At Findlay College the Griffith Memorial Arch serves as the formal gateway to the campus. As freshmen the students marched in through the arch, greeted by a row of faculty on each side of the wide sidewalk leading to historic Old Main. Graduating seniors take their last walk out through the arch, again past rows of faculty and administrators who wish them farewell (Kern 1984: 342).

Similarly, at Brown University, the elaborate Van Wickle Gates are opened only twice a year: inward, toward the campus, on the day of opening convocation, and outward, on the day of commencement. At Wofford College, seniors make a graduation journey "past the posts" into the outside world. While cameras click, the commencement line forms at Main, marches through campus and through the Church Street gate to the city auditorium. Westminster College has venerated classical columns on campus. Students pass through the columns in front of Westminster Hall only twice in their academic careers: once during orientation week and again during graduation.

The stage is set for the big event. Sometimes number magic is invoked for the set-up. At Colgate, lore dictates that thirteen men with thirteen dollars and thirteen prayers founded the college in 1819. "Live true to the memory of those thirteen men of yore" is a line from a song sung at most programs by the Thirteen, a male singing group at the college. So among the thirteen traditions observed today at Colgate is the placement of thirteen chairs on the chapel platform for major convocations. Colgate isn't alone in its fondness for the number thirteen. The ceremonial mace used at the University of Nevada at Reno has thirteen silver coins symbolizing the thirteen years of minting silver in Carson City.

Many outdoor commencement settings are like Emory's—in the main quadrangle, emphasizing four sides, with a commencement platform on the steps of the administration building. Pointing out the symmetry of the setting, the commencement program points out that spectators are seated facing west between the two oldest buildings on the Atlanta campus; to the east are the physics and history buildings constructed in the same style. Looking across the quadrangle from the administration building is the other unifying academic symbol of the library.

Most students gather at commencement in black robes and tasseled mortarboard. The dress has its roots in medieval Europe when monastic orders oversaw higher learning. The monk's tippet became the "hood" worn by master's and doctoral students. When caps came into fashion in the fifteenth century, wearers draped hoods down and back and ornamented them with silk or velvet linings and edgings. Master's students received a cap with a tuft at the center. The tassel used today on American mortarboards derives from the use of the tuft. The mortarboard style follows Oxford University custom in which master's students wear the flat-topped cap.

The wearing of academic dress in America dates to 1754 when George II chartered King's College, now Columbia University, and transferred academic regulations from Oxford and Cambridge. Colonial colleges rejected the scarlet robes of the English institutions for the somber black preferred by Puritan clergy. In 1895, a commission of American educators adopted black as the standard color for academic robes and established a hierarchy of robe design from the unadorned undergraduate robe to the ornamented full robes for the doctoral graduate. With revisions to the code in 1935 and 1960 allowing for variation, many universities have adopted colored robes. Harvard allows degree holders to wear crimson gowns and Yale parades its blues. Satin linings in hoods given for master's and doctoral students typically use school colors, and soft six- and eight-cornered caps can be worn. Trimming around the edge of the hood varies in color and designates the degree holder's realm of study.

Penn State Harrisburg mace in commencement procession. (Darrell Peterson)

A ceremonial mace leads most graduation processions. The use of the mace comes from the first royal mace presented by Queen Elizabeth I to Oxford University in 1589. Not about to be outdone, Cambridge received the royal mace from King Charles II in 1629, and thereafter the mace has been a fixture at academic convocations (Heckscher 1970: 9-10).

American universities adopted the mace during the nineteenth century when ceremonies became more elaborate in imitation of European convention. Representing masculine strength as well as regal authority, the mace usually has a finial at the bottom with a shaft capped by an ornamented head. At Penn State Harrisburg, the top is a crown engraved with the school mascot, the Nittany Lion. The bottom takes the shape of a flame. A faculty member authoritatively carries the mace into commencement with the head up, and flame up on the way out to recognize the light of knowledge acquired. At Bethany, the president of the senior class serves as mace bearer, and commencement concludes with the transfer of the mace to the president of the incoming senior class.

Inviting comment is Emory's mace, which includes a relief rendering of a human skeleton lovingly dubbed "Dooley." This "Dooley-chosen" lord of misrule has Emory's spring carnival named after him, and has class-ending powers. Bedecked in top hat, cane, and cape, the spirit of Emory has been known to enter classrooms during his special week and announce "class dismissed!" Beginning humbly as a teaching aid in the biology department at the turn of the century, the caped cadaver regularly took part in campus pranks and later contributed to student publications.

Baylor University celebrates Sam Houston, its famous neighbor and friend from the past, with a gold-headed walking stick as one of four elements of the university's mace (Keeth 1985: 41). Variations on the mace are Georgia's sword and Berkeley's baton. The ceremonial scepters often have symbols and legends attached to them. Berkeley's baton is said to be made from the wood taken from Old North Hall (Dundes 1968: 27).

Banners or gonfalons (flags, often with streamers, hanging from a cross-piece on an upright staff) representing the university's divisions or schools often give the commencement procession the look of a medieval festival. At Emory, gonfalons for the arts and sciences show lamps of knowledge; nursing has a globe and red cross against an apricot background; and business administration luxuriously carries Medici bezants (representations of coins) on sapphire.

The traditional uniformity of robes marks the graduates as initiates ready for a special community. Since the 1960s, however, one sees personalized messages pasted onto mortarboards. "Thanks Mom and Dad," "It's Over," "$."

Asking students why they disrupted prescribed dress, a campus reporter at Penn State heard "I've been here for four years. I want to be noticed in this crowd"; "I definitely want to do something to say 'Look Mom and Dad'"; and "We want to tell the world the essence of our senior year" (Repcheck 1988: 5). Looking to quantify the trend, four psychologists found that women were more likely to be adorned than were men, and Bachelor of Arts candidates more likely than Bachelor of Science (Harrison, et al. 1986: 863-74). Women, they offered, "are more likely than men to distinguish themselves and attract attention through individualization of attire" (p. 872). B.A. students, priding themselves on their imagination and expressiveness, were more willing than B.S. seniors to trumpet their individual creativity. The messages also convert the attire prescribed by authority to one controlled by students, especially as adolescents today are more likely to express themselves through secular rather than ritual clothing (Harrison, et al. 1986: 873). Still, the number of expressive gestures is small (twelve percent in their sample), and if the psychologists are right, the number decreased during the conservative late 1980s.

Personalized mortarboard. (Darrell Peterson)

Besides the caps, robes receive special treatment from students. Hawaiian graduates sport floral leis on their robes. Other students wear shorts and other sportswear underneath the robe. "I need a job" and other signs can occasionally be sighted pinned to robes. Bottles of champagne have been known to be carried in under robes and popped during long commencement speeches (Toelken 1986: 527). Colorful balloons fly up from under robes into the air, sometimes carrying students' messages (Repcheck 1988: 5). Students quip about the association of the black robes with funerary rites. "College women," Barre Toelken reports, cynically talk of these "black robes of mourning, imposed as an outward show of penance and punishment for those who have not succeeded in finding a mate during their four years at college" (1986: 522). Students also ascribe their attire to mourning for students who died in the battle for grades, killed by deadly exams and courses.

Commencement may attract cynicism because at many large institutions it is hardly an engaging ritual. Graduates are recognized simply by quickly standing together in the midst of a huge arena. Students may also question the significance of commencement for them, when the proceedings often involve political speeches and awards to celebrities and donors. Stephens College seniors answer with a mock commencement kicking off commencement week. The event includes "Commencement Bingo" which calls for class members to listen for graduation jargon such as "beginning," "challenging," "opportunity," and "future" to fill out their cards. This parodying of commencement is hardly new, although during the nineteenth century it was more a sign of class rivalry than jaded attitudes. Sophomore and Junior "exhibitions" showcased mock commencement orations, and broadsides called "burlesques" or "slubs" parodied the commencement program (Brubaker 1987: 220-22; Dundes 1968: 20-21; Moffatt 1985: 5, 23; Stadtman 1970: 164-65; Hall 1968: 46, 344-45).

Small colleges boast that students receive personal attention, reflected in the handing out of diplomas to students walking on stage as their names are called out. The walk on stage is a transitional passage to the new status of graduate. The student receives the diploma and shakes hands with administrators. At women's colleges such as Hood and Stephens, the chief administrator may receive a "secret gift" in return. In 1989, Hood's president received a plastic Lego block from 283 graduates. In years past, students handed her pennies, marbles, pieces of a jigsaw puzzle, and goldfish in plastic bags. At Stephens, the president received birthday candles and shoe laces (she was a jogger). The students connect the tradition to their "Secret Santa" custom which values tokens of affection. The president of Hood found that the "secret gift" tradition has a therapeutic value for students. "I haven't had to shake a clammy hand in four years," she explained. "It helps them relax" (Torok 1989: 3).

After students receive their diploma on stage, the sober tone of the event

Receiving diplomas on stage at Penn State Harrisburg. (Darrell Peterson)

dictates that the audience keep religiously silent. Yet the trend is to announce joy by applause and shouts from family members. During the long procession, audience members don't seem to mind the commotion because it provides some comic relief. At Penn State Harrisburg's commencement in 1989, the house came down when one student's brother yelled "Get a job!"

Displays are especially conspicuous at the service academies. Here's a description of the 1989 graduation at Annapolis: "Clad in their formal white uniforms, midshipmen punched their fists in the air, danced across the stage and held their diplomas aloft as they accepted their degrees. Their families and friends competed to be the loudest cheering section…" (Robinson 1989b: 2). If receiving the degree is the post-separation stage in the transition, the pre-incorporation ritual is the moving the tassel from the right to the left on the mortarboard. Placement on the left in American society is considered an odd, but select location. Thus graduates announce entrance into an esoteric community. Despite the air of restraint on stage, some students additionally hoist their diploma and jump for joy.

In addition to diplomas, advanced degree students receive their hoods. By tradition, the student carries the hood to the stage or has it placed on a platform there. In the ceremony, a dean places the hood over the student. Law school graduates at the University of Texas have the unusual distinction of also

Changing position of tassel after receiving diploma. (Darrell Peterson)

''I did it!'' (Darrell Peterson)

receiving sunflowers. The custom has its origin in a university-wide student meeting in 1900 to approve the wearing of caps and gowns to graduation. The organizers neglected to invite the law students and in protest, the law students wore silk hats and sunflowers pinned on their lapels. Students probably chose the flowers because they grew in abundance near the campus. But later, tongue-in-cheek pronouncements about their symbolism emerged. One account held that the sunflower belongs to a family with world-wide distribution, and so do lawyers. Another opined that "as the sunflower always keeps its face turned to the sun, the lawyer turns to the light of justice" (Berry 1983: 122). Today the "Sunflower Ceremony," attended by law graduates and their relatives, occurs on commencement day. The associate dean pins a sunflower on each graduate, and the graduates in turn present sunflowers to relatives and friends (Berry 1980: 301).

Some colleges have additional ceremonies after commencement. Adrian College has held an outdoor cane ceremony every year since 1921. Each year, seniors use this opportunity to symbolically transfer leadership for the college to the juniors, and this next class to graduate affixes its colors to the "shepherd's crook," thus linking it to an unbroken chain of college alumni. The ribbons on the cane represent the colors of every graduating class in all the shades of the rainbow. The old cane carries the date 1887 and the words *Non Sine Labote*, or "climb without falling." The cane—and the custom of affixing class colors—dates to 1887, when it was a trophy of "cane rush" war between the classes. Today, as a crook, it carries a peaceful message in a ceremony by the college tower. At Wofford College, graduating seniors, nearly three hundred of them, receive Bibles personally autographed by each member of the faculty and staff in a ceremony.

The end of commencement is a hat-raising event at the service academies. Traditionally the graduates toss their hats high in the air accompanied by cheers (Robinson 1989b: 1-2). Less honored by tradition are tossing antics at Harvard. When recognized, students in some fields throw a symbolic item up in the air. Business students throw dollar bills while liberal arts students toss their caps (survey response, 1989).

After the ceremony come hugs and dinners from family—signs of incorporation. The graduation is thus a beginning of a new status, a new venture—in short a rebirth into society. In the old-time college, this symbolism was more manifest because the college acted as a parent during the student's four years. With this role reduced and the size of graduating classes so much larger, commencement has lost much of its ritual meaning.

Hooding ceremony at University of Nevada at Reno.

Cane Ceremony at Adrian College, 1980.

Thanks to Mom and Dad after graduation. (Darrell Peterson)

While commencement once marked the culmination of a week full of activities, most graduation ceremonies now are restricted to the day of commencement and involve only the seniors. Some of the changes in commencement can be attributed to loss of cohesiveness in student bodies. Students now divide into a wide spectrum of majors, interests, ages, and cultural backgrounds. It's no wonder the most elaborate and traditional ceremonies in my survey occurred at small, relatively homogeneous women's colleges or religious schools. They tend to retain the social function of commencement as a final passage of transition, rather than as a public-relations "pep rally," as some observers have asserted about public university graduations (Hodges 1989: 32).

Still another factor in the deritualization of commencement is the possible devaluation of the degree itself, as more and more Americans treat a college education less as a special status marking learning than a necessary license to practice. Some calls for restoring meaning to graduation suggest shifting emphasis to ceremonies run by constituent schools, departments, or residence complexes, and having the ceremonies become more student-centered (Hedges 1989: 32).

Using what's been learned

The value of the college degree after graduation comes up in a good bit of folk humor. Many of the older anecdotes concern the farmboy transformed by college. In one such story a farmer asks a fellow farmer and father of a recent graduate, "Well, since Tom has a college degree, can you see any change in the way he plows?" "No, he plows the same, but he talks different," was the reply. "How do you mean," the first farmer pressed. "Well, when he gets to the end of a row, instead of saying 'Whoa, Gee, or Haw,' he says, 'Halt, Rebecca, pivot and proceed'" (Mitchell 1976: 347). In Pennsylvania Dutch country people tell the dialect-joke about the farmer who asks his son what he learned in college, usually at Franklin and Marshall or Muhlenberg. "I used to say 'no-ess' instead of north and 'sow-ess' instead of south, but now I can say *'beau-ess'*!"

Another farmer questioning his son at the dinner table about what he learned in college is told "the study of logic." Asked to demonstrate, the son vows to prove that three chickens lie on the plate when it appears that only two are there. The son sticks his fork in one and says, "Here's one, right?" "Yes," says the boy's dad. Poking the other one, the boy says, "And this is two?" "All right," the father follows. "Well, don't one and two make three?" the grad beamed. "Tell you what," said the old man. "I'll give Mom one of the chickens to eat and I'll take the other, and you can have the third. How's that?" (Copeland 1940: 408).

Raconteur Billy Edd Wheeler tells the traditional joke about a farmer from West Virginia who sent his son off to college. "As soon as the boy came home after graduation the farmer couldn't wait to take him down to the country store and show him off. The boy was a little embarrassed by it all, but he loved his dad and was grateful to him for helping finance his education. So he went along with it. As soon as they got to the store, the farmer proudly exclaimed, 'Here's my son, fellers, home from college with a degree in algebra!' He turned to his son and said, 'Well, don't be bashful, boy, say something to them in algebra.' The son blushed and said, 'Okay...pi-r-square.' The farmer got very flustered at that, blushed himself, and said, 'Don't be silly, boy! Pie are round. *Cornbread* are square!'" (Jones and Wheeler 1987: 54-55). The joke also appears as an Aggie joke about the A&M grad who worked himself up to the position of personnel manager of a company and interviewed his first job applicant, who was from Baylor. "What was your major at Baylor?" he asks. "Mathematics," the applicant answers. "Well, say something in Mathematics," the Aggie demands. "Pi-r-square," he offers. "Wrong," says the Aggie, "Pie are round, cornbread are square" (Wassell 1973: 8).

Another farmer-and-college-boy joke transformed into a rivalry joke is the one about the farmer going into the town bank for a meeting with a loan executive. The bank executive asked him, "Are you a farmer?" "Why sure, how did you know?" the farmer replied. Proud of his perceptiveness, the exec explained, "I smelled the manure on your shoes." After the meeting, the farmer asked the exec, "Did you go to Harvard?" Flattered, the executive said, "Certainly, how did you guess?" "I noticed your class ring when you picked your nose," the farmer shot back (Mac Barrick Memorial Folklore Archives, Shippensburg University, 1986).

In North Carolina, one hears a related joke about a State grad and another fellow on an airplane. "And as they were about to get off, the State grad says, 'I bet you went to Carolina.' The other guy says, 'I sure did. How did you know? Was it my noticeable macho appeal, my high level of intelligence, my good taste for food and women, or what?' 'No,' says the State grad. 'I saw UNC on your class ring when you picked your nose" (Beezley 1981: 112; cf. *Best* 1976: 4; Mitchell 1976: 480-81, 712).

There's also the old farmyard joke now told about three college students instead of three ethnic travelers. "One from A&M, one from SMU, and one from the U. of Texas," a version offers, "applied for a job at a farm. The farmer had only one opening, and said he'd employ the one who could stay in the pig sty longest. After one hour the Mustang came out of the sty, gasping, and fainted. After two hours, the Teasipper crawled out on his hands and knees and collapsed. Three hours later, the pigs came out" (*Best* 1976: 29; cf. Clements type G4.5, Baughman motif X691.5.1; Bronner 1989: 141-42; McCosh 1979: 244).

Another ethnically styled joke is about the University of Texas grad who had a former Baylor student and several Aggie alums working for him. The Baylor grad stood on a table with his right arm raised, saying, "I'm a light bulb." The Texas boss, figuring he was insane, fired him. Later that day, all the Aggies started walking out. "Where are you going?" asked the Texas grad. "You don't expect us to work in the dark, do you?" replied one of the Aggies (*Best* 1976: 114; cf. Clements type E3.6).

The honor of college women comes up in a widely circulating, and variable, joke about the salesman who makes his pitch in, say, Arkansas when the subject of the University of Alabama comes up. "The only people who go to Alabama are whores and football players," he triumphantly declares. His client coolly informs him that his wife went to Alabama. "Oh," he sputters, "What position did she play?" (survey response, 1990; cf. Dundes and Pagter 1987: 156; *Best* 1976: 25).

Many of today's jokes shift the humor to question the value of a degree at a time when masses of students attending universities suggest the lowering of standards and narrowing of knowledge. At West Virginia, students walk around in T-shirts emblazoned with the message "I are a college student" (Birnbach 1984: 423). This humor is sometimes coupled with the observation that academic success in college does not insure prosperity in life, and that in fact, those who fail at school often come back as millionaires (Hand et al. 1981: 143).

From Wisconsin, for example, comes the story of the math major who graduated only by the skin of his teeth and the charity of his teachers. At his class's twenty-fifth reunion he drove up in a Cadillac, wore expensive clothes, and showed all the trappings of wealth. When amazed classmates asked him about his secret to success, he explained that he had invented a little gadget which he manufactured in his own plant. "It cost only $2 to make," this former math major said, "I sold it for $4, and with that 2 percent profit, I built a great business" (Wyman 1979: 82).

Engineers, accused of pursuing profitable careers despite a lack of imagination and literacy, are the most frequent butts of photocopied humor. One sheet shows an overgrown oaf holding a diploma in one hand and a slide rule in the other. The caption reads, "Golly, six weeks ago I could not even spell 'Enjanear'—NOW I ARE ONE!" Another caricature of an engineer shows an ugly nerd, affluently dressed and carrying a rolled diploma under one arm. In a crude hand, the caption announces: "Six munce ugo I cutnt evn spel injuneer—an now I are one… " (Dundes and Pagter 1987: 212-14).

There's also the joke about the college graduates registering for rooms at a hotel. The first signed "L.B." after his name. "What does the L.B. stand for?" the clerk asked. He eloquently explained, "I am a law school graduate and the initials indicate that I have earned my degree as a Bachelor of Law." The second man put B.J. next to his name, and when the clerk asked him about the initials, he answered that he received a Bachelor of Journalism degree. The third fellow signed his name with an "S.I." "What on earth does S.I. mean?" the clerk asked. "Hey, I got my degree in civil engineering," the fellow declared (*Best* 1976: 12).

Satirical readings of acronyms answer the social question: what do these initials *really* mean? "USC" becomes "University of Spoiled Children," and "ISU" turns into "Inebriated State University"; "LSAT" and "MCAT," exams taken by many graduating seniors, change into "Legally Sadistic Admissions Test" and "Most Costly Aptitude Test" (Howe 1989: 176-77; cf. "Feedback" 1984-85: 261-62). Another way for students to assert control of formal institutional symbols, the satirical readings are also a modern sign of the proliferation of organizational doublespeak (see Howe 1989: 171-82; Bronner 1986b: 116;

Lowe 1982: 131-39).

Freely using wordplay, the "Master's Degree in Drinking" is offered in photocopied form around the country. The bogus diploma is bestowed on the student who has excelled in fractions, particularly fifths. Some wisecracks about degrees target women. One hears about coeds getting the MRS. degree, and about women who earn the Ph.T., or "Pushing Him Through," for supporting a man pursuing his degree (Copeland 1940: 407; Egan 1985: 130, 132; Birnbach 1984: 104, 141; "Going" 1986). And so we return to the folkloric progression of B.S., M.S., and Ph.D.—or "Piled Higher and Deeper."

More than mere adolescent irreverence, this humor and the deritualization of graduation speak to the distance between the expansive university and the student seeking a culturally compassionate community. The distended university in today's folklore feels cold and corporate. To be sure, in many colleges today a strong feeling of community, fostered by traditions, permeates student life. And after letting go of traditions in the 1960s, some colleges today are reviving customs that offer students a feeling of belonging. Even so, reports regularly surface of a woeful number of students wandering directionless in the maze of today's mass university (Boyer 1987; Bloom 1987).

College folklore and cultural meaning

Students seek to strengthen their social identity, value system, and emotional growth, but find that the academic setting once noted for assisting this cultural passage has alienated rather than involved them. Increasingly students turn to one another for support, but struggle to create group harmony in a mass society stressing the uprooted, competitive individual. Students speak of this new "self" as taking so many roles that confusion about who "one really is" results. They find themselves seeking identity yet often fearful of commitment, and looking for social guidance but often unsure of where to find it. As a result, student lore today appears more privately and spontaneously generated, rather than publicly and predictably shared.

In the isolated realm of the old-time college, custom conveyed a social and cultural consistency. Today's lore can seem highly variable and even contradictory (Albas 1989: 603-13). It makes sense, as today's colleges are a diverse lot with a varied constituency. Unlike the old popular stereotype of the rah-rah college man decked out in raccoon coat and waving a college banner, today's student is harder to caricature. Sweatshirt-clad couch potatoes share the stage with suit-attired dream-chasers. Students feel the burden of undertaking the serious business of being in school, while realizing that it is not considered a "real job." Students today share anxieties about professional advancement, about grades, about "making it." But more than ever, they belong to any number of permeable student "worlds" divided by major or profession, social and political interest, and racial and ethnic affiliation, among other lines (Horowitz 1987). In the absence of publicly shared ritual, privatized folklore often serves to culturally identify the connections within these hazy social worlds.

The widening representation of different age groups at many universities is particularly striking. By the twenty-first century, many predict, part-time adult learners on metropolitan campuses will predominate. Will that mean that college will take on even less a role as cultural passage between adolescence and adulthood than it does now in its corporate, non-parental position?

Many students will find cultural passage in small separated groups that promote social ritual and lore within a rising culture of diversity. Fraternities, sororities, teams, dorms, clubs, and ethnic and religious organizations are reporting upswings in student involvement from the rebellious days of the 1960s. The rise of these separated groups sometimes creates a renewed tension, however, between the call for an open, tolerant society based on the volition of the individual and the need for social support from a distinctive community that culturally instills values and offers a feeling of human control.

After graduation, being an alum of a college may become a kind of special social identity to be shared with a broad network or to be compared with others in a profession or region. Many colleges offer an association to grads who look to the publicly visible institution as a tie that binds. And when grads get together they often perpetuate lore based on their reminiscences. Yet much has been made lately of the increased marginality of college life to the student's total experience and later loyalties, especially at large campuses (Horowitz 1987: 263-88). So one has to wonder about the educational and social process that is supposed to be college life as the attitude spreads that going to college is a matter of certification rather than of development.

Colleges may pack so much lore and attract so much criticism precisely because they are expected to bring out the best in our increasingly complex society and in ourselves, although they are rarely equipped for the task. Places of intense work and play, discovery and routine, today's colleges intensify many of the organizational pressures found generally in modern life. Students call on socially significant tradition to provide outlets for imagining, and imaging, the workings of life "out there." They use their folkloric occasions to relate to one another and share their private fears, joys, and hopes, often at the expense of the organizational giant. The problems dealt with in student lore are not just the college student's to bear, they are society's. Beyond the statistics and surveys chronicling student attitudes, folklore gives a very human profile of college, and modern, life. It reminds us of the dimensions of cultural meaning we inherit and create.

Afterword

What's new on campus? One sign of how much is new and how much stays the same is the folklore posted on the Internet and other computer services, communication links that students increasingly use as a basic tool of college life. The services have a wide assortment of "lists" and "newsgroups" on subjects attracting discussion from world-wide participants on-line. A newsgroup I've been especially checking is "alt.folklore.college," "a great place to get a reality check on anything that a 'friend' told you," so the newsgroup's introduction states. It's an offshoot of alt.folklore.urban, which has over 100,000 subscribers logging on (Furr 1995). Folklore can be found in other places in "cyberspace" from newsgroups such as humor, computers, and science. Computer links are adding another dimension to the transmission of, indeed the need for, folklore in collegiate culture (Jennings 1990; Fox 1983).

The discussions bring up the latest stories on the minds of students, even though many of the newest subjects relate to traditions around for a good while, such as the belief that when a college student commits suicide, the roommate gets As for the semester (Fox 1990). The predominance of legends and beliefs on collegiate folklore newsgroups relates to a central point I made about the individualistic nature of university life. In contrast to publicly and ritually shared traditions of passage common in the old-time college, the modern university fosters a questioning through conversational folklore of individuals stumbling through a maze of a mass society. The open-ended structure of legends invites commentary and often, cultural guidance about what it all means.

Many of the roommate legends focusing on the presence of violence and the vulnerability of women have been updated, for example, with reference to fear of AIDS. At the core of the story is a woman inflicted with AIDS who intentionally passes it to men. "AIDS Mary," as she is sometimes called, invokes the image of the famed Irish servant woman Mary Mallon, nicknamed "Typhoid Mary" by the press. From 1906 to 1915 she was accused of spreading typhoid to families for whom she cooked, even after tests showed that she carried the disease. She denied the presence of the disease, however, and angrily blamed ethnic antagonisms for her troubles (Kraut 1994: 101). As most of today's students know Mary, she is a striking woman who picks up men. In the morning, her partner sees a note written in red lipstick left on the bathroom mirror: "Welcome to the world of AIDS." In discussions of the story on-line and in dorms, one learns of different interpretations by men and women. When I was visiting professor at the University of California at Davis in 1990, I surveyed the large class of close to a hundred students and found that more than seventy percent had heard the story and other references testified to the prevalence of the narrative cycle (Fine 1987; Smith 1990; Goldstein 1992). Discussing the story with the class, I found that women often believe a revenge factor is present. AIDS Mary is getting back at men for infecting her, or the sexual injustice or power imbalance she feels. Some of the beliefs given in response to the legend follow from this interpretation. One frequently reported message from women was that a fraternity held a blood drive and most of the frat donors tested HIV positive (see Ellis and Mays 1992). Another was the view that fraternities had the highest rape rates on campus. Men tend to view the legend as a warning about anonymous sex, or perhaps the lure of attractive women over which they have no control. Some report that women have the upper hand in relationships. In a variation told by women, the man rapes the woman, sometimes on the first date, only to discover the scary message (Fine 1987; Brunvand 1989: 195-202). The story contains dramatic techniques of the story of the roommate who enters a dorm room in the middle of the night and considerately leaves the light off. In the morning she finds her roommate murdered and a note, "Aren't you glad you didn't turn the light on?" Sometimes the message is written in blood on the wall, and one might infer a connection of the blood to the "red lipstick" found so often in the AIDS Mary legend. The discussion of AIDS Mary draws attention to the theme of a deathly scare found in many cautionary legends, but in addition, it sets sexual practices against the background of gender power and the assumption of a free atmosphere for sex on campus.

A male counterpart of the AIDS Mary story is making the rounds (dubbed AIDS John or AIDS Harry by some folklorists). The setting is often a spring break vacation where a college woman meets a man described as kind and good-looking. They get to know each other and engage in sex. As the moment nears for her to return to school, he gives her a gift and instructs her not to open it until she gets back. She is emotionally touched by this classy move, but later becomes impatient or suspicious. On the plane she opens the package and discovers a tiny coffin, sometimes a dead rose, with a note saying "Welcome to the world of AIDS." Appearances are deceiving, the legend suggests, especially in a sexually active society. Another story concerns a woman attracted to a handsome fellow in a dark bar. She takes him home, and to her horror in the morning light she discovers AIDS-related sores on his face. The story has the signs of a cautionary tale for women, especially in light of acceptance of the sexual aggressiveness of women related in the story.

Newly found power of women appears in a cycle of stories concerning women's revenge against rape. Frances Cattermole-Tally has recorded several legends about women who attack a man with a dildo, so that he feels the pain of rape. In one variant, several women surround the macho man and he is at first delighted by the prospect of sex until they hold him down and attack him. Tellers explain the inattention to the attack in the media by reporting that he was too ashamed to report the event to the police. In a campus version, sorority sisters attack a frat rat accused of getting women drunk and taking advantage of them. The man at first laughs at them, but soon cries for mercy as the attack begins. The sisters throw the dildo weapon into the fraternity house as a warning. In some versions, a female hero strolls dangerous areas and invites trouble. She cuts down would-be rapists with martial arts and violates them with the dildo. In Chicago, the story is told that the female heroine "Amazalia, aged nineteen," during periods of the full moon . . . would go to Hyde Park at midnight and stroll around." She is "still at large," tellers report, because her male victims are too embarrassed to press charges" (Cattermole-Tally 1990: 45).

AIDS shows up in a contamination legend that I first heard in 1993 at Penn State. The story brings up a legendary student obsession—pizza. Supposedly a pizza delivery man infected with AIDS ejaculated on a pizza delivered to students. In many accounts, students describe a revenge motive, or a suggestion that they are being punished for their sexual appetite. The target of the pizza has significance, not only because of student fondness for the saucy food, but also because it is communally shared, gleefully grabbed with the hands, and generally associated with the intimate informality of eating at home. It suggests epidemic proportions and sexual overtones. In the story, something wrong is suspected because the food tastes bad or someone gets sick. Sometimes a tag to the story is given as "the pizza was analyzed at a local hospital or that the delivery man was arrested." There is a hint, too, that the "kind of people who work at the place" become suspect, suggesting some assumptions of class difference or corporate negligence. One student newspaper trying to disclaim the story went to great lengths to assure students that the pizza deliverers were often students themselves and the establishment was locally owned (King 1993).

The pizza contamination rumor, to this day unsubstantiated, circulated so widely that many student newspapers reported dropoffs in pizza delivery business for a while (King 1993). It followed a cycle of rumors about tainted mayonnaise on hamburgers bought at a fast-food franchise. The burger contamination rumor might have drawn on newspaper coverage during the 1980s of a case of typhoid fever in suburban Maryland traced to an immigrant worker at McDonald's, dubbed Typhoid McMary by the press, who had removed plastic gloves when mixing vegetables (Kraut 1994: 97). According to rumors, a fast-food worker with AIDS sought revenge by ejaculating in a jar of mayonnaise; the tainted mayo then gets passed to customers on hamburgers (Langlois 1991). It is one of many examples of contamination legends told by consumers about fast-food chains, such as the batter-fried rat or worms in the fast-food burger, maybe because of the unnaturalness connected to a mass cultural phenomenon of corporate preparation and mass consumption of fast food (Fine 1992). There is also an occupational lore shared by fast-food workers relating to retribution against difficult customers. In one on-line "conversation" I recorded, a report of a delivered pizza contaminated with semen was followed by the following exchange: "I used to know a guy from Burger King who would spit on burgers of people that pissed him off in the drive thru ... I knew some people at Domino's that would do that ... HAHA ... HEH!" (April 11, 1993). Folklorist Jan Brunvand additionally mentioned in 1984 an "urban legend" about an employee of a donut chain who masturbated into the batter (121).

Added twists in the AIDS contamination legends are the revenge and invisibility of the virus, although a rumor circulating around 1986 about invisible traces of LSD placed in paper tattoos popular among children invites comparison of these themes (Brunvand 1989: 55-64). There might be a connection to rumors reported in England where semen is detected by customers in curry or yogurt sauce served in Indian or Chinese restaurants. In versions from England reported on-line (June 8 and November 26, 1992), the semen (without the feature of AIDS) is revenge by the establishment on customers complaining about service or food quality. After reporting the story, one British student commented, "I suppose it all stems from the British general distrust of all things foreign, especially what they put in food" (June 8, 1992). Do American contamination legends, then, speak to a fear of items made too fast and on a massive scale, or consumed too voraciously? To be sure, a number of American contamination legends, even some recent rumors about Vietnamese restaurants, refer to ethnic prejudice, but the AIDS cycle may very well be a variant that is especially concerned with the vulnerability of the healthy population (particularly sexually active youth) to the deadly virus, especially in a society aware of deadly drug tampering and terrorism.

The mystery behind the sudden appearance of AIDS in contemporary society has inspired rumors of conspiratorial origin. Folklorist Patricia Turner has documented a pattern of such rumors among African-Americans that include frequent references to a governmental experiment in biological warfare to diminish the gay or black population (Turner 1993: 151-63). Suspected culprits include the Central Intelligence Agency, Center for Disease Control, and Pentagon. Other sources point fingers at the World Health Organization, Ku Klux Klan, Hitler scientists, and Soviet communists (Smith 1990; Ellis and Mays 1992). Postings on the Internet regarding these conspiracy stories and collections from oral tradition by folklorist Paul Smith show that the beliefs are common to both blacks and whites. At the top of Smith's list are "it has originated in green monkeys in Africa" and "it has spread from specific ethnic groups—such as Haitians" followed by "an out-of-control germ warfare virus that escaped" (Smith 1990: 124-25). Does the bias that certain groups are being punished for their sexual freedom (or in Turner's words, "persistent beliefs about black sexual licentiousness") underlie the rumors? My observation on-line has been that when the conspiratorial rumors are posted, they typically are responses to the mystery of such a deadly virus spreading in an age of science, or a mistrust of big government and its covert operations. Turner, however, was interested in the way that the story complemented other conspiracy rumors among blacks such as those for fried chicken franchises and tropical fruit drinks which were believed to be part of a Ku Klux Klan plot to sterilize black men. She cites texts that indicate a distinctive meaning to blacks: "The AIDS virus was created in a CIA laboratory. The CIA brought it to Africa to test on blacks, thinking they could watch it, but it got out of control. This is why doctors cannot come up with a vaccine that will work on it. It has to be man-made." Turner comments that "Here again we find, as in the Atlanta child killer legend and the castrated boy legend, the rationale that the powerful group needs the oppressed group's bodies for their own enrichment" (Turner 1993: 158).

Homosexual sex became a topic of discussion through one legend that particularly made the rounds among college men in the 1990s. In most versions, a male student goes to a doctor or student health center to complain of headaches, nausea, or soreness in the rectal area, or a combination of these. The narrator of the story might explain that the student figures that it is a case of hemorrhoids. The student is surprised as well as outraged when the doctor insists that his problem is caused by anal sex. Returning to the room, the student searches his roommate's possessions and finds a bottle of ether or chloroform. Sometimes the student takes the doctor back to the room and the doctor discovers the knockout drug. The implication is that the student had been an unwilling sexual partner for his roommate when he was sleeping. Folklorist Jan Harold Brunvand collected variations such as traces of ether or chloroform discovered in the student's blood, and implications that the student had been infected with AIDS. Brunvand pointed out that the "new" campus legend had connections to stories reported as far away as Australia and as long ago as 1886 about men who return with a sore rear end from a party where liquor was flowing freely (Brunvand 1993: 310). This reference may explain one on-line remark that students sometimes faked evidence of homosexual activity as a prank on a passed-out, drunk roommate. Some commentators piped in with examples dating back some years about drugged seduction among soldiers and dentists (Ellis 1990). The story may also have been influenced by a campus cautionary tale about a woman who wakes up in a fraternity house after a party and discovers that she had been gang raped after having had a drug slipped into her drink (Greenberg 1973). The stories suggest a fear of rape (as signs of violence in a sexually open society and individual vulnerability among hostile strangers), and in the case of the male version, evidence of homophobia. The setting of the university is significant because of the uncertainty about the background of roommates. Little is known about roommates in the modern setting, and that adds to the mystery in the story. In G. Legman's famous collection of sexual humor, the hotel of the 1930s where strangers congregate is the setting for a "well-known joke" about a bellboy plied with champagne by a homosexual guest (Legman 1975: 156). Now the university appears in narrative as a place where people are strangers to one another. As in the college game of "Killer" reported earlier in this book, the individual in the "gay roommate" story must be on the lookout for hidden dangers from anyone, even those supposedly close to him. In folklore, the university appears less socially predictable than the old-time college.

I shouldn't give the impression that sex is all students talk about when they share their stories with one another. Probably the largest file that librarian and folklorist Alan Mays passed along to me from on-line discussions of college folklore concerns a category of belief and legend I called "building follies." There are fresh rumors to add to the persistent beliefs that libraries were sinking or collapsing (or floors emptied of books) because architects or engineers failed to account for the weight of the books (see Brunvand 1993: 299-301). Students reported that one on-line from the University of Massachusetts, University of Connecticut, Yale University, Syracuse University, Brown University, University of Chicago, University of Pennsylvania, Stanford University, University of Calgary, University of Waterloo, University of Saskatchewan, and University College of Wales. Another favorite "sinking" building rumor explains that the structure was negligently put on top of an underground stream or near a lake (marsh, river, or swamp), and sometimes the additional detail is given that the same architect planned ten other campus buildings! In an interesting twist, a Rensselaer student offered a variant that the library was designed with the concrete floors bowed upwards so that when the books were added the weight would level the floor. But the construction crews thought it was a mistake and built the floors level. Now the floors all bow downwards. The library is a central symbol of learning on campus, and the neglect of the building, the stories imply, says something about tarnish on the ideal of knowledge on campus and administrative bungling of educational management. Sometimes there's a commentary on the source of the problem—budget cuts—that is timely because of the cant of belt tightening that students and faculty hear from administration.

Some building stories suggest that when the scholars are put to work, they don't perform very well. "While at Montana State University," one posting of 1991 stated, "I remember hearing rumors that many of the buildings on campus were designed by the architectural/civil engineering programs. Several of them had major flaws. One of the dorms was constantly raining large chunks of itself onto the sidewalk below." There's a kind of student justice when the flaws emerge in the engineering building. "Here at Pitt," a reply came on-line, "the sinking building is Benedum, the engineering building. Supposedly, it was built above an underground river, and is now slowly sinking." Here's one from the same "thread" (computer slang for a conversation on-line about a particular topic) that combines the beliefs about the roles of engineering and library on campus: "At SMU [Southern Methodist University], when the CS (computer science) floor was being added to the Engineering Library they forgot to take into account the thickness of the walls. That is why you have to go through one office to get to another." Some of the stories arise as explanations for designs that seem to students to be odd or unnecessary. Others imply a knock on the privileged status of engineering programs on campus (undeserved, the stories suggest), similar to the way that humor about campus athletes question the rise of athletics as big business over the mission of liberal arts education. Some stories also explain the relative position of other groups on campus, or the priorities of the school, such as this one posted by Michael Covington on December 3, 1991: "Yale University has a miserable graduate dorm called Helen Hadley Hall that was built in the 1950s. It is poorly ventilated and very hot in the summer. Reliable sources say it was designed to be air-conditioned and then at the last minute the air conditioning was deleted as a cost-saving measure. The important thing about Hadley is that it was built for graduate women at a time when the undergraduate school (Yale College) was still all-male. And it is widely recognized as an indicator of the low status of women at Yale at the time." If such stories suggest that students don't put too much stock in the wisdom of seasoned professionals, especially those hired by universities, other fresh postings imply that students of the 1990s, accused often of being politically apathetic, wonder whether the rebellious students of another generation influenced the institutional look of their buildings. On September 20, 1994, an Ohio State student asked, "Ever notice that the buildings on West Campus have almost no windows? Like prisons? This is because they were built when riots were common in the early 1970s. A related story says that the South Campus area used to have lots of brick walkways, which are now covered with asphalt. They were paved over because the rioters were digging up the bricks and throwing them at buildings." A reply came from Edward (Alex) Sobie at the University of Oregon who reported that Bean complex has only two exits from the quads. The explanation? "This feature, rumor goes, was to allow police to block off the building in case of student riots." Sobie, who works for the Housing Department, and therefore heard the rumor often, decided to investigate. According to the architectural firm, the design owed to budget and technical constraints rather than a prison model or fear of riots, although the firm built a women's prison after completing the dorm project. Students from Georgetown, Brandeis, State University of New York at Binghamton, State University of New York at Buffalo, University of Washington, University of Illinois at Chicago, Columbia, City College of New York, Wesleyan (Connecticut), University of California at Santa Cruz, University of California at San Diego, Michigan, Swarthmore, Boston, San Francisco State, and Sonoma State appeared surprised that their school wasn't the only one with the rumor. Students frequently reported the additional belief in the presence of secret underground tunnels from the administration building so that administrators could escape if a riot occurred. Some students added variations that also comment on what they consider a bizarre architectural environment: the University of California campus at Santa Cruz was built to move troublesome Berkeley students, a graduate center at Brown was designed by an architect for the Nazis, a Penn State hall was a secret atomic test site, dormitories at Pitt and Flagler were failed hotels, and a residence hall at Rhodes was designed to confuse intruders or rapists. Sometimes strange-shaped buildings attract trouble, such as the round of rumors of a psychic predictions around Halloween time that a mass murder would occur on a college campus in a U (also reported as T and L) shaped building (sometimes with the added characteristic of a cemetery or river near the building). As was the case with other predictions, Halloween passed without any murderous incidents on campus. In previous versions of the rumor, predictions heard supposedly on Carson or Donahue talk shows (now Oprah is the favorite reference) centered on a freshman or women's dorm (see Ellis 1991; Brunvand 1993: 116-19).

Sometimes the explanation for the appearance of a building is the whim of an eccentric donor, or the administration bending backwards to please a rich benefactor. The student center at Brandeis, for example, by one posted account, "looks almost like a moonbase, with pods/wings connected by underground and above-ground passageways." According to Ted Frank, two rumors circulated to explain the design. One was that it minimized the chance of a student takeover, and the other was that it allowed the administration to solicit six large donations for each of the wings. A student from Washington University reported that he often heard that the reason that there were so many dogs running freely on campus was that "some alum left a substantial sum to the school on the condition that the dogs would be allowed...." Students elsewhere explain the presence of an anachronistic swim test by a condition of a deceased donor. Responding to a rumor at Harvard that the swim test was a memorial to a victim of the icy depths around the Titanic, students from Cornell and Bryn Mawr recalled a story about endowments that carried the condition of the swim test established by alums who drowned. Similar to the story of the donor's revenge (see the story of Penn's Irvine Auditorium) is the posting about the University of North Carolina library dome. "Seems that the guy who gave the money for the bell tower on campus originally wanted to endow the library but was turned down. So, he just gave the money for the tower, on the condition that he get to design the tower and select its location." According to the legend, the dome design appeared to be a "dunce cap" if viewed from the Chancellor's office. Such narratives with remarks about administrative "selling-out" for donations with Faustian implications and penny-wise and pound-foolish "budget cuts" reiterate the perception that money rather than mission drives the modern university.

In many new student narratives these days the administration gets hit hard, even harder, it seems to me, than the absent-minded professors of yore. Professors often join students in the new campus coalition against the corporate administration. They appear in humor to be as victimized as much as students by budget cuts and bureaucracy. Bill Prokasy of Georgia offered the following example making the rounds in 1993:

A new dean had just arrived at Modern University and thought she might well profit from a discussion with her predecessor who had recently resigned. During a luncheon meeting she asked the former dean how he had managed crises. His response was to give her three envelopes with the instruction to open #1 with the first crisis, #2 with the second crisis, and #3 with the third crisis. She accepted the envelopes and the rest of the luncheon was spent on pleasantries. Things went extremely well for her during the first six months. However, she then discovered a major problem in the budget: the year was only half over and it was clear that she was going to overspend her budget by 10%. The ruckus she caused by pulling funds back from departments, failing to commitments, etc., was such that she was facing her first major crisis. She opened envelope #1 to find that it stated "Blame the prior dean for poor planning." This she did, and the crisis was muted. The next year her curriculum committee recommended, and she implemented, a reduction in course requirements for graduation. Faculty from the affected departments were enraged, as they felt that they had not been appropriately consulted. The new dean, sensing her second crisis, opened envelope #2 which said: "blame a faculty committee." To her amazement, this worked and the committee had to shoulder the blame for poor consultation. Later that year she was preparing budgets for the following year and realized that she would not have enough funds to provide raises for faculty and staff because of some unanticipated capital costs. This caused a real uproar across the college. Confronting her third crisis, she opened envelope #3. It said: "Prepare three envelopes."

Playing up the tainted image of deans and administrators, Neil Sapper of Amarillo College reported on-line the following variation of an old ethnic joke gaining circulation in 1993: "Two anthropologists were on a field trip when they were surrounded by cannibals. Terrified, they were herded into a compound with the other fresh meat. They still could not escape the habits of their adult lives, so they were entranced by a sign that posted current prices: Professors-$5, Associate Professors-$3, Assistant Professors-$2, Instructors-$1, Deans-$0.25. In their bemusement, they summoned a guard to ask why deans were so cheap. 'Is the meat tougher than other academics?' 'No, about the same. But have you ever tried to clean one?'" (see Clements 1969, type G6.4). Another play on a traditional ethnic slur is told about the dean's brains that are the most expensive in a restaurant. When asked the reason for the high price, the server replies, "Do you know how many deans' brains it took to make up that one!" (see Baker 1986: 111).

If deans and administrators are gaining in the disrepute of college humor lately, then exams are building on their past legendary fame, or infamy. In this day of large lecture classes in universities, the favorite on-line story is still the one I discussed about the exam-taker in a large class who shoves his paper into a pile of papers and runs out of the room after asking the professor "Do you know who I am?" and hearing that the professor doesn't recognize him. I found a common variation reported on-line in 1994 worth mentioning. Often the scenario is a take-home exam which is turned in late by the student. Unlike other versions in which the exam-taker is a cheater, in this variation the student knows his stuff but is striking out at the bureaucratic rigidness of rules as well as the theme of the university's impersonality. Another late student who knows more than expected is the subject of a story that aroused a vigorous argument on-line as to its veracity. It's the account of a student who arrives late for a class and sees several math problems placed on the board. He is unaware that the professor had given them as unsolvable problems and he assumes that they are part of a test or homework. He ends up solving one or more of them. Jan Brunvand has claimed to find the source of the story in the well-documented experience of famed Stanford University mathematician George B. Dantzig, but the appeal of student one-upmanship to generations of collegians has resulted in many localized, and dramatic, narratives of the solution of the "unsolvable" problem. (Brunvand 1989: 278-83). The folkloric "truth" of the story now resides in the perception of classroom expectations it reveals.

Other variations of the legendary philosophy exam that asks "Why" with the reply "Why Not" were reported on-line. From the University of Dublin, Tampere University of Technology (Finland), Monash University (Australia), and the University of Maine came accounts of the essay theme "What it means to be brave" (or "courage," "the most 'difficult/harrowing experience' you ever had," or "laziness"). The highest grade went to the student who simply wrote "This!" From Stanford and Harvard came the variation of the exam calling for students to "Make up an appropriate final exam for this course and answer it. You will be graded on both parts." The answer that a clever student offered was: "The exam is 'Make up an appropriate final exam for this course and answer it. You will be graded on both parts.' The answer is 'The exam is make up an appropriate final exam for this course and answer it ....'" In response to this thread in 1994, Jared Thaler of the University of California at Davis remembered the story of the college entrance exam that asks for one word that describes yourself and an explanation. The student's response was "Terse." He was admitted. Even more minimalist is the philosophy exam that simply read "?" The high grade went to the response "!" This example prompted a discussion of whether tests prepare students for "real life." Reflecting the interpretation of the popularity of these narratives as an indication of student frustration over the importance placed on exams, one student offered that "people who are good in school have learned a bunch of strategies for dealing with all the stupid things governing tests" (November 24, 1993). Giving insight to some student views of the "exam game," another student replied "Test taking IS like real life in that you are no more likely to succeed in tests using an inflexible set of strategies than you are in real life. I never learned any such strategies, anyway—most teachers have their own bizarre variations to the rules, and you always had to be on the lookout" (November 24, 1993).

If most collegiate folklore seems to favor students getting the upper hand over professors, there are a few stories that feature teachers who get their point across to their pupils. In one account, "a professor was known for being an easy grader. The grades he gave for a survey course were based entirely on two exams, and the stuff on the exams was entirely covered in the textbook. So showing up for class wasn't a big deal. However, this started to get out of hand. As word of the course spread, each term there was a larger block of students who would show up infrequently or not at all, except for exam days. Finally, it got so bad that about half of the students one term never showed before the midterm. The day of the midterm everyone came in, and a graduate assistant handed out exams. 'Prof X is sick, so he asked me to give you your exams.' There was only one question in the exam booklets: 'which one of the pictures below is of Professor X?'" "Obviously," Cindy Kandolf who offered the story added, "the students who never showed up didn't know and had to guess. Many failed, while the students who had been showing up regularly got As" (May 17, 1991; rec.humor, alt.folklore.urban).

Students have a great reputation for making excuses, and every semester it seems that grandmothers fall victim right around finals (why not grandfathers?). Probably the best known exam legend involving famed excuses is one that might be called "The Flat Tire Excuse," although on-line in the rec.humor newsgroup it is known as "The Bastard Professor."

One weekend this past winter, four college students went away for a weekend while midterms were going on. However, it was not until late Sunday night that they realized that they all had a Philosophy exam the next morning at 8 AM. This proved to be most unfortunate as none had even cracked a book for the course, and even if they had studied they would never be able to make it back to school in time for the exam. So, one of the students called their professor and told him that they had gotten a very bad flat tire, where the rim was bent. The mechanic said that he would not be able to repair it until Monday afternoon. Well, the professor was very understanding and told them to take their time getting back and to call him when they were on campus again. Well, the students thought this was great. They came leisurely back on campus Monday afternoon and called the professor. He said they could take the exam the next morning in the auditorium. Come the next morning, all four students arrived in the auditorium and were seated in each of the four corners of the room. The professor then proceeded to give the following instructions: "I know that you have all had a chance to talk with the other students in the class in order to find out what was on the exam. Well, fear not, because this is a very different exam. In fact, you will be very happy to know that there is only one very simple question on this exam. Are you ready to begin?" All of the students nod. "Okay, you will have ninety minutes. The question is: Which tire?" (Alec Peterson, July 31, 1994, alt.folklore.urban).

The majors in question often change in the telling. From Marshall University came an account of two engineering students kept in separate rooms while they were given the simple question. Sometimes there's the explanation that the students were doing very well in the course and therefore decided to party before the final. At Duke it was known as an anecdote about a renowned chemistry professor (February 17, 1994; Michael Burstin, rec.humor). Typical of many versions, that one has the question "Which tire?" worth 95 points following a science problem that the students master for 5 points. Meanwhile in alt.folklore.science, posters are discussing what statistics would suggest for the best guess.

The computer that has made possible broad waves of folkloric transmission is also the subject of folklore. There might be numskull tales of naive computer users, wonder stories of love and hate, by and for machine, and rumors about a modem tax and exploding components. There is a good bit of humor such as the riddle joke for the new Pentium chips that replaced the faulty ones—Repentium. Not so funny are cautionary tales about disastrous "crashes," slang for computer malfunctions. The stories abound, especially among dissertation writers, about the need for "back-ups" and not putting too much faith in the computer, just as a previous generation was regaled with sad tales of students who failed to make copies and their professors who lost them (Brunvand 1993: 322-24). As one academic veteran recalled, "Certainly we passed around a lot of cautionary tales about people who had to wait another semester to get their degrees because their computer crashed, was hit by lightning, and their only draft of their thesis was lost" (February 25, 1992, Stephanie Hall, Folklore List).

The scariest legends for computer users may be those about computer viruses that bear a resemblance to the narrated fear of AIDS I mentioned earlier (Jennings 1990: 143-58; Lundgren 1994; Ellis 1995). The computer virus is a program that can replicate itself and cause damage in the host computer. Beliefs circulate that dangerous viruses are rapidly spreading and are difficult to detect. They're more fear-inducing than program "bugs" (comparable to contaminating "cooties" of American lore?) which also concern computer users. Suggesting a thickening plot, many narrators of computer lore blame the spread of the deadly viruses on "insane geniuses," "technoterrorists," or "oddball misfits" seeking attention or pointing to the dark side of the good that computers bring. A favorite thread is the revenge factor that motivates the clever or deranged "hacker," the term used for amateurish computer users who live for the machine and vie with professionals for inventiveness. Occasionally one hears a distinction between the "hacker" who engages in nondestructive mischief and the "cracker" who is mean-spirited (Leibowitz 1990). Karla Jennings reports that although statistics show that hackers are just as likely to be women as men, narratives tend to emphasize the man seeking retribution for a woman denying him a date or a rude meter reader by ruining credit files (1990: 151). Bill Ellis, however, documented accounts of a shady female figure named Cathy who reportedly sends a message with the subject line "Good Times." The message contains a virus which, if downloaded, will destroy the user's hard disk (Ellis 1995). "Good times" is a euphemism for sex, and in the manner of AIDS Mary legend, Cathy hands down punishment for falling for the temptation of the subject by wiping out the sexually suggestive "hard drive." After investigating the incidence of the virus, Ellis found that "more people were affected by the alert than by any 'Good Times' file." The "Good Times" virus scare of 1994 (which followed an overblown panic widely reported in the press about a deadly "Michelangelo" virus) then inspired in-group humor (the group of computer users, that is) in the form of a number of parodies such as on-line chain letters and alerts threatening exploding components (Ellis 1995).

The computer is not just for hackers or nerds anymore. Students everywhere are logging on, and becoming "computer folklore" literate. They know in-group slang from FAQs (Frequently Asked Questions) to functions. Internet users have shared ways to show emotion (combinations of parentheses and dashes that form smiles and smirks) in the faceless medium. The forms that have emerged in the process of creating traditions on-line bear watching. Student users appear more likely to construct diagrams that identify themselves at the bottom of their messages often accompanied by sayings that play on tradition. Leaving messages much like writing graffiti on a wall, a student from Rensselaer offered, "It is better to lurk and be thought a moron than to post and remove all doubt." Another from the University of Missouri-Rolla typed in, "There is nothing to see here. Move along" at the end of a message. Streaking across the bottom of a screen in dashes and slashes, a Valparaiso student's diagram was accompanied by the proclamation, "Only the tough can run a Code in the Buff." The potential folkloric reach of an international network inspires an occasional cry of "This seems ripe for some sort of rumor ... anyone heard any? Wanna make one up?" (April 10, 1994; alt.folklore.urban).

Adjustments to new technology, concerns for health, relations of groups, and questions of morality—indeed, the very conception of tradition—are among the issues confronted in today's collegiate folklore. On and off line, students revise and devise narratives to give expression to their fears, hopes, and uncertainties. Folklore offers views of the cultural scenes in which students act in the dorm, classroom, computer network, and campus. It is equally invaluable for showing connections to the larger organizations—regions, ethnic groups, and nations—of which students are a part. A watchful eye for continuing legacies and new developments in folklore offers insight into the beliefs, the perceptions, the attitudes that underlie the many forms of society and culture.

References

Aarne, Antti. 1964. *The Types of the Folktale: A Classification and Bibliography.* Translated and enlarged by Stith Thompson. Second revision, Helsinki: Folklore Fellows Communications, no. 184.

Acheson, Susan. 1987. "'Scoping': Modern Folklore." Danielle Roemer Papers, Northern Kentucky University.

Acri, Kimberly. 1989. "The Folklore of the TKE Little Sisters [St. Francis College]." Penn State Harrisburg Folklore Archives (89-003).

Adams, John A., Jr. *We Are the Aggies: The Texas A&M University Association of Former Students.* College Station: Texas A&M University Press.

Adams, Virginia, Katie Armitage, Donna Butler, Carol Shankel, and Barbara Watkins, comps. 1983. *On the Hill: A Photographic History of the University of Kansas.* Lawrence: University Press of Kansas.

"Agony, Then Ecstasy: End of Senior Theses." 1989. *New York Times,* March 26 (sec. 1, part 2): 31.

Albas, Daniel, and Cheryl Albas. 1989. "Modern Magic: The Case of Examinations." *Sociological Quarterly* 30: 603-13.

Alter, Jonathan. 1983. "Nightmare in California." *Newsweek,* June 20: 28.

Altick, Richard D. 1937. "Pranks and Punishment in an Old Pennsylvania College." *Pennsylvania History* 4: 241-47.

Aman, Reinhold. 1984-85. "Queries." *Maledicta* 8: 281-84.

_____. 1986-87. "Bawdy Books.*170 Maledicta* 9: 141-42.

_____. 1988-89. "Kakologia: A Chronicle of Ribald Riddles and Wicked Wordplays." *Maledicta* 10: 247-316.

Amick, Blair. 1980. "Parking Legends." Indiana University Folklore Archives.

Anderson, Kelly. 1987. "Steppin' Out: Black Greek Pledges Show Unity in 26-year Tradition." *State News* (Michigan State University, East Lansing), April 13: 1.

Anderson, William A. 1977. "The Social Organization and Social Control of a Fad." *Urban Life* 6: 221-40.

Andrews, Gigi Babinec. 1988. "Reflections on Brenau 'Tradition.'" *Brenau Magazine* (Brenau College, Gainesville, Georgia) 2 (1): n.p.

Anthony, Ted. 1989. "A Vexing Mystery: 20 Years Later, Pattee Stabbing Still Perplexes the State Police." *Daily Collegian* (Pennsylvania State University, University Park), November 28: 1, 4.

Baker, Ronald L. 1978. "The Phone in the Mausoleum: A Local Legend." *Midwestern Journal of Language and Folklore* 4: 70-76.

_____. 1982. *Hoosier Folk Legends.* Bloomington: Indiana University Press.

_____. 1983. "The Folklore of Students." In *Handbook of American Folklore,* ed. Richard M. Dorson, pp. 106-14. Bloomington: Indiana University Press.

_____. 1986. *Jokelore: Humorous Folktales from Indiana.* Bloomington: Indiana University Press.

Barlow, Sharon. 1989. "The Ghosts of Wesleyan." *Wesleyan Pharos* (West Virginia Wesleyan College, Buckhannon), April 14: 4.

Barnes, Daniel R. 1966. "Some Functional Horror Stories on the Kansas University Campus." *Southern Folklore Quarterly* 30: 305-12.

Barrick, Mac E. 1974. "The Growth of Graffiti." *Folklore Forum* 7: 273-75.

Bart, Peter. 1983. "Prigging Out." *Rolling Stone,* April 14: 88-92, 94-95.

Battreall, Greg. 1987. "The Michael A. Frang Legend." Indiana University Folklore Archives (87-027).

Baughman, Ernest. 1945. "The Cadaver Arm." *Hoosier Folklore Bulletin* 4: 30-32.

_____. 1945b. "The Fatal Initiation." *Hoosier Folklore Bulletin* 4: 49-55.

_____. 1966. *Type and Motif-Index of the Folktales of England and North America.* The Hague:

Mouton.

Baum, S. V. 1958. "Legend-Makers on the Campus." *American Speech* 33: 292-93.

Beckwith, Martha Warren. 1923. "Signs and Superstitions Collected from American College Girls." *Journal of American Folklore* 36: 1-15.

Beezley, William H. 1980. "Locker Rumors: Folklore and Football." *Journal of the Folklore Institute* 17: 196-221.

———. 1981. "Better Ag Than Fag!--And Other North Carolina Jokes.*170 North Carolina Folklore* Journal 29: 112-19.

———. 1985. "Counterimages of the Student Athlete in Football Folklore." In *American Sport Culture: The Humanistic Dimensions*, ed. Wiley Lee Umphlett, pp. 212-25. Lewisburg, Pennsylvania: Bucknell University Press.

———. 1988. "'Nice Girls Don't Sweat': Women in American Sport." In *The Sporting Image: Readings in American Sport History*, ed. Paul J. Zingg, pp. 337-52. Lanham, Maryland: University Press of America.

Belanger, Greg. 1988. "Chuck and His Brothers." *Washington Monthly* 20 (10): 42-43.

Bellah, Robert N., Richard Madsen, William M. Sullivan, Ann Swidler, and Steven M. Tipton. 1985. *Habits of the Heart: Individualism and Commitment in American Life.* New York: Harper and Row.

Berberoglu, Linda, and David Hilliard. 1986. "Halloween Scare Fits Description of 'Modern Legend.'" *Daily Item* (Sunbury, Pennsylvania), October 30: 1.

Berger, Joseph. 1988. "Honor Code: Rewards and Pitfalls of an Ideal." *New York Times*, March 9 (sec. B): 9.

Berry, Margaret C. 1980. *The University of Texas: A Pictorial Account of Its First Century.* Austin: University of Texas Press.

———.. 1983. *UT Austin Traditions and Nostalgia.* Rev. ed., Austin, Texas: Eakins Press.

The Best of 606 Aggie Jokes. 1976. Dallas, Texas: Gigem Press.

Betterton, Don. 1988. *Alma Mater: Unusual Stories and Little-Known Facts from America's College Campuses.* Princeton, New Jersey: Peterson's Guides.

Birnbach, Lisa. 1984. *Lisa Birnbach's College Book.* New York: Ballantine Books.

Bishop, Morris. 1962. *A History of Cornell.* Ithaca, N.Y.: Cornell University Press.

Blankman, Edward J., and Thurlow O. Cannon. 1987. *The Scarlet and the Brown: A History of St. Lawrence University*, ed. Neal S. Burdick. [Canton, New York]: St. Lawrence University.

Bledstein, Burton. 1976. *The Culture of Professionalism: The Middle Class and the Development of Higher Education in America.* New York: W. W. Norton.

Bloom, Allan. 1987. *The Closing of the American Mind: How Higher Education Has Failed Democracy and Impoverished the Souls of Today's Students.* New York: Simon and Schuster.

Boas, Louise. 1971. *Woman's Education Begins: The Rise of the Women's Colleges.* 1935; reprint, New York: Arno.

Boeltcher, Alexandra. 1980. "Initiation Rites Common at MSU." *State News* (Michigan State University, East Lansing), May 27: 1-2.

Boewe, Charles. 1987. "Who's Buried in Rafinesque's Tomb?" *Pennsylvania Magazine of History and Biography* 111: 213-35.

Boney, F. N. 1984. *A Pictorial History of the University of Georgia.* Athens: University of Georgia Press.

Boone, Lalia Phipps. 1959. "Gator (University of Florida) Slang." *American Speech* 34: 153-57.

Boorstin, Daniel J. 1965. *The Americans: The National Experience.* New York: Vintage Books/ Random House.

Boswell, George W. 1976. "Ole Miss Jokes and Anecdotes." *Tennessee Folklore Society Bulletin* 42: 72-82.

———. 1979. "Irony in Campus Speech." *Tennessee Folklore Society Bulletin* 45: 154-60.

Botkin, B. A., and William G. Tyrrell. 1962. "Upstate, Downstate." *New York Folklore Quarterly* 18: 304-14.

Boyer, Ernest L. 1987. *College: The Undergraduate Experience in America.* New York: Harper and Row.

Brackett, Frank Parkhurst. 1944. *Granite and Sagebrush: Reminiscences of the First Fifty Years of Pomona College.* Los Angeles: Ward Ritchie Press.

Bradley, Charlotte, Ruth Coleman, and Anita Peck, comps. 1925. *Barnard College Song Book.* New York: A. S. Barnes.

Brandes, Stanley H. 1985. *Forty: The Age and the Symbol.* Knoxville: University of Tennessee Press.

Bratcher, James T. 1972. "The Professor Who Didn't Get His Grades In: A Traveling Anecdote." In *Diamond Bessie and the Shepherds,* ed. William M. Hudson, pp. 121-23. Publications of the Texas Folklore Society, no. 36. Austin, Texas: Encino Press.

Brenneis, Donald. "'Turkey,' 'Wienie,' 'Animal,' 'Stud': Intragroup Variation in Folk Speech." *Western Folklore* 36: 238-46.

Briscoe, Virginia Wolf. 1981a. "Bryn Mawr College Traditions: Women's Rituals as Expressive Behavior." Ph.D. diss., University of Pennsylvania.

_____. 1981b. "Readin', Ritin', and Ritual." *Center for Southern Folklore Magazine* 4 (1): 11.

Britton, Ruth. 1987. "The Folklore of College Students at Penn State." Penn State Harrisburg Folklore Archives (88-004).

Bronner, Simon J. 1984. "Folklore in the Bureaucracy." In *Tools for Management,* ed. Frederick Richmond and Kathy Nazar, pp. 45-57. Harrisburg, Pennsylvania: PEN Publications.

_____. 1985. "'What's Grosser Than Gross?': New Sick Joke Cycles." *Midwestern Journal of Language and Folklore* 11: 39-49.

_____. 1986. *Grasping Things: Folk Material Culture and Mass Society in America.* Lexington: University Press of Kentucky.

_____. 1986b. *American Folklore Studies: An Intellectual History.* Lawrence: University Press of Kansas.

_____. 1989. *American Children's Folklore,* annotated edition. Little Rock, Arkansas: August House.

Bronson, John. 1968a. "Pranks, Customs Alive in Past." *Daily Collegian* (Pennsylvania State University, University Park), May 10: 1.

_____. 1968b. "Extensive Class Rivalry Part of University History." *Daily Collegian* (Pennsylvania State University, University Park), May 15: 1, 4.

Brubaker, John H., III. 1987. *Hullabaloo Nevonia: An Anecdotal History of Student Life at Franklin and Marshall College.* Lancaster, Pennsylvania: Franklin and Marshall College.

Brunvand, Jan Harold. 1960. "Sex in the Classroom." *Journal of American Folklore* 73: 250-51.

_____. 1962. "Further Notes on Sex in the Classroom." *Journal of American Folklore* 75: 62.

_____. 1981. *The Vanishing Hitchhiker: American Urban Legends and Their Meanings.* New York: W. W. Norton.

_____. 1984. *The Choking Doberman and Other "New" Urban Legends.* New York: W.W. Norton.

_____. 1986. *The Mexican Pet: More "New" Urban Legends and Some Old Favorites.* New York: W. W. Norton.

_____. 1989. *Curses! Broiled Again! The Hottest Urban Legends Going.* New York: W. W. Norton.

_____. 1993. *The Baby Train, and Other Lusty Urban Legends.* New York: W. W. Norton

Bryan, W. F. 1954. "A Modern Ballad." *North Carolina Folklore* 2 (1): 8-9.

Burson, Anne C. 1980. "Model and Text in Folk Drama." *Journal of American Folklore* 93: 305-16.

_____. 1982. "Pomp and Circumcision: A Parodic Skit in a Medical Community. *170 Keystone Folklore,* n.s., 1 (1): 28-40.

Calkin, Nancy, and William Randel. 1945. "Campus Slang at Minnesota." *American Speech* 20: 233-34.

"Campus Comedy." 1962. *Reader's Digest,* October: 180I.

"Campus Comedy." 1963. *Reader's Digest,* June: 217-18.

"Campus Comedy." 1966. *Reader's Digest,* October: 56.

Cannon, Anthon S., collector. 1984. *Popular Beliefs and Superstitions from Utah.* Edited with introduction and notes by Wayland D. Hand and Jeannine E. Talley. Salt Lake City: University of Utah Press.

Carey, George G. 1971. *Maryland Folk Legends and Folk Songs.* Cambridge, Maryland: Tidewater Publishers.

_____. 1988. "Mysteries, Legends, and Tall Tales. *170 Busline, The Five College Magazine* (North Amherst, Massachusetts), Fall: 6-9.

Carlinsky, Dan, ed. 1971. *A Century of College Humor.* New York: Random House.

Carnegie Foundation for the Advancement of Teaching. 1987. *A Classification of Institutions of Higher Education.* Princeton, New Jersey: Carnegie Foundation.

Carter, Virginia. 1930-31. "University of Missouri Slang." *American Speech* 6: 203-6.

Cattermole-Tally, Frances. 1990. "Male Fantasy or Female Revenge?: A Look at Some Modern Rape Legends." In *A Nest of Vipers: Perspectives on Contemporary Legend* 5, ed. Gillian Bennett and Paul Smith, pp. 41-48. Sheffield, England:Sheffield Academic Press.

Chambers, E. O. 1983. "The Mona Lisa Legend of City Park, New Orleans." *Louisiana Folklore Miscellany* 5 (3): 31-39.

Chesworth, Jo. 1976. "Shapeless in the Hands of Fate." *The Penn Stater* (Pennsylvania State University, University Park) 62 (4): 1-5.

_____. 1980. "Swampy's Son Revives a Legend." *The Penn Stater* (Pennsylvania State University, University Park) 67 (1): 8-9.

Christner, Becky. 1967. "A Collection of Songs and Traditions of Alpha Chi Omega Sorority at UCLA." Wayne State University Folklore Archive (1974/18).

Chronicle of Higher Education. 1989. *Almanac.* Washington, District of Columbia: Chronicle of Higher Education, (September 6).

Clarke, Malea. 1987. "Determination of the Caloric Equivalent of a Single M&M and Evidence of a Population Control Strategy." *Journal of Irreproducible Results* 32 (5): 28-29.

"A Class in Itself? Mastering the Art of the 'Gut' Course." 1989. *New York Times,* March 5 (sec. 1, part 2): 52.

Clawges, Patricia. 1989. "The Folklore of Law Students: Coping with Impersonality and Intimidation." Penn State Harrisburg Folklore Archives (89-047).

Clements, William M. 1969. *The Types of the Polack Joke.* Folklore Forum Bibliographic and Special Series, no. 3.

_____. 1969b. "The Chain." *Indiana Folklore* 2 (1): 90-96.

Clerval, Henry. 1986-87. "Clap Books." *Maledicta* 9: 139-41.

Closson, David L. 1977. "The Onomastics of the Rabble." *Maledicta* 1: 215-33.

Cochran, Carolyn. 1981. "Candlelights on the Indiana University Campus." Indiana University Folklore Archives.

Cohen, Hennig. 1951. "Going to See the Widow." *Journal of American Folklore* 64: 223.

Cohen, Hennig, and Tristam Potter Coffin, eds. 1987. *The Folklore of American Holidays.* Detroit, Michigan: Gale Research Company.

"College Holidays." 1856. *Williams Quarterly* (Williams College, Williamstown, Massachusetts) 3 (4): 378-80.

Collins, Hently. 1988. "Fraternity Rites Stir Sexual Violence, Conference Told." *Philadelphia Inquirer,* October 29: 3-B.

Collison, Michele. 1990. "8 Major Black Fraternities and Sororities Agree to End the Practice of Pledging." *Chronicle of Higher Education,* February 28: A31.

Conkin, Paul, assisted by Henry Lee Swint and Patricia S. Mile. 1985. *Gone with the Ivy: A Biography of Vanderbilt University.* Knoxville: University of Tennessee Press.

Consider the Years: 1883-1983, Houghton College. 1982. Houghton, New York: Houghton College.

Copeland, Lewis, and Faye Copeland, eds. 1940. *10,000 Jokes, Toasts, and Stories.* Garden City, New York: Garden City Books.

Costner, Sharon. 1975. "'State' Jokes on the Carolina Campus." *North Carolina Folklore Journal* 23: 107-11.

Cottom, Daniel. 1989. *Text and Culture: The Politics of Interpretation.* Minneapolis: University of Minnesota Press.

Cowan, Helen. 1989. "The Worst Way to Get a 4.0 at College: A College Legend." Angus Gillespie Papers, Rutgers, Douglass College, New Brunswick.

Cowley, W. H., and Glenn A. Reed. "Academics Are Human." 1977. *Change* 9 (8): 33-38.

Craig, Allen. 1974. "Songs of Pi Kappa Alpha Fraternity." Wayne State University Folklore Archive (R1975/34).

Cramer, C. H. 1976. *Case Western Reserve: A History of the University, 1826-1976.* Boston: Little, Brown.

Crane, Beverly. 1977. "The Structure of Value in 'The Roommate's Death': A Methodology for Interpretive Analysis of Folk Legends." *Journal of the Folklore Institute* 14: 133-49.

Crawford, Michael L. 1974. "Legends from St. Mary-of-the-Woods College." *Indiana Folklore* 7: 53-75.

Dalkoff, Breena. 1974. "Rituals of a Fraternity House." Indiana University Folklore Archives (74/52).

Danielson, Larry. 1979. "Folklore and Film: Some Thoughts on Baughman Z500-599.*170 Western*

Folklore 38: 209-19.

Daughrity, Kenneth L. 1930-31. "Handed-Down Campus Expressions." *American Speech* 6: 129-30.

Davidson, Levette Jay. 1943. "Moron Stories." *Southern Folklore Quarterly* 7: 101-4.

Davie, James S., and A. Paul Hare. 1974. "Button-Down Collar Culture: A Study of Undergraduate Life at a Men's College." In *Anthropology and American Life*, ed. Joseph Jorgensen and Marcello Truzzi, pp. 262-81. Englewood Cliffs, New Jersey: Prentice-Hall.

Dawson, Jim. 1971. "Ed Diddle Stories." Western Kentucky Folklore Archive (1972-4).

de Caro, F. A., and Richard Lunt. 1968. "The Face on the Tombstone." *Indiana Folklore* 1 (1): 34-41.

Dégh, Linda. 1968. "The Hook." *Indiana Folklore* 1 (1): 92-100.

_____. 1968b. "The Boy Friend's Death." *Indiana Folklore* 1 (1): 101-6.

_____. 1969. "The Haunted Bridges Near Avon and Danville and Their Role in Legend Formation." *Indiana Folklore* 2 (1): 54-89.

_____. 1969b. "The Roommate's Death and Related Dormitory Stories in Formation." *Indiana Folklore* 2 (2): 55-74.

_____. 1971. "The 'Belief Legend' in Modern Society: Form, Function, and Relationship to Other Genres." In *American Folk Legend: A Symposium*, ed. Wayland D. Hand, pp. 55-68. Berkeley: University of California Press.

DeParle, Jason. 1988. "About Men." *Washington Monthly* 20 (10): 38-46, 48.

Dickinson, M. B. 1951. "Words from the Diaries of North Carolina Students." *American Speech* 26: 181-84.

Dodge, Willard A., Jr., Reuben B. Moulton, Harrison W. Sigworth, and Adrian C. Smith, Jr. 1982. Legends of Caltech. [Pasadena]: Alumni Association, California Institute of Technology.

Domowitz, Susan. 1979. "Foreign Matter in Food: A Legend Type." *Indiana Folklore* 12: 86-95.

Donovan, Dan. 1989. "Mass Murder Rumors on American Campuses." *Foaftale News*, no. 12: 1-2.

Dorson, Richard M. 1949. "The Folklore of Colleges." *American Mercury* 68: 671-77.

_____. 1959. *American Folklore*. Chicago: University of Chicago Press.

_____. 1967. *American Negro Folktales*. Greenwich, Connecticut: Fawcett Publications.

Douglas, Paul. 1987. "Bizz-Buzz, Turtles, Quarters, and One Horse Club: The Role of Drinking Games among High School and College Students." *Alcohol Health and Research World*, Summer: 54-57, 92.

Doyle, Charles Clay. 1973. "Title-Author Jokes, Now and Long Ago." *Journal of American Folklore* 86: 52-54.

D'Pnymph, Sue. 1988. *Eat Beans, They Make You Astute*. Research notes by James Withers. Little Rock, Arkansas: Privately printed.

Dresser, Norine, and Theodor Schuchat. 1980. "In Search of the Perforated Page." *Western Folklore* 39: 300-6.

Duda, Ambrose. 1987. "Drinking Games of Male Students Attending Western Oregon State College." Western Oregon State Folklore Archives.

Dundes, Alan. 1961. "Mnemonic Devices." *Midwest Folklore* 11: 139-47.

_____. 1964. "Here I Sit—A Study of American Latrinalia." *Kroeber Anthropological Society Papers*, no. 34 (Spring): 91-105.

_____. 1968. "One Hundred Years of California Traditions." *California Monthly* 78(5): 19-32.

_____. 1971. "On the Psychology of Legend." In *American Folk Legend: A Symposium*, ed. Wayland D. Hand, pp. 21-36. Berkeley: University of California Press.

_____. 1980. *Interpreting Folklore*. Bloomington: Indiana University Press.

_____. 1987a. *Cracking Jokes: Studies of Sick Humor Cycles and Stereotypes*. Berkeley: Ten Speed Press.

_____. 1987b. "The American Game of 'Smear the Queer' and the Homosexual Component of Male Competitive Sport and Warfare." In *Parsing through Customs: Essays by a Freudian Folklorist*, pp. 178-96. Madison: University of Wisconsin Press.

_____, and Robert A. Georges. 1962. "Some Minor Genres of Obscene Folklore." *Journal of American Folklore* 75: 221-26.

_____, and Carl R. Pagter. 1975. "Bar Dice in the San Francisco Bay Area." *Kroeber Anthropological Society Papers*, nos. 51-52 (Spring-Fall): 1-18.

_____. 1978. *Work Hard and You Shall Be Rewarded: Urban Folklore from the Paperwork Empire*. 1975; reprint, Bloomington: Indiana University Press.

_____. 1987. *When You're Up to Your Ass in Alligators: More Urban Folklore from the Paperwork Empire.* Detroit: Wayne State University Press.

Dundes, Alan, and C. Fayne Porter. 1963. "American Indian Student Slang." *American Speech* 38: 270-77.

Dundes, Alan, and Manuel R. Schonhorn. 1963. "Kansas University Slang: A New Generation." *American Speech* 38: 163-77.

Dunn, Tom. 1973. "Class Scraps Begat Bruises and Arnica." *The Penn Stater* (Pennsylvania State University, University Park) 59 (5): 8-9.

Earley, James. 1987. *On the Frontier of Leadership.* Tacoma, Washington: University of Puget Sound, 1987.

Editors of Guinness. 1982. *Guinness Book of College Records and Facts.* New York: Sterling.

Egan, Robert. 1985. *From Here to Fraternity.* New York: Bantam

Eikel, Fred, Jr. 1946. "An Aggie Vocabulary of Slang." *American Speech* 21: 29-36.

Eliot, Charles William. 1969. *Harvard Memories.* 1923; reprint, Freeport, N.Y.: Books for Libraries Press.

Ellis, Bill. 1983. "Legend-Tripping in Ohio: A Behavioral Survey." *Papers in Comparative Studies* 2: 61-73.

_____. 1990. "Gay Roommates and Unethical Dentists." *Foaftale News,* no. 18: 7.

_____. 1991. "Nostradamus and Massacres." *Foaftale News,* no. 24: 8-10.

_____. 1995. "Good-Times Cathy Computer Virus." *Foaftale News,* no. 36: 4-5.

_____, and Alan Mays. 1992. "AIDS." *Foaftale News,* no. 27: 8-9.

Ellis, Junius. 1987. "At Witty Caltech, Pranks Aren't Purely a Laughing Matter." *Smithsonian* 18 (6): 100-2, 104, 106-8, 110, 112-13.

Emrich, Duncan. 1972. *Folklore on the American Land.* Boston: Little, Brown.

Ernstberger, Mary J. 1983. "Little Bo Peep." Indiana University Folklore Archives.

Eschholz, Paul A., and Alfred F. Rosa. 1970. "Course Names: Another Aspect of College Slang." *American Speech* 45: 85-90.

"Everybody into the Water Even at 50 Degrees." 1989. *New York Times,* May 7 (sec. 1, part 2): 54.

Fagan, Susan Martin. 1981. "Ten Words for a Dollar—A New Campus Custom." *Western Folklore* 40: 337-43.

"Feedback." 1984-85. *Maledicta* 8: 257-67.

Fine, Gary Alan. 1979. "Cokelore and Coke Law: Urban Belief Tales and the Problem of Multiple Origins." *Journal of American Folklore* 92: 477-84.

_____. 1983. *Shared Fantasy: Role Playing Games as Social Worlds.* Chicago: University of Chicago Press.

_____. 1987. "Welcome to the World of AIDS: Fantasies of Female Revenge," *Western Folklore* 46: 192-97.

_____. 1992. *Manufacturing Tales: Sex and Money in Contemporary Legends.* Knoxville: University of Tennessee Press.

_____. and Bruce Noel Johnson. 1980. "The Promiscuous Cheerleader: An Adolescent Male Belief Legend." *Western Folklore* 39: 120-29.

Fish, Lydia. 1972. "The Old Wife in the Dormitory—Sexual Folklore and Magical Practices from State University College." *New York Folklore Quarterly* 28: 30-36.

Fitton, Mary Louise. 1941. "Hanover College Has Hoosier Folklore Background." *Yearbook of the Society of Indiana Pioneers,* pp. 17-26.

_____. 1942. "College Folklore." *Hoosier Folklore Bulletin* 1 (2): 40-41.

Forrest, Rex. 1940. "Ranking the Professors." *American Speech* 15: 445.

Fox, William S. 1983. "Computerized Creation and Diffusion of Folkloric Materials." *Folklore Forum* 16: 5-20.

_____. 1990. "The Roommate's Suicide and the 4.0." In *A Nest of Vipers: Perspectives on Contemporary Legend, Volume 5,* ed. Gillian Bennett and Paul Smith, pp. 69-76. Sheffield: Sheffield Academic Press.

Franks, Ray. 1982. *What's in a Nickname? Exploring the Jungle of College Athletic Mascots.* Amarillo, Texas: Ray Franks Publishing Ranch.

"Fraternity Pledges Are 'On Line' in Rite of Passage." 1989. *New York Times,* April 9 (sec. 1, part 2): 39.

Free, James. 1982. "Fraternity Jokes, Pranks, and Bore-Asses." Indiana University Folklore Archives (85-009).

Freedman, Mervin B. 1967. *The College Experience.* San Francisco: Jossey-Bass.

"A Fummer's Guide to the Universe." 1988. *F&M Today* (Franklin and Marshall College, Lancaster, Pennsylvania) 18 (1): 36.

Furr, Joel. 1995. "Stalking Chicken Little: Myth, Reality, and Absurdity in Alt.Folklore." *Internet World* 6 (2): 86-89.

Gach, Vicki. 1973. "Graffiti." *College English* 35: 285-87.

Gadson, A. Denita. 1989. "Greek Power: African-American Greek-Letter Organizations Wield Massive Influence after School Days." *Black Collegian* 20 (1): 34-36, 136-37.

Gammage, Jeff. 1989. "Groups Keep in Step with Tradition." *Philadelphia Inquirer,* July 9: 2-B.

Gardner, Robert G. 1972. *On the Hill: The Story of Shorter College.* Rome, Georgia: Shorter College, 1972.

Garfinkel, David. 1986. "High Jinks at Cal Tech." *Business Week Careers* 4 (4): 52-54.

Gates, Charlene. 1976. "Graffiti and the Environment of the Folk Group: University Music Majors." *Folklore Forum* 9: 35-42.

Geeslin, Ned, and S. Avery Brown. 1989. "With a Campus Legend in Peril, Members of a Fraternity Vow to Save the Endangered M.I.T. Smoot." *People Weekly,* April 24: 93-95.

Gilkey, Carolyn F. 1990. "The Mathematician and the Engineer: Scientists and the Professional Slur." *Western Folklore* 49: 215-20.

Girdler, Lew. 1970. "The Legend of the Second Blue Book." *Western Folklore* 29: 111-17.

Glavan, Joyce. 1968. "Sorority Tradition and Song." *Journal of the Ohio Folklore Society* 3: 192-98.

Glazer, Mark. 1987. "The Cultural Adaptation of a Rumour Legend: 'The Boyfriend's Death' in South Texas." In *Perspectives on Contemporary Legend, Volume II,* ed. Gillian Bennett, Paul Smith, and J. D. A. Widdowson, pp. 93-108. Sheffield, England: Sheffield Academic Press.

Glimm, James York. 1983. *Flatlanders and Ridgerunners: Folktales from the Mountains of Northern Pennsylvania.* Pittsburgh, Pennsylvania: University of Pittsburgh Press.

Gluck, Michael. 1989. "Coin Ingesting Complicating a Tavern Game." *Western Journal of Medicine* 150: 343-44.

"Going Back in Time." 1986. *F&M Today* (Franklin and Marshall College, Lancaster, Pennsylvania) 15 (2): n.p.

Golden, Gail D. 1974. "Contemporary Bathroom Graffiti." Wayne State University Folklore Archive (R1974/104).

Goldstein, Diane E. 1992. "Welcome to the Mainland, Welcome to the World of AIDS: Cultural Viability, Localization and Contemporary Legend." *Contemporary Legend* 2: 23-40.

Goodman, Norman, and Kenneth A. Feldman. 1975. "Expectations, Ideals, and Reality: Youth Enters College." In *Adolescence in the Life Cycle: Psychological Change and Social Context,* ed. Sigmund E. Dragastin and Glen H. Elder, pp. 147-69. Washington, D.C.: Hemisphere Publishing.

Goss, Michael. 1984. *The Evidence for Phantom Hitch-hikers.* Wellingborough, Northamptonshire: Aquarian Press.

Graham, Joe S. 1985. "Old Army Went to Hell in 1958: Aggie War Stories from the Corps of Cadets." In *Sonovagun Stew: A Folklore Miscellany,* ed. Francis Edward Abernethy, pp. 105-21. Publication of the Texas Folklore Society, no. 46. Dallas: Southern Methodist University Press.

Graves, Oliver Finley. 1979. "Folklore in Academe: The Anecdote of the Professor and the Transom." *Indiana Folklore* 12: 142-45.

Gray, Joseph M. 1969-70. "The Folk Tradition of the Sweetheart Tree." *Pennsylvania Folklife* 19 (2): 14-17.

Greenberg, Andrea. 1973. "Drugged and Seduced: A Contemporary Legend." *New York Folklore Quarterly* 29: 131-58.

Grider, Sylvia. 1980. "The Hatchet Man." In *Indiana Folklore: A Reader,* ed. Linda Dégh, pp. 147-78. Bloomington: Indiana University Press.

Griscom, Andy, Ben Rand, and Scott Johnson. 1984. *The Complete Book of Beer Drinking Games.* New Haven, Connecticut: RJ Publications.

———, and Michael Balay. 1986. *Beer Games II: The Exploitative Sequel.* New Haven, Connecticut: Mustang Publishing.

Grotegut, Eugene K. 1955. "Going to See the O'Reilly Sisters." *Western Folklore* 14: 51-52.

Hafferty, Frederic W. 1988. "Cadaver Stories and the Emotional Socialization of Medical Students." *Journal of Health and Social Behavior* 29: 344-56.

Haglund, Elizabeth, ed. 1981. *Remembering: The University of Utah.* Salt Lake City: University of Utah Press.

Hale, Allean Lemmon. 1968. *Petticoat Pioneer: The Story of Christian College, Oldest College for Women West of the Mississippi.* Rev. ed., St. Paul, Minnesota: North Central Publishing Company.

Hall, B. H. 1968. *A Collection of College Words and Customs.* Cambridge, Massachusetts: John Bartlett, 1856; reprint, Detroit: Gale Research Company.

Hall, Gary. 1973. "The Big Tunnel: Legends and Legend-Telling." *Indiana Folklore* 6: 139-73.

Hancock, Elsie. 1988. "Zoos, Tunes, and Gweeps: A Dictionary of Campus Slang." *F&M Today* (Franklin and Marshall College, Lancaster, Pennsylvania) 18 (1): XII-XVI.

Hand, Wayland D. 1958. "Going to See the Widow." *Western Folklore* 17: 275-76.

_____, ed. 1961. *The Frank C. Brown Collection of North Carolina Folklore, Vol. 6: Popular Beliefs and Superstitions from North Carolina.* Durham, North Carolina: Duke University Press.

_____, Anna Casetta, and Sondra B. Thiederman, eds. 1981. *Popular Beliefs and Superstitions: A Compendium of American Folklore from the Ohio Collection of Newbell Niles Puckett.* 3 vols. Boston, Massachusetts: G. K. Hall.

Hankey, Rosalie. 1944. "Campus Folklore and California's 'Pedro!'" *California Folklore Quarterly* 3: 29-35.

Hansen, William B., and Irwin Altman. 1976. "Decorating Personal Places: A Descriptive Analysis." *Environment and Behavior* 8: 491-504.

Harrison, Albert A., Robert Sommer, Margaret H. Rucker, and Michael Moore. 1986. "Standing Out from the Crowd: Personalization of Graduation Attire." *Adolescence* 21: 863-74.

Hartikka, H. D. 1946. "Tales Collected from Indiana University Students." *Hoosier Folklore* 5: 71-82.

Healy, Dorothy. 1972. "Footnote for Just Before Christmas Exams." *The Mirror* (Westbrook College, Portland, Maine) 12 (1): 21.

Heckscher, William S. 1970. *Maces: An Exhibition of American Ceremonial Academic Scepters in Honor of the Inauguration of President Terry Sanford, October 18, 1970.* [Durham, North Carolina]: Duke University Museum of Art.

Hedges, James L. 1989. "It's Time for a Change: The Commencement Ceremony Has Lost Much of Its Historical Value and Power." *Chronicle of Higher Education,* June 28: A32.

Hendricks, George D. 1959. "Folk Process on the Campus." *Sing Out!* 9 (Fall): 25-26.

Hickerson, Joseph. 1958. "College Songs in the Indiana University Folklore Archives." *Folklore and Folk Music Archivist* 1 (2): 2.

_____. 1963. "The Indiana University Folklore Archives Song Index." *Folklore and Folk Music Archivist* 6 (1): 3-6.

Hine, Thomas. 1980. "Penn's Art and Architecture Reflect the History of the Cityscape." *Philadelphia Inquirer,* February 24 (sec. I): 1.

Hobbs, Alexander. 1973. "Downie's Slaughter." *Aberdeen University Review* 45: 183-91.

Hoffman, Frank A. 1962. "The Daisy Chain." *Journal of American Folklore* 75: 264-65.

Holden, Reuben A. 1967. *Yale: A Pictorial History.* New Haven, Connecticut: Yale University Press.

"Homicide on the Campus." 1966. *Time,* May 13: 70.

"Hoop-de-doo." 1989. *Sun* (Baltimore, Maryland), April 17 (sec. A): 3.

Hornbein, George, and Kenneth A. Thigpen, Jr. 1982. *Salamanders: A Night at the Phi Delt House.* 16 mm film. State College, Pennsylvania: Documentary Resource Center and Filmspace.

Horowitz, Helen Lefkowitz. 1984. *Alma Mater: Design and Experience in the Women's Colleges from Their Nineteenth Century Beginnings to the 1930s.* New York: Alfred A. Knopf.

_____. 1987. *Campus Life: Undergraduate Cultures from the End of the Eighteenth Century to the Present.* New York: Alfred A. Knopf.

Howe, Nicholas. 1989. "Rewriting Initialisms: Folk Derivations and Linguistic Riddles." *Journal of American Folklore* 102: 171-82.

Hoy, Jim, and Tom Isern. 1987. *Plains Folk: A Commonplace of the Great Plains.* Norman: University of Oklahoma Press.

Hufford, David. 1989. "Customary Observances in Modern Medicine." *Western Folklore* 48: 129-43.

Huguenin, Charles A. 1961. "Burial of Calculus at Syracuse." *New York Folklore Quarterly* 17: 256-62.

_____. 1962. "A Prayer for Examinations." *New York Folklore Quarterly* 18: 145-48.

Hunter, Carolyn. 1977. "Folklore on the Prudish Campus, or Watch Out for the Dean of Women."
    Southwest Folklore 1: 11-29.
Hunter, Edwin R., and Bernice E. Gaines. 1938. "Verbal Taboo in a College Community." *American
    Speech* 13: 97-107.
"If M.I.T. Frosh Ted Larkin Knows His Studies Cold, He Can Credit a Textbook Case of Prank-
    sterism." *People Weekly,* February 28: 34-35.
"It's Funny Business at Business School." 1989. *Wall Street Journal,* February 10 (sec. B): 1.
"J," Mr. 1981. *Still More of the World's Best Dirty Jokes.* New York: Ballantine Books.
Jachimiak, Pam. 1978. "Graffiti from Women's Restrooms." Indiana University Folklore Archives
    (78/4).
Jackson, Bruce. 1972. "'The Greatest Mathematician in the World': Norbert Wiener Stories." *Western
    Folklore* 31: 1-22.
Jacob, Philip E. 1957. *Changing Values in College: An Exploratory Study of the Impact of College
    Teaching.* New York: Harper and Row.
Jarnagin, Bert, and Fred Eikel, Jr. 1948. "North Texas Agricultural College Slang." *American Speech*
    23: 248-50.
Jeakle, Bill, and Ed Wyatt. 1989. *How to College in the 90s.* New York: New American Library.
Jennings, Karla. 1986. "Computer Folklore." *American Way,* November 1: 16.
_____. 1990. *The Devouring Fungus: Tales of the Computer Age.* New York: W. W. Norton.
Johnson, Jerah. 1960. "Professor Einstein and the Chorus Girl." *Journal of American Folklore* 73:
    248-49.
Johnson, John William. 1980. "Killer: An American Campus Folk Game." *Indiana Folklore* 13: 81-101.
Jones, Loyal, and Billy Edd Wheeler. 1987. *Laughter in Appalachia: A Festival of Southern
    Mountain Humor.* Little Rock, Arkansas: August House.
Jones, Suzi. 1977. *Oregon Folklore.* Eugene: University of Oregon and the Oregon Arts Commission.
Judge, Roy. 1986. "May Morning and Magdalen College, Oxford." *Folklore* 97: 15-40.
Kahn, E. J., Jr. 1969. *Harvard: Through Change and Through Storm.* New York: W. W. Norton.
Kaylor, Earl C., Jr. 1976. *Truth Sets Free: Juniata Independent College in Pennsylvania, Founded
    by the Brethren, 1876: A Centennial History.* South Brunswick, New Jersey: A. S. Barnes.
Kannerstein, Gregory. 1967. "Slang at a Negro College: 'Home Boy.'" *American Speech* 42: 238-39.
Keeth, Kent, with Harry Marsh. 1985. *Looking Back at Baylor: A Collection of Historical Vignettes.*
    Waco, Texas: Baylor University.
Kelley, Janet Agnes. 1949. *College Life and Mores.* New York: Bureau of Publications, Teachers
    College, Columbia University.
Kenwill, Margaret. 1886. "Home and Social Life." *Southern Workman* 15 (June): 70.
Kern, Richard. 1984. *Findlay College: The First Hundred Years.* Nappannee, Indiana: Evangel Press.
Keseling, Peter C., and John Kinney, eds. 1956. *Summa Cum Laughter: The Best Cartoons and Jokes
    from College Humor Magazines.* New York: Waldorf Publishing.
Kett, Joseph. 1977. *Rites of Passage: Adolescence in America, 1790 to the Present.* New York: Basic
    Books.
Kinder, Franz, and Boaz the Clown, eds. 1989. *Metafolkloristica: An Informal Anthology of Folk-
    lorists' Humor.* Salt Lake City, Utah: Franz Kinder and Boaz the Clown.
King, Laura. 1993. "Local Pizza Delivery Business Fights Rumors." *Arkansas Traveler* (August 4).
Klein, Robert. 1975. *"Fraternity Folklore: A Study of the Pledge and Rush Traditions of Theta Chi
    Fraternity at the University of Michigan."* Wayne State University Folklore Archive (R1975/14).
Koppe, Richard, William Irvine, and John Burns, comps. and eds. 1950. *A Treasury of College
    Humor.* New York: William Penn Publishing.
Krattenmaker, Tom. 1989. "'Animal House' May Be Getting a Den Mother." *Sunday News* (Lan-
    caster, Pennsylvania), April 9 (sec. AA): 9, 12.
Kratz, Henry. 1964. "What Is College Slang?" *American Speech* 39: 188-95.
Krause, Betsy. 1989. "Traditions." *Oregon Stater* (Oregon State University, Corvallis), June: 9-12.
Kraut, Alan M. 1994. *Silent Travelers: Germs, Genes, and the "Immigrant Menace."* 170 New York:
    Harper Collins.
Kreston, Rosemary. 1973. "Folklore in the Helen Newberry Joy Residence for Women." Wayne State
    University Folklore Archive (1973/205).
Kuethe, J. Louis. 1931-32. "Johns Hopkins Jargon." American Speech 7: 327-38.

Kurian, George Thomas. 1984. *The New Book of World Rankings.* New York: Facts on File.

La Barre, Weston. 1979. "Academic Graffiti." *Maledicta* 3: 275-76.

Langlois, Janet. 1991. "'Hold the Mayo': Purity and Danger in an AIDS Legend." *Contemporary Legend* 1: 153-72.

Langway, Lynn, and Janet Huck. 1980. "An Outbreak of Campus KAOS." *Newsweek,* June 9: 103.

Lasch, Christopher. 1979. *The Culture of Narcissism: American Life in an Age of Diminishing Expectations.* New York: W. W. Norton.

Lavin, J. A. 1962. "The Clerk of Oxenford in Oral Tradition." *New York Folklore Quarterly* 18: 61-64.

Lawrence University. 1988. *Time and Traditions.* Appleton, Wisconsin: Lawrence University.

Lears, T. J. Jackson. 1981. *No Place of Grace: Antimodernism and the Transformation of American Culture, 1880-1920.* New York: Pantheon.

Leary, James P. 1978. "The Notre Dame Man: Christian Athlete or Dirtball?" *Journal of the Folklore Institute* 15: 133-45.

_____. 1982. "A Trickster in Everyday Life." In *The Paradoxes of Play,* ed. John W. Loy, pp. 57-64. West Point, New York: Leisure Press.

Leacock, Stephen. 1935. *Humor: Its Theory and Technique.* New York: Dodd, Mead.

Lecocq, James Gary. 1980. "The Ghost of the Doctor and a Vacant Fraternity House." In *Indiana Folklore: A Reader,* ed. Linda Dégh pp. 265-78. Bloomington: Indiana University Press.

Leddy, Betty. 1948. "La Llorona in Southern Arizona." *Western Folklore* 7: 272-77.

Lee, Dorothy Sara, ed. 1981. *Franklin County Folklore.* Chambersburg, Pennsylvania: Wilson College.

Legman, G. 1964. *The Horn Book: Studies in Erotic Folklore and Bibliography.* New Hyde Park, New York: University Books.

_____. 1968. *Rationale of the Dirty Joke: An Analysis of Sexual Humor, First Series.* New York: Grove Press.

_____. 1975. *Rationale of the Dirty Joke: An Analysis of Sexual Humor, Second Series.* New York: Breaking Point.

Leibowitz, Brian M. 1990. *The Journal of the Institute for Hacks, Tomfoolery, and Pranks at MIT.* Cambridge: MIT Museum.

Levine, Robert. 1987. "Waiting Is a Power Game." *Psychology Today,* April: 24-33.

Lewis, Margaret Jane. 1970. "Some Nicknames and Their Derivations." *Mississippi Folklore Register* 4: 52-57.

Ligotti, Gregory S. 1987. "Blue Book Legends." Wayne State University Folklore Archive (R1987/3).

Lockwood, Sheree. 1978. "Desk-Top Graffiti at UVM." Folklore and Oral History Collection, University of Vermont Library.

Long, George. 1977. *The Folklore Calendar.* 1930; reprint, London: EP Publishing.

Longenecker, Gregory J. 1977. "Sequential Parody Graffiti." *Western Folklore* 36: 354-64.

Lowe, Donald M. 1982. *History of Bourgeois Perception.* Chicago: University of Chicago Press.

Lundgren, Terry D. 1994. "Computer Virus Folklore." *Journal of End User Computing* 6 (2): 19-23.

Lycan, Gilbert L. 1983. *Stetson University: The First 100 Years.* DeLand, Florida: Stetson University Press.

Manley, Robert N. 1969. *Centennial History of the University of Nebraska, Vol. I: Frontier University (1869-1919).* Lincoln: University of Nebraska Press.

Martin, William. 1990. "Greek Pledging Process: Hardly 'Ritualistic.'" *Chronicle of Higher Education,* January 10: B3.

Mason, Melissa Caswell. 1977. "Sorority Serenading: Its Pretext and Defense." *Folklore and Mythology Studies* 1: 51-52.

Matthews, Gail. 1986. "Mercedes Benzene: The Elite Folklife of Physical Chemists." *Folklore Forum* 19: 153-74.

Maurer, Marilyn. 1976. "College Folksongs." Indiana University Folklore Archives (75/124).

Maxwell, Kimera. 1987. "Traditions, Myths, and Legends Live On." *Spotlight* (Emporia State University, Emporia, Kansas), December: 11.

"May Day Queen Leona Crowns Virgin's Statue." 1939. *Mount Mary Times* (Mount Mary College, Milwaukee, Wisconsin), May 8: 1.

Mays, Alan E. 1980. "'The Shithouse Poet Strikes Again': A Collection of Latrinalia from Men's Rest Rooms at the Pennsylvania State University, October-November, 1980." Penn State Folklore Archives (Penn State Room, Pattee Library, University Park).

McCallum, John Dennis, and Charles H. Pearson. 1971. *College Football, U.S.A., 1869-1971*. Greenwich, Connecticut: Hall of Fame Pub.

McCarthy, Barbara. 1975. "Traditions." In *Wellesley College, 1875-1975: A Century of Women*, ed. Jean Glasscock, pp. 235-64. Wellesley, Massachusetts: Wellesley College.

McCosh, Sandra. 1979. *Children's Humour*. London: Granada Publishing.

McCulloh, Gordon. 1987. "Suicidal Sculptors: Scottish Versions of a Migratory Legend." In *Perspectives on Contemporary Legend, Volume II*, ed. Gillian Bennett, Paul Smith, and J.D.A. Widdowson, pp. 109-16. Sheffield, England: Sheffield Academic Press.

McGeachy, John A., III. 1978. "Student Nicknames for College Faculty." *Western Folklore* 37: 281-96.

McNeil, W. K., comp. and ed. 1985. *Ghost Stories from the American South*. Little Rock, Arkansas: August House.

McPhee, M. C. 1927-28. "College Slang." *American Speech* 3: 131-33.

Mechling, Jay. 1988. "On the Relation between Creativity and Cutting Corners." *Adolescent Psychiatry* 15: 346-66.

_____. 1989. "Mediating Structures and the Significance of University Folk." In *Folk Groups and Folklore Genres: A Reader*, ed. Elliot Oring, pp. 287-95. Logan: Utah State University Press.

_____, and David Scofield Wilson. 1988. "Organizational Festivals and the Uses of Ambiguity: The Case of Picnic Day at Davis." In *Inside Organizations: Understanding the Human Dimension*, ed. Michael Owen Jones, Michael Dane Moore, and Richard Christopher Snyder, pp. 303-17. Newbury Park, California: Sage Publications.

Meley, Patricia. 1990. "Adolescent Legend Trips as Teenage Cultural Response: A Study of Lore in Context." M.A. thesis, Penn State Harrisburg.

Metler, Beverly. 1979. "Wells Plans May Day Mirth." *Syracuse Herald-Journal*, April 30.

Miller, Russell E. 1966. *Light on the Hill: A History of Tufts College, 1852-1952*. Boston: Beacon Press.

Mills, Randolph V. 1951. "Oregon's Pigger: A College Tradition." *Western Folklore* 10: 298-309.

Minot, John Clair, and Donald Francis Snow. 1901. *Tales of Bowdoin*. Augusta, Maine: Press of Kennebec.

Mitchell, Carol Ann. 1976. "The Differences Between Male and Female Joke Telling as Exemplified in a College Community." Ph.D. diss., Indiana University.

_____. 1985. "Some Differences in Male and Female Joke-Telling." In *Women's Folklore, Women's Culture*, ed. Rosan A. Jordan and Susan J. Kalcik, pp. 163-86. Philadelphia: University of Pennsylvania Press.

Mitchell, Roger E. 1982. "Campus Drug Lore and the Sociology of Rumor." *Midwestern Journal of Language and Folklore* 8: 89-108.

Moffat, Michael. 1985. "Inventing the 'Time-Honored Traditions' of 'Old Rutgers': Rutgers Student Culture, 1858-1900." *Journal of the Rutgers University Libraries* 47: 1-11.

_____. 1985b. *The Rutgers Picture Book: An Illustrated History of Student Life in the Changing College and University*. New Brunswick, New Jersey: Rutgers University Press.

_____. 1986. "The Discourse of the Dorm: Race, Friendship, and 'Culture' among College Youth." In *Symbolizing America*, ed. Herve Varenne, pp. 158-77. Lincoln: University of Nebraska Press.

_____. 1989. *Coming of Age in New Jersey: College and American Culture*. New Brunswick, New Jersey: Rutgers University Press.

Mohler, Owen. 1977. "Purdue University ... Tradition." *Purdue Exponent* (Purdue University, West Lafayette, Indiana), June 14: 8B.

Monteiro, George. 1964. "Parodies of Scripture, Prayer, and Hymn." *Journal of American Folklore* 77: 45-52.

_____. 1964. "Religious and Scriptural Parodies." *New York Folklore* 2: 150-66.

Mook, Maurice A. 1961. "Quaker Campus Lore." *New York Folklore Quarterly* 17: 243-52.

Moore, Alexis. 1989. "Getting into 'Step.'" *Philadelphia Inquirer*, July 8 (sec. D): 1, 5.

Moore, Danny W. 1974. "The Deductive Riddle: An Adaptation to Modern Society." *North Carolina Folklore Journal* 22: 119-25.

Moore, Jack B. 1961. "Go Ahead, Ma'm: Washington and Lee Student Lore." *North Carolina Folklore* 9 (2): 32-34.

Moore, Michael Dane. 1979. "Linguistic Aggression and Literary Allusion." *Western Folklore* 38: 259-66.

Morgan, Hal, and Kerry Tucker. 1987. *More Rumor!* New York: Penguin.

Morris, Robert S. 1969. "The Lemon Squeezer Legend, 1857-1969." *Trinity Alumni Magazine* (Trinity College, Hartford, Connecticut), Summer: 13-17.

Newchurch, Karen. 1985. "The Georgia Tech Legacy." *Georgia Tech Alumni Magazine* (Atlanta, Georgia) 60 (2): 12-14.

Nichols, Raymond. 1983. "Foreword." In *On the Hill: A Photographic History of the University of Kansas*, comp. Virginia Adams, Katie Armitage, Donna Butler, and Carol Shankel. Lawrence: University Press of Kansas.

Nilsen, Don L. F. 1981. "Sigma Epsilon Xi: Sex in the Typical University Classroom." *Maledicta* 5: 79-91.

Nomani, Asra Q. 1989. "Steeped in Tradition, 'Step Dance' Unites Blacks on Campus." *Wall Street Journal*, July 10 (sec. A): 1, 4.

Ockerlander, Lynda. 1975. "Methods of Cheating." Indiana University Folklore Archives (76-071).

Ohlidal, Susan. 1981. "The Ghost of Norland Hall." In *Franklin County Folklore*, ed. Dorothy Sara Lee, n.p. Chambersburg, Pennsylvania: Wilson College.

Olesen, Virginia, and Elvi Whittaker. 1968. "Conditions under Which College Students Borrow, Use, and Alter Slang." *American Speech* 43: 222-28.

Oliphant, J. Orin. 1965. *The Rise of Bucknell University.* New York: Appleton-Century-Crofts.

Pankake, Marcia, and John Pankake. 1988. *A Prairie Home Companion Folk Song Book.* New York: Viking.

Parini, Jay. 1989. "The More They Write, The More They Write." *New York Times Book Review*, July 30: 1, 24.

Parker, Garland G. 1971. *The Enrollment Explosion: A Half-Century of Attendance in U.S. Colleges and Universities.* New York: School and Society Books.

Parler, Mary Celestia. 1984. "Folklore from the Campus." [1958]. In *The Charm Is Broken: Readings in Arkansas and Missouri Folklore*, ed. W. K. McNeil, pp. 25-29. Little Rock, Arkansas: August House.

Parochetti, JoAnn Stephens. 1965. "Scary Stories from Purdue." *Keystone Folklore Quarterly* 10: 49-57.

Parsons, James J. 1988. "Hillside Letters in the Western Landscape." *Landscape* 30 (1): 15-23.

Pattee, Fred Lewis. 1928. "Penn State Traditions." *Old Main Bell* (Pennsylvania State College, State College) 5 (1): 3-7.

_____. 1953. *Penn State Yankee: The Autobiography of Fred Lewis Pattee.* State College: Pennsylvania State College.

Pederson, Daniel. 1986. "10 Minutes of Madness." *Newsweek*, September 1: 18-19.

Peterson, Walter F. 1964. "Downer's Rite of Spring: The Hat Hunt." *Historical Messenger* (Milwaukee, Wisconsin: Milwaukee County Historical Society) 20 (2): 31-36.

Piehler, G. Kurt. 1988. "Phi Beta Kappa: The Invention of an Academic Tradition." *History of Education Quarterly* 28: 207-29.

Pimple, Kenneth D. 1986. "The Inmates of Eigenmann: A Look at Door Decoration in a Graduate Dormitory." *Folklore Forum* 19: 5-35.

Pingry, Carl, and Vance Randolph. 1927-28. "Kansas University Slang." *American Speech* 3: 218-21.

Plowman, Gisela J. 1944. "Pedroing at California." *California Folklore Quarterly* 3: 277-83.

Posen, I. Sheldon. 1974. "Pranks and Practical Jokes at Children's Summer Camps." *Southern Folklore Quarterly* 38: 299-309.

Poston, Lawrence, III. 1964. "Some Problems in the Study of Campus Slang." *American Speech* 39: 114-23.

_____. 1965. "On the Persistence of Some Older Student Slang Terms." *American Speech* 40: 77-78.

_____, and Francis J. Stillman. 1965. "Notes on Campus Vocabulary, 1964." *American Speech* 40: 193-95.

Preston, Michael J. 1973. "The Traditional Ringing at Temple Buell College." *Western Folklore* 32: 271-74.

_____. 1982. "The English Literal Rebus and the Graphic Riddle Tradition." *Western Folklore* 41: 104-121.

Primiano, Leonard. 1976. "Student Life at a Pennsylvania Dutch College." *Pennsylvania Folklife* 26 (1): 34-38.

Procter, Harvey T., Jr. 1966. "Collection of Good Luck Charms and Tales during Final Exam Week from Six College Students." Wayne State University Folklore Archive (1966/86).

Proctor, Samuel, and Wright Langley. 1986. *Gator History: A Pictorial History of the University of Florida.* Gainesville, Florida: South Star Publishing.

Prosser, William L. 1957. "Needlemann on Mortgages." *Journal of Legal Education* 9: 489-94.

"Proving That Slime Is on Their Side, Santa Cruz Students Make the Slug Their Mascot." 1986. People Weekly, June 16: 85.

Quinto, Louis B. 1989. "Pledgeship: Who Needs It?" *Shield and Diamond [of Pi Kappa Alpha]* 100 (4): 27-28.

Rader, Benjamin G. 1983. *American Sports, from the Age of Folk Games to the Age of Spectators.* Englewood Cliffs, New Jersey: Prentice-Hall.

Raftery, Kathleen. 1989. "Vomit Is a Five Letter Word." Elizabeth Tucker Papers, SUNY Binghamton.

Randolph, Vance. 1928. "A Survival of Phallic Superstition in Kansas." *Psychoanalytic Review* 15: 242-44.

————, collector. 1957. *The Talking Turtle and Other Ozark Folk Tales.* Notes by Herbert Halpert. New York: Columbia University Press.

Raphael, Ray. 1988. *The Men from the Boys: Rites of Passage in Male America.* Lincoln: University of Nebraska Press.

Repcheck, Diane. 1988. "Zaniness Abounds at Commencement." *Daily Collegian* (Pennsylvania State University, University Park), April 29: 5.

Reuss, Richard A. 1965. "An Annotated Field Collection of Songs from the American College Student Oral Tradition." M.A. thesis, Indiana University.

————. 1974. "'That Can't Be Alan Dundes! Alan Dundes Is Taller Than That!': The Folklore of Folklorists." *Journal of American Folklore* 87: 303-17.

Reynolds, Neil B. 1961. "Lore from Union and Princeton." *New York Folklore Quarterly* 17: 253-56.

Rice, George W., and David F. Jacobs. 1973. "Saltpeter: A Folkloric Adjustment to Acculturation Stress." *Western Folklore* 32: 164-79.

Robertson, Lynda. 1989a. "6-Foot-8 Navy Plebe Ends Year's Agony with Long Reach." *Sun* (Baltimore, Maryland), May 27 (sec. A): 1, 8.

————. 1989b. "Naval Academy's Class of '89 Embarks for Military Life." *Sun* (Baltimore, Maryland), June 1 (sec. B): 1, 2.

Roemer, Danielle. 1971. "Scary Story Legends." *Folklore Annual of the University Folklore Association* 3: 1-16.

Rogers, James. 1970. "The Folklore of Faculty Nicknames at the Academy." *Keystone Folklore Quarterly* 15: 74-80.

Rollins, Alfred B., Jr. 1961. "College Folklore." *New York Folklore Quarterly* 17: 163-73.

Rosemeyer, Cathy. 1976. "Stories of 625 North Jordan." Indiana University Folklore Archives (77-152).

Roskin, David. 1988. "Elmo: The Ghost of Mitchell Hall." University of Delaware Folklore Archives.

Rosnow, Ralph L., and Gary Alan Fine. 1976. *Rumor and Gossip: The Social Psychology of Hearsay.* New York: Elsevier.

Roth, Philip. 1988. *The Facts: A Novelist's Autobiography.* New York: Farrar, Straus, and Giroux.

Rountree, Pam. 1985. "Ramblin' Wreck." *Georgia Tech Alumni Magazine* (Atlanta, Georgia) 60 (2): 16-18.

Rudolph, Frederick. 1962. *The American College and University: A History.* New York: Vintage Books/Random House.

Russell, Jason Almus. 1929-30. "Colgate University Slang." *American Speech* 5: 238-39.

Russo, John. 1990. "'Reel' vs. Real Violence." *Newsweek,* February 19: 10.

Sackett, S. J. 1964. "Student Slang in Hays, Kansas." *American Speech* 39: 235.

Safire, William. 1982. *What's the Good Word?* New York: Times Books.

Salmon, Mike. 1983. "The Banging of the Doors: An Analysis of a Folkloric Event [Purdue University]." Danielle Roemer Papers, Northern Kentucky University.

Sampson, Anthony, and Sally Sampson, comps. 1985. *The Oxford Book of Ages.* New York: Oxford University Press.

Samuelson, Sue. 1979. "The White Witch: An Analysis of an Adolescent Legend." *Indiana Folklore* 12: 18-37.

"Scatological Lore on Campus." 1962. *Journal of American Folklore* 75: 260-62.

Schaeper, Thomas J., Jonathan D. Merrill, and John Hutchison. 1987. *The St. Bonaventure University Trivia Book*. St. Bonaventure, New York: St. Bonaventure University.

Schechter, Harold. 1988. *The Bosom Serpent: Folklore and Popular Art*. Iowa City: University of Iowa Press.

Schultz, William Eben. 1929-30. "College Abbreviations." *American Speech* 5: 240-44.

Sebastian, Hugh. 1934. "Negro Slang in Lincoln University." *American Speech* 9: 287-90.

_____. 1936. "Agricultural College Slang in South Dakota." *American Speech* 11: 279-80.

Sechrest, Lee, and A. Kenneth Olson. 1971. "Graffiti in Four Types of Institutions of Higher Learning." *Journal of Sex Research* 7: 62-71.

Senn, Mary C. 1983. "Mona Lisa, Is That You?" *Louisiana Folklore Miscellany* 5 (3): 27-30.

Sennett, Richard. 1977. *The Fall of Public Man: On the Social Psychology of Capitalism*. New York: Vintage.

Sentman, Ron. 1972. "Logic Problems of College Students." Indiana University Folklore Archives (14/183).

Seventh Generation of 101 Aggie Jokes. 1988. Dallas: Gigem Press.

Sherman, Constance D. 1962. "Oberlin Lore." *New York Folklore Quarterly* 18: 58-60.

Shidler, John Ashton. 1931-32. "More Stanford Expressions." *American Speech* 7: 434-37.

_____, and R. M. Clarke, Jr. 1931-32. "Stanfordiana." *American Speech* 7: 232-33.

Shulman, Max, ed. 1955. *Max Shulman's Guided Tour of Campus Humor: The Best Stories, Articles, Poems, Jokes, and Nonsense from Over Sixty-Five College Humor Magazines*. Garden City, New York: Hanover House.

Shutan, Lynn. 1972. "The Folklore of Stephens College." Indiana University Folklore Archives (75/42).

Sigler, Scott. 1988. "Does Olivet Need Ghostbusters?" *The Echo* (Olivet College, Olivet, Michigan), October 27: 1.

Simmons, Donald G. 1967. "Some Special Terms Used in a University of Connecticut Men's Dormitory." *American Speech* 42: 227-30.

Sims, Dunny. 1944. "Moron Jokes." In *From Hell to Breakfast*, ed. Mody C. Boatright and Donald Day, pp. 155-61. Publications of the Texas Folklore Society, no.19. Dallas: Southern Methodist University Press.

Smith, Grace P. 1937. "'Rushing' in the Sixties?" *American Speech* 12: 156-57.

Smith, Paul. 1990. "'AIDS: Don't Die of Ignorance': Exploring the Cultural Complex." In *A Nest of Vipers: Perspectives on Contemporary Legend V*, ed. Gillian Bennett and Paul Smith, pp. 113-42. Sheffield, England: Sheffield Academic Press.

Smith, Warren Hunting. 1972. *Hobart and William Smith: The History of Two Colleges*. Geneva, New York: Hobart and William Smith Colleges.

Snyder, Henry L. 1949. *Our College Colors*. Nashville, Tennessee: Southern Publishing Company.

Sobel, Eli. 1951. "'Going to See the Widow' Again." *Journal of American Folklore* 64: 420-21.

Sparks, Linda, and Bruce Emerton, comps. 1988. *American College Regalia: A Handbook*. New York: Greenwood Press.

Spectorsky, A. C., ed. 1958. *The College Years*. New York: Hawthorn Books.

Spradley, James P., and Brenda J. Mann. 1975. *The Cocktail Waitress: Woman's Work in a Man's World*. New York: John Wiley and Sons.

Stadtmann, Verne A. 1970. *The University of California, 1868-1968*. New York: McGraw-Hill.

Starr, Mrs. Morton H. 1954. "Wisconsin Pastimes." *Journal of American Folklore* 67: 184.

Stec, Kathleen. 1985. "The Folklore of College Students: Cheating." Mac Barrick Memorial Folklore Archives, Shippensburg University.

Stephanoff, Alexander. 1970. "College Interviews as a Folklore Genre." *Keystone Folklore Quarterly* 15: 106-13.

Stuller, Jay. 1987. "Fight, Fight, Fight, Fight, Banana Slugs, Banana Slugs." *Audubon* 89 (2): 128-30, 132-35.

Suffern, Betty. 1959. "'Pedro' at California." *Western Folklore* 18: 326.

Sykes, Charles J. 1988. *ProfScam: Professors and the Demise of Higher Education*. New York: St.

Martin's Press.

"Symbols of Campus Community." 1989. *Educational Record* 70 (3-4): 36-38.

T., M. 1976. "Fraternity Lore." Penn State Folklore Archives (Penn State Room, Pattee Library, University Park).

_____. 1979. "The Pattee Murder." Penn State Folklore Archives (Penn State Room, Pattee Library, University Park).

Taboada, Margaret. 1967. "The Sorority Song Tradition [UCLA]." Wayne State Folklore Archive (R1973/244).

Taylor, Archer. 1947. "'Pedro! Pedro!'" *Western Folklore* 6: 228-31.

Tenth Generation of 101 Aggie Jokes. 1988. Dallas: Gigem Press.

Theroux, Alexander. 1986. "Nerd U.: What Is It about MIT, Anyway?" *New England Monthly*, October: 60-65.

_____. 1987. "Caution: Geniuses at Work and Play." *Reader's Digest*, October: 215-18, 220.

Thigpen, Kenneth A., Jr. 1971. "Adolescent Legends in Brown County: A Survey." *Indiana Folklore* 4: 141-215.

Thompson, Stith. 1966. *Motif-Index of Folk-Literature.* Rev. ed., 6 vols. Bloomington: Indiana University Press.

Tiger, Lionel. 1969. *Men In Groups.* New York: Vintage Books.

Till, Gerry Marie. 1976. "The Murder at Franklin College." *Indiana Folklore* 9: 187-95.

Tillson, William. 1961. "How the Boilermakers Did Not Get Their Name." *Midwest Folklore* 11: 105-14.

_____. 1962. "Purdue Classroom Recollection." *New York Folklore Quarterly* 18: 55-57.

Toelken, Barre. 1986. "The Folklore of Academe." In *The Study of American Folklore: An Introduction*, by Jan Harold Brunvand, pp. 502-28. 3rd ed. New York: W. W. Norton.

Tolley, William Pearson. 1989. *At the Fountain of Youth: Memories of a College President.* Syracuse, New York: Syracuse University.

Topping, Robert W. 1988. *A Century and Beyond: The History of Purdue University.* West Lafayette, Indiana: Purdue University Press.

Torok, Tom. 1989. "You've Got to Hand It to Her." *Philadelphia Inquirer,* May 27 (sec. A): 3.

"Tradition Crumbles, Students Grumble." 1989. *New York Times,* July 23 (sec. 1, part 2): 35.

"Tradition Is Basis of May Day Contests." 1935. *Lamron* (Western Oregon State College, Monmouth) 12 (April 27): 1.

Traditions Cluster of the New Dimensions in Total Teaching Program. 1981. *Traditions: Roanoke College Yesterday and Today.* [Salem, Virginia]: Roanoke College.

Tucker, Elizabeth. 1978. "The Seven-Day Wonder Diet: Magic and Ritual in Diet Folklore." *Indiana Folklore* 6: 141-50.

Turner, Patricia A. 1993. *I Heard It Through the Grapevine: Rumor in African-American Culture.* Berkeley: University of California Press.

Turrell, William. 1961. "Editor's Page." *New York Folklore Quarterly* 17: 162, 237, 242, 309-11.

Underwood, Gary N. 1975. "Razorback Slang." *American Speech* 50: 50-69.

_____. 1976. "Some Characteristics of Slang Used at the University of Arkansas at Fayetteville." *Mid-South Folklore* 4: 49-54.

"University of Wisconsin Basketball Prospects 1988." 1986-87. *Maledicta* 9: 37-38.

Utt, Walter C. 1968. *A Mountain, A Pickax, A College.* Angwin, California: Alumni Association, Pacific Union College.

Van Gennep, Arnold. 1960. *The Rites of Passage,* trans. Monika B. Vizedom and Gabrielle L. Caffee. Chicago: University of Chicago Press.

Vizedom, Monika. 1976. *Rites and Relationships: Rites of Passage and Contemporary Anthropology.* Beverly Hills, California: Sage Publications.

"V.M.I.'s 'Brother Rats' May Get Some Sisters." 1989. *New York Times,* June 4 (sec. 1, part 2): 47.

Von Hoffman, Nicholas. 1966. *The Multiversity: A Personal Report on What Happens to Today's Students at American Universities.* New York: Holt, Rinehart and Winston.

Wadler, Joyce. 1983. "Mary in the Lavender Pumps." *Rolling Stone,* April 14: 25-28, 33, 36, 113, 116-17.

Walden, Keith. 1987. "Respectable Hooligans: Male Toronto College Students Celebrate Hallowe'en, 1884-1910." *Canadian Historical Review* 68: 1-34.

Washburn, B. E. 1955. "College Folklore at Chapel Hill in the Early 1900's." *North Carolina Folklore* 3 (2): 27-30.

Washburn, Jane. 1976. "Changes in Alpha Mu Chapter Customs." Indiana University Folklore
    Archives (75/145).
Wassell, Gayle. 1973. "Aggie Jokes and Riddles." Special Collections, University of Arkansas Libraries.
Watkins, Martin A. 1968. "Some Notes on Flunk Notes." *American Speech* 43: 76-77.
Waymire, Susan. 1978. "Myths and Legends of Indiana University." Indiana University Folklore
    Archives (79/047).
Weales, Gerald. 1957. "Ritual in Georgia." *Southern Folklore Quarterly* 21: 104-9.
Welch, Kelley. 1982. "Dirty Sorority Folksongs." Indiana University Folklore Archives (86/1).
White, William. 1943. "Whitman College Slang." *American Speech* 18: 153-55.
_____. 1955. "Wayne University Slang." *American Speech* 30: 301-5.
Whitney, Gertrude Churchill. 1962. "Frogs and Their Imitators." *New York Folklore Quarterly* 18: 141-
    44.
Wilgus, D. K. 1972. "More Norbert Wiener Stories." *Western Folklore* 31: 23-25.
Wilson, Robin. 1990. "Worried about 'Anything Goes' Moral Code, Colleges Are Stepping In to Help
    Students Shape Values." *Chronicle of Higher Education,* January 3: A1, A28.
Windham, Kathryn Tucker, and Margaret Gillis Figh. 1969. *13 Alabama Ghosts and Jeffrey.*
    Huntsville, Alabama: Strode Publishers.
Winger, Matt. 1975. "Methods of Cheating." Indiana University Folklore Archives (76-075).
Wise, James. 1977. "Tugging on Superman's Cape: The Making of a College Legend." *Western
    Folklore* 36: 227-38.
Wolfe, Suzanne Rau. 1983. *The University of Alabama: A Pictorial History.* University: University of
    Alabama Press.
Woodward, Kenneth L. 1984. "The Lessons of the Master." *Notre Dame Magazine* (Notre Dame,
    Indiana) 13 (2): 14-21.
Worthington, Chesley. 1965. "From the Folklore of Brown University." *Brown Alumni Monthly*
    (Brown University, Providence, Rhode Island) 65 (8): 52-57.
Wylie, Jeanne Porter. 1933. "Student Customs in the University of Arkansas." M.S. thesis, University
    of Arkansas.
Wyman, Walker D. 1979. "Academic or Campus Folklore." In *Wisconsin Folklore,* pp. 81-91. River
    Falls: University of Wisconsin-Extension Department of Arts Development.
Yale Daily News. 1990. *The Insider's Guide to the Colleges.* New York: St. Martin's Press.
Yohe, Charles. 1950. "Observations on an Adolescent Folkway." *Psychoanalytic Review* 37: 79-81.
Young, Frank W. 1962. "The Function of Male Initiation Ceremonies: A Cross-Cultural Test of an
    Alternative Hypothesis." *American Journal of Sociology* 67: 379-96.

Index

A

B

Cornell, Ezra (Cornell University), 179
Cornell University, 46-47, 101, 139, 179
Corps of Cadets (Texas A&M University), 82
Coulter, Hope (Harvard University), 40
Courtship: kissing belief, 185-86; slang, 187
Courtyard Carni (Viterbo College), 94
Crane, Beverly, 172
Crooks. *See* Canes
Crum Creek Regatta (Swarthmore College), 96
C.W. Post Campus of Long Island University. *See*
    Long Island University, C.W. Post Campus

D

Daisy chains, 212. *See also* Bluebonnet chains; Ivy
    chains
Dégh, Linda, 169, 173
Delaware, University of, 24, 43, 132, 177
Delta Delta Delta, 42, 139
Delta Gamma, 139, 188
Delta Sigma Theta, 136
Delta Tau Delta, 42
DePauw University, 127, 134
Derby Days, 142
Detroit, University of, 58
Detweiler, Chris (Pennsylvania State University at
    Harrisburg), 44
De Voto, Bernard (Harvard University), 48
Dickinson College, 47, 173
Dickinson School of Law, 29
Dictionary, 44
Diddle, Ed (Western Kentucky University), 195
Diets: jokes, 190; legends, 189; photocopy humor,
    190
Diplomas, 219-20
Ditch Day (California Institute of Technology), 104
Dixon, Jeane, 173-74, 175
Donahue, Phil, 173
Dooley (Emory University), 217
Doorknob signals, 186
Door slams, 37
Dorson, Richard M., 28, 36, 38, 46, 48, 185
Douglas, Paul (Towson State University), 123
Drinking games: Bizz-Bizz, 121; Cheers, 123; Hi
    Bob, 123; Liar's Dice, 123; Mexicali, 123; Quar-
    ters, 1240; Thumper, 121; Turtles, 122; Up and
    Down the River, 122. *See also* Alcohol
Drugs, 28, 128, 176, 190, 191, 203. *See also*
    Alcohol; LSD
Duke, James (Duke University), 179
Duke University, 98, 133, 179, 196

Dundes, Alan, 38, 40, 169
Duquesne University, 39, 79
Dutch Treat Week (North Texas State College), 99
Dykstra, Reverend Mr. (Hope College), 39

E

Earlham College, 95, 108, 116
Easter, 91, 177
Eastern Michigan University, 30, 120, 185, 208, 213
East Stroudsburg University of Pennsylvania, 173
Edman, Irwin (Columbia University), 46
Eeyore (University of Texas), 93
Egbert, James (Michigan State University), 152
Einstein, Albert, 59
Elmira College, 104
Emory University, 215, 217
Emporia State University, 76
Engagement customs: bell ringing, 188; candlelight-
    ing ceremony, 187; poling, 188; ponding, 119;
    shower, 188; swirlie, 188
Engineering students 87, 101, 104, 114, 121, 228
Ergman, John P., Memorial Festival (University of
    California at Berkeley). 92
Ethnic stereotypes, 141, 194
Eureka College, 120
Everett, Edward (Harvard University), 158
Examinations: beliefs, 29-30; jokes, 35-37, 193;
    legends, 27-29, 32-27; parodies, 62-63, 66;
    photocopy humor, 63-66

F

Female students: bluebonnet chains, 213; class
    competitions, 79, 100; daisy chains, 212; Dutch
    Treat Week, 99; freshman initiation, 79-81;
    graffiti, 202; ivy chains, 12; May Day, 104-110;
    Sadie Hawkins Day, 99; Secret Santa, 91; status,
    182; virgin legend, 182. *See also* Jokes, coeds;
    Jokes, feminists; Jokes, women; Photocopy
    humor, coed letter; Professors, female; Sororities;
    Women's colleges
Fijis. *See* Phi Gamma Delta
Finagle's Laws, 68
Findlay College, 90, 214
Fine, Gary Alan, 190
Fitton, Mary Louise, 117
Flaw Day (Duke University), 98
Florida, University of, 86, 146
Florida State University, 174
Flunk Day (Coe College), 103